STREET CHILD

A Memoir

∞∞∞

JUSTIN REED EARLY

TABLE OF CONTENTS

Prologue

PART I

NOTE FROM THE AUTHOR

This memoir is inspired by my life story and is a work of nonfiction. I have been very careful to articulate events honestly and faithfully as I recall them, sometimes researching my own past to ensure facts are accurate. Some names, descriptions and event locations have been changed to respect the privacy of others. Many events are combined and several participants are not mentioned to allow the story to flow uncomplicated. No one was omitted disrespectfully. These events, conversations and depictions are solely from my recollection and have been recreated in the spirit of raising awareness of various issues including (but not limited to) homelessness, child trafficking, drug addiction and racism and the negative affects they have among our the worldly population. I also describe some common dangers of homelessness and street life. Though everything written is real and the timeline is genuine – I know that I am unable to provide exact reenactments of conversations and dates though I have tried my best to capture clarity.

DEDICATION

To the Source that creates and delivers my fate…
To the Family that inspired a street child:
Lou Ellen Couch
Roberta Joseph Hayes
Cameron David Early
Lloyd George Early
To my sweet Honeychild, you were this man's best friend.

Special thanks to my StreetTeam, Marilyn Kentz, Rob Woronoff, Cathy Renna, Cindi Creager, Rainie Cole, and everyone who continues to take the time to bring this true story to life.

Chapter Zero

THE PROLOGUE
(a couple years back...)

"It is easier to build strong children, then to repair broken men..."

- Frederick Douglass

The California sun was edging west toward the Pacific Ocean as I drove down the canyon through Baldwin Hills on the southern edge of the City of Angels. This exciting portion of La Brea Avenue, also known as the La Brea Green Belt, cuts through a deep crevice in the mountain in a curvy descent, which reveals the mountainous beauty of Los Angeles. In the distance, amazing views flow into the infamous Hollywood Hills about eight miles to the north. As I continue down the hill, I see the sun twinkling towards the Hollywood sign set on the top of the distant hills, compelling views of the California earth tease in and out.

Though it was still morning on a beautiful October day, the sun was already bright and seemed hotter than in recent years. This warm weather swing was emphasized as I had made the bone-headed mistake of buying a black car with radioactive interior. The rich custom red leather amplified the heat of the sun, which was beaming directly into the driver's window onto my arm, face and eyes. My first mid-life crisis status symbol, an entry-level BMW coupe, seemed to cause the sun to shine twice as bright.

I cracked the car window a few inches hoping the outside breeze would bring coolness as the air conditioning didn't seem to be doing it's job, or maybe I haven't quite figured out how to work it properly. As the hot breeze entered the car I could smell the scent of fresh cut grass from the recently manicured rolling hills. There was also a familiar smell of a flower or a tree, but I couldn't quite grasp its identity. I looked around carefully as I managed the curves yet didn't see anything I would recognize. The smell was obviously from my early childhood, and it would have been something that would have thrived in rainy Seattle. I always found these flashbacks interesting and wondered their purpose. In this case, I think it was just to be reminded that I have a lengthy past, full of sustenance.

I was heading to my office in Beverly Hills from my condo in Inglewood, near South Los Angeles, to put in a few extra hours work, which I have been doing since becoming a bit of a workaholic. It was clear since being hired, that my boss liked the type of employee that was willing to work long hours and go above and beyond the standard call of duty. Desperate for success and not quiet versed on how to deal with my personal head-drama effectively while sitting still, I would do whatever it took to please and impress my superiors and stay busy enough to keep my mind off my life and past.

Keep it moving at all times.

I recently celebrated my 40th birthday and am grateful to be alive. Whenever people hear my story they call me a miracle. It seems a bit too "heroic" for me and makes me uncomfortable. I am clearly not a hero.

I *am* a survivor. I am everything I had been taught to be in order to survive a very challenging and interesting experience.

During my younger years I did the bad behavior thing very well. I strived to be and developed into the worst possible child to battle my internal emotional and physical pain and to manufacture much needed attention. Many of these behaviors extended into my young adult life. Ask any therapist or social worker that evaluated me and they would tell you I had more 'issues' than People Magazine. Admittedly, I still have some of those issues, which I keep very close and deep inside me. Sometimes I wonder if I will ever be ready to rid myself of them. Quite frankly, most who came in contact with me *knew* that I would die on their watch, but thankfully I enjoy an amazing God who assigned a very skilled team of angel's and heroes who have stuck by me for many years affording me many sometimes undeserved second chances…

A thousand, second chances.

After fielding several calls already on my fancy Beemer Bluetooth, a call came in from a Washington, DC area code. "Hi Justin, It's Vicki Wagner," the voice from the other end reverberated throughout every speaker in my car. Vicki was an outreach worker in the 1980's and became the Executive Director of the largest homeless youth agency, Youth-Care in Seattle before being selected to lead the largest National Agency, which was based in Washington, DC. She had recently moved to the East Coast with her family.

"Would you have any interest serving on our Board of Directors? As you may know the Board is currently made up with mostly non-profit agency staff from all over the United States. I would like to get a homeless youth and a formerly homeless youth on the Board for better representation of the population we serve."

Glamorous? *I think not.* But, Board of Directors does sound pretty astute and could contribute to my "Jack of all trades, master of none" resume.

"Unfortunately, it's an unpaid position and the meetings are mostly in DC. So you would have to pay for your own travel. If you can come to the next Board Meeting they would like to meet with you and hopefully vote you onto the Board. We would love to have your insights."

Insights? Which ones?

Insanity? Immorality? Alleged Immortality?

"I would love to. Email me the details of the next meeting and I will make it happen, thanks for calling." I hung up the phone and giggled at how professional she always sounded. This woman practically raised me but was always wrapped so tight in boundaries she never let her emotions show and was always to the point. She was an excellent executive but not the most nurturing social worker. I was glad she found her calling.

It's hard to believe I was a homeless street child more than a quarter of a century ago but even more so that it was this experience and perspective that I was going to be able to offer in my new capacity. I spent many years on the streets, at one point more than half of my life. Interestingly, in many ways I am still that little street child. The physical, mental and emotional battle scars remain and although some have healed significantly, many remain indefinitely.

As I contemplated my new mission in the non-profit world as a member of this agencies governing board, I began to recall and relive my younger life on the streets. The characters, friends and heroes from my past came back to life. I could hear them, see them, touch and even smell them vividly. I have never forgotten them.

There was no way I could.

They were as much a part of my life and success as anyone else, tattooed in my heart and soul in ways deeper and clearer than the Polynesian ink tattoo sleeves on my arms, which were strategically designed to cover the many physical scars of my experience. But this time my head was articulating memories so vividly that I knew it was time I started to direct these thoughts and memories into a new experience.

Little Justin would begin to put his pen to paper.

Still deep in the thoughts of my new mission my phone rang again, this time with my mother on the line. I knew something had to be up when she called as I usually initiated the communication. As a result of my motivation, we have remained in contact in the years since my street life, but once I did what I needed to do in order to live a productive life, I didn't need parents anymore. I was a grown man when I 'came to life'.

I respect her and love her dearly. I still make a point to check on her at least once per week out of respect for the woman who gave me life. But there still remains a cloud of unspoken regret that we both failed terribly as parent and child. God forbid anyone talk honestly about it, we surely never have. In fact everything that has happened in our lives is top secret, never happened, never talked about. Even my closest friends would think the relationship with my mother is as normal as the setting on a dishwasher.

As I suspected, there was nothing normal or casual about her reason for calling.

"Your father is coughing up blood. He had an abnormal x-ray and has already been given an MRI. We get the results tomorrow. They are concerned he has lung cancer." I was trying to read her tone, concentrating on what my next move should be because I am not terribly bothered or surprised that my father is having this serious health problem. "Do you want me to come up and support you?"

"You don't have to do that," She sighed suspiciously.

"I am going to book the next flight. I can drive you to his appointment." I felt guilty because I wasn't offering the ride to be of service to my father. I just wanted to be in the same room to rejoice when the professional opinions and estimated length of survival were discussed regarding his final termination.

I started praying not only for him to *have* lung cancer, but that is inoperable, untreatable, advanced beyond any possible medical miracles and that is was absolutely impossible to cure.

Amen.

I hung up my cell as I pulled into the driveway at my office. I immediately put the manual shifter into reverse and began the drive home to pack my bags.

∞∞∞∞

The two and a half hour flight seemed to take forever because my head was spinning faster than this jets turbine engines.

I admitted to myself that it was not acceptable to pray for anyone's death, not even my evil father. This doesn't mean I am going to speak to him, it just means that I won't lower myself to wish for his death.

As the Alaska Airlines flight started its descent, I could see the full view of Downtown Seattle and some of the buildings that were around when I was a kid. There were many new buildings but the infrastructure was noticeably intact. The skyline and the lack of sunlight brought back memories too. The grey-ness and the blah-ness was something that I didn't miss. But was it really the weather that I associate with the wrong-ness of this otherwise beautiful city? Memories began to flow deeper as I thought of my friends from the "streets of the lost". Many of them did not survive their experience. They didn't have a chance.

To many, we were the *bad* kids. The worst delinquent children, who enjoyed living up to our reputations by keeping everyone away from our fragile hearts. As badass as we thought we were, deep inside we just wanted to be loved. We wanted to be loved and protected by our imaginary loving families and we wanted to be happy. We wanted to be doctors and lawyers and we wanted to succeed. We dreamt big dreams but without any means. Our most important task was surviving in the moment with each moment multiplying hours into days, weeks, and if we were lucky – years. Where was the next meal coming from? Where would we sleep tonight? How would we hustle enough money for this and that? Most importantly, how would we medicate these feelings of uselessness and abandonment?

My eyes began to burn as I thought of these children.

I won't ruin this story for you but children who are raised by the streets are considered "high-risk" which, by definition means *Being particularly subject to potential danger or hazard'*. That being said, it should be no surprise that many kids living on the streets die horrible and sometimes senseless – but mostly *preventable* deaths. There is so much that can be been done to help them and to manifest a successful path for them. They are the reason I am writing this book today.

The wheels of the plane landed sloppily onto the runway startling my emotions back to black. I composed myself and wiped the salty ocean from my face so no one would see - *me*.

After a series of challenging tragedies of their own, my parents had moved to Northern Washington from Seattle to their new home near Blaine, which is close to the Canadian border. It is a good two-hour drive of the most amazing rich greens, mountains of trees and farms with moss-covered barns. There were a couple of overpriced outlet malls but I didn't bother to stop at them anymore. You can get better deals on Rodeo Drive in Beverly Hills.

Interstate 5, which runs from the Northern tip of Washington State to the Mexican border, is enjoyable until its time to pull off a few exits before Blaine. That's when things get a little bare. Hidden trailer parks. Trailer trash. Mostly white people, and lots of them. I don't have anything against my race, but in this remote area it is not as common for communities to be as culturally aware and accepting of people who aren't just like them.

I have a diverse cultural flavor from my upbringing that I am proud of. I talk differently then they do. I listen to hip-hop, R&B, and Gospel. I say this because at times I was ashamed of myself and was relentlessly teased and tormented by my Caucasoid counterparts for being a sellout. Nowadays it seems everyone younger than me acts and talks like me. Thank god for Justin Timberlake. As the years have passed cultural assimilation has become more ubiquitous, so I don't stand out as much as I used to and friends don't tease me as much. Now they all call me Justin TimberFake, which is better than Vanilla Ice, which I still get from time to time.

I drove in to my parent's driveway via the gravel road that ran through the manufactured home section of Birch Bay, an intimate humble vacation town situated on the northern edge of the Puget Sound. Clam digging, crabbing and fishing are the most popular pass times when in season.

My mother greeted me at the door. I kissed her on the cheek and said nothing to him. The medical appointment was scheduled for the early afternoon so I urged them to begin what I hoped would be a quiet drive to the hospital in Bellingham where his prognosis would be given. I noticed him drinking out of a wine glass but was shocked when he had the audacity to get inside the car with it. We still hadn't said one word to each other.

"You can't bring that in my car," I said firmly as nice as I could so he wouldn't have a hissy fit. He snapped, "Why the hell not? I'm not driving, and even if I was I'm not drunk!"

"It doesn't matter who's driving, I haven't been in jail in almost fifteen years, and I am not about to go back now," I waited for his response.

Three, two, one, "You're a god damn loser!" He gave me his 'I'm Dr. Evil' look and pointed at me with his spare finger. The look lasted a while as I stared back without blinking.

It was interesting how he would project on me that I was such a disappointment like he was such a brilliant, loving and tolerant father and I should have turned out better. What was even more interesting is that I would buy into that and feel like I was a bad person. Words are very powerful and when negativity is relayed repeatedly, it's easier for one to accept and believe it as true. It took a long time to reprogram all the negative garbage that was dumped on me over the years. But I would be lying if I said it didn't bother me at all. It still does.

He caught my firm stare, and noticed my refusal to enter the car with a wine glass in it. Frustrated, he got out of the back seat and set his wine glass on the entry stoop by the front door after take one long final swig, emptying the glass. He returned to the car without saying another word. I could tell by the look on his face that he was *pissed*.

He mumbled loudly as he got back into the car, "Jesus Christ!" His temper was childish and pathetic, but at least I won the first battle.

∞∞∞∞

The specialist brought the three of us to the back office to show us copies of the MRI that was done before I arrived. There were so many slides. Each millimeter represented another invasive internal view of his organs. With a press of a button on the keyboard, the doctor was able to show the insides of his entire human entity. The doctor took us through his pancreas, liver, heart and finally his lungs. Then I saw something I knew was abnormal and it was huge.

The doctor was the first to break the silence. "Surgery is not an option. Not when there is cancer involved in both lungs," his voice was compassionate. Trying to avoid looking into anyone's eyes, I kept mine on the thick white cloudy bubble on the screen while the doctor continued, "The tumor on the upper part of the lung is pressing up against an artery. If we do not treat it immediately, there is a significant chance the artery will rupture."

"What about chemo?" I asked, more for my mother than myself. The ornery patient interrupted. "No! I don't want any *goddamn* chemo! I don't want it and I'm not doing it." The doctor was taken aback by his blunt foulness. My mothers' husband was never one to mince words. With the doctor's diagnosis and the size of the tumors, it seemed chemo would have only bought him a few months.

Once a stunning man, his looks now matched his attitude and hatred for life, and me. His face was red and he had large rosacea pustules on his nose. His body was deteriorating, but not from the cancer. His downfall was alcohol, and at seventy-six years of age - over sixty years of daily drinking was taking its toll on his health. Cancer just might be his savior.

It was definitely going to be mine.

∞∞∞∞

I was sitting out on the back patio having a talk and a cigarette with my mom when my dad came strolling out with his wine. I wasn't exactly keeping count, but I reminded myself that he had one in his hand when I arrived earlier in the morning.

He glanced at me with his 'I'm possessed by the devil' look and started speaking in his fatherly way. "What the hell are you smoking for? You are one fucking idiot! Jesus Christ, you asshole. You're *still* a goddamn loser!"

This is the point in the story where I would lose my temper and throw all of my negative feelings and vicious attacks back at him so he would know how hurtful he is and what a terrible father he was. But I have grown and have learned that lowering myself to his level would make me as bad as he, a prospect I couldn't swallow. I remained silent.

I looked at my mother who had on her 'I wish I attended Al-Anon when I had a chance' face. As usual, she was hoping the familiar invitation to fight would simply go away. Disturbed at the behavior of her husband and used to it at the same time, she nervously lit another cigarette. He didn't seem to have a judgment with her ignition.

My throat was expanding and swelling with things I had wanted to say for a very long time. I *really* wanted to stay quiet, but like a loose bowel on the brink of explosive diarrhea, words started to leak out uncontrollably.

"Well, Dad," cringing that I had to actually said the 'D' word, "it's not like I had many good role models growing up. I'm sure I would have turned out worse if I had been raised by you." I turned to my mother for validation. She was sitting on a cheap plastic patio chair, unimpressed with my calm cutting choice of words. With my back to my father, I noticed Mom's hand pop up as if to warn me of the swiftly moving shadow. Then it hit me - literally.

Drink still in hand he gave me an angry punch to the face with his empty fist. "You will not talk to me like that you fucking faggot!"

Is that was this is about?

Amazingly, only a little wine spilled out of his glass. My mother jumped up and began to scream, "No, Lloyd! You can't do this now! No!"

Truth be told, the physical aspect of his punch was nothing - it didn't hurt me or even mark my face. But the emotional pain and anger enveloped my thoughts and pierced through my body like a knife through flesh. As I tried to compose myself, he came at me again. This time, I grabbed his fist to stop him from hitting me. Then his other hand rose - still holding onto his drink - and I grabbed it. With both of his arms in my hands protecting myself from any additional blows, I looked him straight in the face. I had to fight the temptation to cut loose. What would happen if I were to pay him back for all the rage he had so easily dumped on me?

"You will not put your hands on me. Do you understand?" I paused to keep myself in control, "I am a grown ass man and you will not *ever* put your hands on me again." My anger was reeling and the "faggot" comment had me seething. I had heard this word all of my life, mostly from mean bigoted bullies. *Mostly from him.*

He tried to look away, knowing any further interaction would result in an embarrassing loss. "*Lloyd*, do you hear me?" I shook him, forcing him to look at me.

Although my voice was quiet, my teeth were clenched and my anger pierced his impaired awareness. My hands began to tremble, tightening around his forearms. He tried to pull away from my grip as wine dripped off both of our arms.

"You're just a loser. Get the hell out of my house".

I pulled him close enough and spit my heated final words into his face, "*Go to hell dying man!* Now you've killed all *three* of your son's!" Without missing a beat, I pushed him. He fell backwards where his ass humbly met the ground. He hit the cement patio with a thud and when he finally released his trusty wine glass, it shattered.

He struggled to get up as I walked in the house to pack my suitcase. I was surprised that my mother followed me instead of helping her dying husband who was still on the ground, bleeding from minor cuts from the broken glass.

"Justin, please don't leave. He is dying. The cancer is in his brain now." She begged. "Mom, his *life* is cancer. He is a belligerent bigot. This is how he has spoken to me my entire life! I will *never* forgive him. I have to leave."

With tears pouring down her face, she validated my entire life experience. "I am so sorry you have gone through all of this." I felt my mom's sincerity and appreciated such a bold and possibly incriminating apology, but I never understood how she stayed with this man for all these years especially knowing in my heart how much she loved me, and my brothers. He came back into the house and darted toward me like he was going to ambush me again. "Get out of my house *NOW!*"

I pushed him away with my suitcase to avoid having to hurt him more physically. As I walked to the front door with my things, my mother followed me.

Still crying she asked, "Are you hungry?"

"No, Mom." I answered in disbelief.

My father turned on his heels and retreated to the den. He always ran and hid until things calmed down, knowing soon everyone will act as if nothing had happened to avoid any further confrontation. Not me, not this time. This elephant in the living room had outgrown our lives. I was at my limit and maybe with my lowest blow about my brothers, he was finally at his.

When he realized that I was really leaving, he came back out. "I did not kill your brothers. Don't ever say that. *I didn't kill them,*" he shut the door to hide his distraught face.

I put my bags in the trunk, got into the car and began my drive towards the freeway feeling vindicated. Something I said must have gotten to him.

It was about time.

I'm talking to you; it's your son,
Father I can't believe all the things we have done,
To each other…

The problem I find, in all my years
The danger is high, though your love is near
So what can be done to heal each other?

I hold my head up high to ease the pain, But quite frankly Lord,
I don't know how much more this world can take,

Yes we truly need more love… for each other…

KEM - "Each Other"

STREETCHILD

Chapter 1

EARLY BEGINNINGS

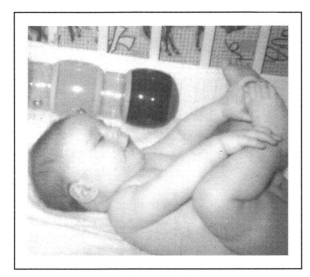

Pictured: Justin

Pictured: Early boys: (L-R) Cameron, George, Justin

The Early's were an average, attractive American middle class family. My father Lloyd was a handsome man with a rough charm that submissive obedient women appreciated. He was tall and looked a bit like Desi Arnez from 'I Love Lucy'. He had dark hair, longer on the top, which was combed in messy perfection. My mother Carol was a looker in her own right. She had a conservative sensibility and was very pretty with wavy light brown hair and striking blue eyes. My father and mother had two children prior to my arrival in September of 1969. My brothers, Cameron and Lloyd George (we call him George), were six and four years my senior, respectively. We lived in a lovely historic home on a quiet street in suburban Bellingham approximately ninety miles north of the city of Seattle. My brothers were closer in age so I was intentionally left out of their fun. But when they were in a tolerant mood, the three of us would play hard and I cherished attention from the big brothers I adored and looked up to as Gods. On cold rainy days we would make elaborate forts outside to shield the cold drips of wetness and we'd play with our big overly utilized yellow metal Tonka trucks in the yard. Cameron would organize everything and after some fierce GI Joe mud battles, he'd sneak peanut butter and jelly sandwiches into our fort and pretend we were camping in a rain forest. We enjoyed our family unit and connection, even though we knew things weren't perfect. Life was slowly getting darker inside the Early home but we looked good from the outside and felt good enough on the inside. We were blessed with good looks and humorous personalities within our immediate collaboration and among our extended families, which was all that anyone was really concerned with anyway.

Our family moved to Seattle when I was six so my father could start his new career investigating disability cases for the State of Washington. He had been a newscaster for various radio stations during my toddler years, but let go of his passion for broadcasting to continue his passion for the bottle.

As our lives evolved, dad became worse with his daily alcohol consumption. He was obviously unhappy and everyone would surely begin to feel his misery by way of a trickle down effect. Every night was a crapshoot as to whether we would get berated and belittled by our increasingly unpredictable father. As the years turned into my pre-teen years and my brother's teenage years, violence in our home replaced our Norman Rockwell portrait. We were no longer the painting that I associated with domestic innocence and humorous family unity. The alcoholic darkness was prevailing and we all knew it yet no one ever mentioned what was really going on. We just went with the flow and looked at each other with constant 'WTF' expressions on our faces. His alcoholic decline was a textbook scenario with no unique characteristics that would redefine alcohol abuse. However, the characters that were met along the way as a result of our journey inspired and contributed to several life changing experiences which began to unfold at my very early age and continue into this present day.

I became afraid of my father as his behavior became increasingly erratic. When I compared our lives to those of my friends and schoolmates, I could see that we were more messed up than most and this was disturbing to my young soul. I felt entitled to a perfect family without the drama of a drunken father and I became angry and opinionated towards him. Was divorce in order? Would Mom leave Dad and take us kids somewhere safe? These scenarios would swirl around endlessly in my still developing brain.

My teenage brother's were known for their good looks. Cameron was tall, had an athletic build and was considered a 'jock' and was popular in High School. George was a bit pudgy and we would tease him relentlessly, "George, George, George of the jungle, *FAT* as he can be!" He grew tired of the insults, joined in on Cameron's physical activities and soon outgrew his baby fat into his own handsome personal design.

Upon entering their teenage years, they began associating with questionable peers, started smoking pot, drinking and being rowdy like most of their friends who came from other everyday families with issues. Their behavior upset my father and he took it personal. Dad thought he could kick their ass into submission and would preach the almighty 'do as I say, not as I do' as loud as his lungs and larynx would permit. He could definitely blow some noise out of his smoked filled lungs. He smoked non-filtered Pall Mall cigarettes and I do not remember a time where he didn't have an extreme hacking cough. It was just part of the norm in our house and Mom smoked too. From the house to the cars, everything smelled like smoke and I couldn't stand being locked up in the car with Dad's chain smoking. He would leave the windows up and the car would fill with white drifting smoke. I am surprised he could see outside the windshield it would get so thick and I wouldn't even consider it second hand smoke. I may as well have been smoking the tobacco out of a bong. The only way to battle this dilemma was to start smoking. My friends and I would steal cigarettes from our parents and nervously inhale, cough and throw up. It was so awful, dizzying and disgusting that we did it again and again and again.

Most of the arguments at home would start with father's brutal comments.

"Cameron, you are a fucking *loser!*" he would taunt my brother for not mowing the lawn properly or for not cleaning his room.

"Fuck you! You are a drunk!" Cameron would respond with his chest in the air, ready for the inevitable fight. Dad would get his fight every time. Cameron and George had graduated into his violent behavior early on, so it wasn't a big surprise when they came right back at him. I thought after getting his ass kicked a few times by his own kids that he would have learned to back off, but his ego and pride would never allow him to fold. The altercations got worse over time and the neighbors began to call the police, who would come with their embarrassing bright red lights spinning - yet do nothing.

At times, I do remember my father as a loving, kind and caring man to his children and wife. He was always intimidating and controlling, but there were moments I would look at him and be in love with the man who was my tallest, most powerful role model. I was proud of my brilliant father and wanted his approval.

From the time we moved to Seattle, I felt him slipping away from us, ever so slowly - yet painfully fast. My biggest problem, already being a needy confused child, was that I didn't *want* my father to love me - I *needed* him to love me. So as he slipped away from our hearts, so slipped my heart from the security and innocence I felt was imminent.

Fights between Dad and Cameron with George sometimes joining in to protect our eldest brother, gradually became the norm. Mom would put our dog Fluffy and I into our Plymouth Volare station wagon and drive around aimlessly, hoping there would be peace when we returned. She had tried her hand at breaking up the fights but it became too much for her. Cameron and George were getting stronger and more experienced in their fight club with dad. Leaving, at least temporarily, was her only alternative. Though I prayed for it every night, I don't think Mom ever considered divorcing him. She was from the generation where leaving the marriage, no matter how bad it got, was not the thing to do. With both sets of grandparents and her seven older brothers and sisters committed to everlasting marriages, divorce was never discussed.

The dysfunction of the Early Family was now just a part of her daily chores and she held her head as high as she could while she co-dependently did her best to take care of her family. Though she wore her 'everything is going to be fine' face well. She too found comfort in drink – especially as the walls began to tumble.

∞∞∞

I found my savior in music. It allowed me to feel, which helped me communicate since we weren't a touchy-feely family. I locked myself in my room, put in my cassettes of Jackson 5, Pat Benetar, Elton John or disco and let myself experience the relative lyrics while learning how to dream outside of the small angry box where I was being raised. I couldn't listen to my happy songs when my brothers were around because they decided disco was for fags.

"Are you a fag, Justin?" they would ask me. "Is that why you're listening to Disco?"

Pictured: Early home, Seattle, WA (Justin in background)

"Um, no, I wasn't listening to Disco," I lied. "And I'm not a fag".

I didn't really know the meaning of fag, but I was taught definitively that fags were *bad*; very, very bad.

Naturally, I wanted to emulate my big brothers whenever they were around because I looked up to them and adored them so much. To avoid the disco drama, I would quickly put on Led Zeppelin and fit right in with my Anglo brothers. I learned that it was less painful to make fun of myself and make them laugh with me rather than have them teasing me relentlessly.

As a young boy I picked up an odd habit that Cameron did most of his life when he would listen to music in his room – 'wiggling my head' is the only way I can describe it. I would lie on my bed, turn the music up loud and wiggle my head repetitively, back and forth to the beat of song.

My mom must have thought I was 'special' when she peaked in to find her youngest boy, rocking and wiggling his head, back and forth relentlessly. I know she was concerned of other things, as I had overheard several discussions of my difference. Escaping and dreaming through lyrics, I had hoped life at home would improve.

I wasn't as masculine as my brothers and was not much into sports. Not that I wanted to wear dresses nor was I having a gender identity crisis. I was just - *me*. I didn't like playing sports – period. I felt comfortable being a boy through and through but the lack of competitive rivalry was problematic and invited homophobic words of hatred that would characterize my young life.

""Faggot!" "Sissy!" "Homo!" flowed freely in my home and culture and seemed to be used frequently in not so secret heated discussions between my parents about me and pertaining to my future. I had never had sex and even though I had been taught what homosexuality was, and how unnatural and wrong it is, I found the word offensive. Especially having it be directed towards or about me. To imply or suspect that I was homosexual without ever being sexual was preposterous and insulting. Sex at this point in my life, was gross anyway. I consciously tried to act more masculine as a result of their grassroots reparative antics.

Mom tried to look after me as best as she could and was much more gentle about allowing me to be authentic. But the loudly spoken law was that my father ruled the house. It angered him when she would try to divert his attention away from me because he knew she was manipulating his anger away from how he wanted me to act. She was extra loving and gave me special treatment. She did what she could to make up for the lack of love from my father and sometimes now my brothers, which made him and them like me even less.

One minute my father would be sitting back in his chair watching Star Trek and the next he would spit out the most offensive remarks toward anyone in his path. If you watched him closely enough, you could see his transitional powers activate beginning with his facial muscles, which would transform to match his internal disgust and distaste for almost everything. He would take his anger out on us and his goal was to humiliate. To make him feel better about him, by making others feel 'less-than' about themselves.

Dad was a classic bully.

As my brothers grew older they would stay away as much as possible but Dad's missiles of verbal abuse didn't need GPS. They found their target every time.

"Loser!" he would blurt out from his chair as I walked by towards the kitchen. He'd take another swig from his cocktail and continue the berating game.

"Who the hell do you think you are? You stupid son of a bitch, you're not *my* son!"

With plans only a ten-year-old could conjure up, I organized my escape. I decided that the next time there was a violent outburst I would go to my favorite aunt's house. I would have went to Nana and Baba's house, but even I knew they were too old now, and Auntie Lynn loved me almost as much as my Nana did. Whenever I was with her an intoxicating feeling of comfort and safety would envelop me. Lynn was my father's younger sister. I felt a connection with her and she empathized with me. I felt protected when I was with her because she made me feel as if I mattered. I was proud that she was my aunt. She was very attractive and classy - yet tough as nails. She had blonde perfectly dyed and styled hair, was thin and beautiful. She had an infectious laugh that made me laugh - which compelled me to love her more. Whenever Lynn was around, Justin was safe. Even my dad knew not to mess with her because she had a little temper of her own.

The time soon came when I simply had enough. On this day I was in the kitchen looking for something to eat. I was staring into the refrigerator when Dad yelled from the other room.

"What the hell are you doing in there?" he lashed out in bully mode.

"Nothin', just looking for something to eat is all."

"Get out of my kitchen!" he screamed.

"I just want to get something to eat!" I snapped back.

"Goddamnit. Did I tell you to get out of the goddamn kitchen? Are you deaf? This is my fucking kitchen and my food! Now get the hell out of there! You will eat when I *allow* you to eat!"

Not wanting to delay the moment, I exploded. I started throwing things at him and he just looked at me dismayed. My brothers came from the other part of the house to try to calm me down, and in total frustration I went after them, too. I felt like I was fighting for my life.

I *was* fighting for my life.

"Justin," Cameron whispered as he held my arm tightly, "You have to calm down. Don't do this, Justin. He is drunk and crazy. I don't want you to get hurt."

I had never seen Cameron fear for me. He too knew that it was the end of the line.

But it was too late.

"Fuck you! *Get offfff meeeeee!*" I screamed while trying to hit anyone within reach of my tiny fists. They pinned me on the ground to restrain me.

My father approached rapidly to pound his fist into my face. It must have felt so good to him, a real relief after ten years of buildup. I could see his immediate regret. We all knew what he did was wrong. I was bleeding and he had hurt me in this painful act of physical violence. He left the kitchen and settled back into his chair in the living room. Instantly, I was now able to finally and fully hate him.

This feeling of betrayal would be imbedded deep in my core.

I knew I was not safe and that my own violent pattern had begun. *What if he gets even more violent and jumps up and hits me again?* I wanted to die when I thought of having to stay any longer.

With brute determination, the sting of his fist and blood still pulsating in my mouth, I moved toward the door. I dared make eye contact with him as he was giving me his 'possessed by the devil' look. I walked quickly and, as he began to get up out of the chair, I shot him my own satanic look right back at him.

I opened the door and walked to toward the street as he jumped up and began to follow.

"If you leave you will not come back! Do you hear me you little faggot?" he said including the epithet to reiterate his power.

"Fuck you!" I screamed back boldly in disbelief.

I felt powerful and for the first time in my life I felt good as I tried to hurt another human with unkind words. I walked about a mile and a half down the hills of Sheridan Heights above Lake Washington to the Lake Forest Park Police station with my bloody mouth and tried to have him arrested. The year was 1980 - a time when police reluctantly involved themselves in domestic issues. They asked if I had anywhere else to go. They called my Auntie Lynn who agreed to come get me.

When I saw her enter through the station house door, I was overwhelmed with relief. I would go away with my savior and then everybody would see how badly my father had been behaving. They would all straighten up and I could eventually go home to a normal family. Or maybe *this* was enough to get Mom to divorce him. Auntie Lynn talked with the officers for a minute and then came over to me.

"You're going to be fine, honey. You can stay with me and your uncle as long as it takes to work this out," she assured.

Just as I started to relax, my angry father burst through the door.

"What the hell do you think you are doing, Lynn?" he began. "You stay out of our goddamn business. This is *my* family business!" he screamed, outraged that she got involved.

He refused. He raged. He would not allow me to be with her. Without his permission, Auntie Lynn had no authority.

My plan was squashed.

This wasn't the first time this had happened. I had been to Lynn's before. I had run-away and I had been told to leave *his* house before.

The police talked with him for some time. They didn't know what to do with me – or him. During the endless moment he was talking with the police, I gathered new strength. "I'm not going with him. I would rather die," I told them in honesty.

"Just take him. There is nothing I can do with him anymore," he said disgusted. Get rid of the problem child. My aunt left, my father left and I was left - alone.

I waited at the Lake Forest Park Police Station for a ride to wherever I was going.

At this point, I wasn't scared or angry. I was relieved.

I didn't know where I was headed but I knew it had to be better than where I had been.

They cry in the dark, so you can't see their tears,
They hide in the light, so you can't see their fears,
Forgive and forget, all the while,
Love and pain become one in the same
In the eyes of a wounded child…

And you shouldn't have to pay for your love with your bones and your flesh…

"Hell Is For Children" – Pat Benetar

Chapter 2

DOWNTOWN

The foster care system was an interesting bureaucracy. At first I didn't understand why all of these good people were taking me into their homes and then acting like they didn't want me there. I had hoped maybe I would get a loving semi-permanent foster family but for months I went from one unwanted situation to more of the same. The other foster kids informed me that some families took foster kids into their homes to supplement their income, or to have income. I became disappointed, disillusioned and highly frustrated and these feelings began to display through my behavior.

If the foster family had their own biological children, it was highly unlikely they would be allowed to associate with the likes of us drifters, and the separation was noticeable and disturbing to me. It was unfair that we would have to be put into a lower 'class' just because our parents didn't want to care for us.

When I walked out of my father's house I knew I had to go somewhere, anywhere, to get away from his virulent words and progressing physical abuse. I thought anything had to be better than home. I would have preferred to go to Auntie Lynn's, or my elderly Nana's though I knew she was too old and fragile to care for me full time. Nana was so fragile that I made a conscious decision not to contact her about recent events. I missed visiting her and watching her face light up whenever I would arrive. She would always come outside onto the porch, give me a huge hug and a kiss and immediately walk me over to her tasty candy bowl. Nana always knew what to say and do to make her grandkids feel special.

I got along pretty well with the other kids and they mostly looked out for me due to my young age. Many of the other kids were African American, which I found fascinating. I was grateful for the opportunity to have this cultural experience especially since the lessons I was taught thus far sponsored passive separation of the races. Nigger, Chink, Fag, Wetback and any other word or gesture that would degrade a person or their people were comically and sometimes seriously utilized, mostly by my father and increasingly by my brothers in household conversations or during a typical spout of road rage. The Early children were being taught passive-aggressive racist beliefs and behaviors.

There was always an alarm within my own spirit that advised me to the inappropriateness of my fathers' behavior towards others. It was only a matter of time before I would have learned to conform to his not so discreet hatred, so it was probably a good thing I got the hell out when I did.

I was tossed around from one troubled situation after another and though I was too young to cope, I somehow always made it to my next home. The families who had the burden feeding and babysitting a ten-year-old with trust issues quickly became exasperated with me and I quickly made sure I didn't fit in anywhere else I was sent. I felt alone and I was developing an inner anger and hatred that began to surface in my behavior. I became unmanageable. I would backtalk my foster parents and social workers in ways I wished I would have my father. Why should I listen to them? I knew their game. They didn't give a crap about me. It was sometimes *too* obvious.

Lost in an abyss of hurt and anger I slowly careened into the worst, most difficult, institutionalized child. It became my new badge of honor and I would continue to refine this skill for as long as I could aggrandize. The worse I acted, the more respect I earned from the other kids. Due to my young age, my repulsive behavior was cute to the other kids and they even encouraged me as a form of entertainment.

It only took a couple months before I had become too much for the foster system as my behavior was out of control. From cussing out the foster parents to destroying furniture I quickly acted my way out of these types of homes.

The next logical alternative for a troubled child such as myself was an institution called The Loft, which was a facility equipped for children with behavioral problems that usually manifested into violent outbursts and emotional tantrums. The Loft was a dormitory style building with the second floor dedicated to troubled youth; north side for boys, south side for girls. This cement palace looked like a convalescent facility and came with a dedicated feelings room; a built-in padded cell equipped with a punching bag that had various sizes of dried blood spots all over from previous raging children.

I would talk back and act out violently often so the staff would tackle me, restrain me and place, force, toss, and throw me into the padded room where I was encouraged to get my anger out on the punching bag and not other humans. I craved the attention I received from making the social workers work hard and they were much more responsive than the bloody bag.

I broke all the rules at The Loft as it seemed more significant. It was my way of showing hatred for rules, hatred for those who make the rules and hatred for the original rule-maker, my father. 'No smoking in the hallway' was simply an invitation as far as I was concerned. Although the minimum age to smoke was 13, they received special permission from my social worker in hopes it would calm me down, or even better prevent me from running away. It was a smart move on their part. Somewhat.

The Loft allotted each child five cigarettes each day. All cigarettes had to be earned by completing chores and by behaving somewhat respectfully. The feel of the smoke entering my lungs, the little buzz I felt and the thought that it would give me cancer made cigarettes all the more attractive.

I would walk boldly out of the dedicated smoking room, down the hall past the staff office with my cigarette prominently in hand and would exhale in the hallway in front of the counselors. "Justin, you know you're not supposed to smoke in the halls, please go back into the smoking room."

I would respond, "Fuck you! You can't tell me what to do!"

That probably would have been enough to make them get my point but ever since I could remember, I never had an OFF-button. I didn't know how to stop. Once I crossed that invisible line, the rage blast was just getting started.

"Shiiiiit, you don't own me, foo! I'll smoke where the hell I wanna smoke!" I would emphasize certain words with a southern drawl so I would sound cool like the black kids. I did learn to restrain my explosive temper enough so I could earn cigarettes. The feeling I got when I smoked felt calming and made me feel like an adult.

I was so full of anger and resentment that I would be unable to control my outbursts for long. These tantrums would escalate until the staff tried to put their hands on me, which was an invitation for war. I would kick, scream, scratch and spit in their faces. Every time they would tackle me and carry me, as I screamed and fought, to the padded cell. Once inside, I would hit the bag until I felt like I was going to pass out. My temper would be so ferocious I would often need bandages for my raw and bloody hands. I wanted to get as much of *my* blood on the bag as I could. I would scream bloody murder at the top of my lungs to the staff that monitored me through the little prison window on the door, "I hate you! FUCK *ALL* of you! I hope you all die *miserable* deaths!" It would sometimes take days for my vocal cords to recover.

Once my tirade of anger was violently merged into the bloody bag, I would emerge from the 'psycho room' refreshed and feeling surprisingly good. My body would produce healing endorphins and I would feel mellow and almost medicated - a calm after the storm. Trained to handle outbursts, the forgiving staff would act like nothing had ever happened, kind of like at home but with nicer people who knew what they were doing. The nice part was they would offer me a Newport cigarette or some candy when all was said and done.

While at The Loft, I met a boy named Kurt, a thirteen-year-old who was much more hip to the runaway street scene than me. I found out his father had been abusive to him, too. It was the first time I got a hint that I was not alone. All the kids in The Loft shared similar problems. We both had a lot of blood on that punching bag. Kurt didn't like The

Loft about as much as I didn't like The Loft, which was probably the biggest thing we had in common.

On a windy partially sunny day in late March, we were talking about how much we needed to get out of The Loft and the next thing I knew, Kurt had it planned. Being only ten years old, I had to defer to his elder brilliance and I was down for anything that would get me out of that hellhole. We decided we would run away from Gasworks Park, an old Gas Refinery on the North side of Seattle's Lake Union, where a group of us were going on a day trip. Once we got there, we scoped it out and were pleasantly surprised when we realized the oblivious counselors were being lazy with our freedom in the park. I noticed a young girl flying a kite with her father and two little boys running around the park playing tag. Other children my age were thinking of nothing but tackling their playmates while my playmate and I waited for the right moment to escape.

The moment came.

Kurt spoke in a serious tone, "Just walk with me normal. Act like we are just lookin' around." I followed his lead and we walked. We didn't look back. We just kept walking and nobody noticed.

It was easier than I thought it would be.

∞∞∞∞

It felt like we were walking forever. I got tired and mad because Kurt walked way ahead of me. I was trying hard to keep up, tagging along as fast as I could.

"Kurt, where the hell are we going?" I asked already tired and frustrated.

"Dude, we're almost there. I got lots of friends. Don't worry about it. Stop whining," he responded unconcerned.

"But we've been walking for two hours," I noted. I was really ticked.

It didn't appear he had a clear plan.

We made several stops along the way to his 'friends' houses, where nobody seemed to live. I was losing faith in Kurt and was beginning to get worried that we would just wander around all night. After I let out another big sigh he said something interesting.

"Don't worry Justin, I can always go pull a trick."

"Fine," I fired back at him, tired and sore from walking. I had no idea what 'pull a trick' meant, nor did I even think or care to ask because I was so tired. The possibility of actually sitting, even for a moment, while he pulled his trick or whatever it was called sounded good. We stopped at a pay phone and thankfully whomever he dialed answered the phone.

We walked back towards where we had come from, across the Aurora Bridge, which spans over Lake Union to the South side. As we approached the first building over the bridge I could see the sign, 'Hillside Motel'.

His friend was waiting for him in a small, dark dingy room in the low budget, run down Motel. The room smelled like mold from the rain and the paint on the walls was peeling. I went in to use the bathroom and it smelled of a urine-mold combination. My family may have been messed up but we were clean and had a nice house. I wasn't used to this blatant deterioration.

Kurt assured me that he would get enough money for a taxi to take us the rest of the way downtown. As tired as I was, I did not want to stay in that nasty room for long.

"We have to do a couple of things," he told me, referring to himself and the old man. "Just be cool and relax and we'll be leaving soon. Just watch TV and don't worry about anything, alright?" Kurt pulled a chair right in front of the television and motioned for me to sit.

"I guess," I said, not too happy about him telling me what to do. The old man didn't say anything, but smiled and stared at me. He grossed me out. I heard them talking about me but their conversation ended with Kurt saying something about me being too young.

I did as I was told and started watching television. I sat there cold, tired and hungry. I couldn't help but notice that something naughty was happening in the bed. I heard moaning noises and could see the bodies moving underneath the sheets. I figured they were doing some stuff they shouldn't be. I couldn't stop thinking, *an old man and a boy*? I had never heard of such a thing. I wasn't sure what grossed me out the most, the sex part or the sound a sixty-year-old makes while inappropriately touching a thirteen-year-old. I didn't know much about sex, but I knew that it was supposed to be between an adult man and an adult woman - period.

They finished their dirty duties and true to his word, Kurt and I immediately left in a taxi. I decided not to say anything about his little tryst. I had learned in my group homes to stay out of other people's business as much as possible. That way I wouldn't get hurt.

But I couldn't stop thinking about the extreme level of wrongness I had just witnessed.

∞∞∞∞

We were let out on the corner of 1st and Pike in downtown Seattle where I saw what would be the symbols of my new home - the big famous clock and a sign for the Pike Place Market. The sun was setting over the Puget Sound reflecting from the ocean water back into the yellow-orange cloudy sky, it was amazing and beautiful.

Life was exciting. I was free from the verbal abuse of my father, free from foster homes, free from group homes and free from rules!

The eventful day was moving into night and I was curious as to how this evening would unfold. I wasn't worried, though. Kurt had it all under control and seemed to have my best interests at heart.

We walked across the street where I saw several older kids congregating in front of a porn shop and strip joint with large neon lights and signs that blinked 'GIRLS, GIRLS, GIRLS'. On the sides of the signs were 'XXX'.

We came up to a small group wearing jeans and ski jackets, most of them smoking cigarettes. They all knew Kurt.

He introduced me to them, Lou Lou, Pinky, Tiny, Little John, White Junior and Black Junior, who seemed cautious and uncomfortable about how young I was. They wanted to know what I was doing there. No one could believe that such a young kid was on the street even though I was only a few years younger than they were.

For a minute I thought they were going to start betting on how old I was and then they did. Pinky guessed thirteen, which made me feel really good. *Someone thinks I'm a teenager?*

It made my day!

Lou Lou, the obvious leader, decided to take control and start her formal investigation.

"Damn man, what are you?" she asked referring to my gender. I wasn't too happy about that question. Whenever my hair grew out it would curl up and people would inadvertently have to contemplate my sex, which really pissed me off. At ten, that was such an offensive mistake. I made a mental note to get a haircut. Lou Lou could tell I was uncomfortable and continued in another direction. "Whatever you are, you are a cute little thing," she said smiling.

I noticed she was missing some of her teeth and thought maybe someone knocked them out. "How old are you?" she asked like a teacher might a new kindergarten student. I looked at her nervously, not sure what to say.

"It's okay, little man. You can tell me."

"I'm ten and a half," I answered trying to disguise my prepubescent high-pitched voice. The whole group started laughing. "And a *half?*" she said with an affectionate giggle. "I'll be sure to note that *half,* little man."

They were still laughing at me, so I joined in. Lou Lou came up and gave me a rough little hug, so I knew she was cool with me. They went back to drinking bottles out of paper bags, and talking with each other. Each of them took turns making sure I knew what or whom they were talking about. I was surprised and pleased how nice they all were and how they seemed to accept me right away. I had never experienced a group of people that were so cool. I just walked up to them that day and I fit in just like that.

A dark skinned boy sauntered up to the group. They all greeted him with deference, like he was somebody important. He bore a close resemblance to Al B. Sure - the good-looking, popular R&B artist of the 80's and 90's. His clean, tight cords and jacket displayed his large frame and I was surprised to find out he was only twelve (and a half). He noticed me immediately and gave me the once over. He looked at me in the face intensely then his face transitioned into an affectionate gentle smile.

Lou Lou made the introduction, "Justin this is my little brother Frankie." I was shocked and disbelieving because Frankie was clearly black.

"What's up," he said with a grin as he caught me staring at him.

Frankie was a serious boy with few words but he smiled sunshine every time he looked at me. His immediate friendship made me feel good.

There was definitely a connection, and I knew we would become fast friends. He was very handsome, confident and sophisticated and I got a good solid vibe from him.

They all talked for a while and I stayed quiet as I observed their roles of who was important. I was trying to figure out where a little kid like me might be useful. Lou Lou and Frankie kept looking at me and engaging me in their conversations.

At the end of the evening, I walked with Kurt to his friend's house on Capital Hill. I was nervous that first night, as I didn't know anyone that well and no longer had the security of the 'bureaucracy'. At least as a ward of the court, I knew I had someone, supposedly, watching over me.

Now I was truly on my own.

I fell asleep wondering what my mother and brothers and even Nana were doing, wondering if they missed me as much and I missed them.

I play the streetlife because there's no place I can go,
Streetlife, It's the only life I know,
Streetlife - And there's a thousand parts to play,
Streetlife - Until you play your life away.

Randy Crawford – "Street Life"

Chapter 3

STREET EDUCATION

Pictured: Justin Early (Credit: Mary Ellen Mark)

I woke up on a smelly over-utilized couch that had endured several rips and stain fading mishaps. The sun was just beginning to focus its rays on the dirty windowsill at Kurt's absent friend's tiny apartment. As I lay on the stinky couch listening to the Capital Hill morning traffic, thoughts of every recent event bombarded my mind. Who knows where his friend was, the apartment seemed more like a crash pad than a personal space as it wasn't kept up very well. My stomach felt uneasy and my nerves were worked as I thought about my new life.

No school. No rules. No family.

This crazy situation wasn't a dream. I had runaway from home in brief intervals but always seemed to make my way back as required by law.

I was no longer *required* to be home. I was *homeless*. It felt odd and I wasn't quite sure how things were going to play out, but the mystery of it also seemed to calm me.

I was in survival mode.

We got up and helped ourselves to a piece of rotten banana and headed down the hill to the Pike Place Market, about a half-mile towards the Puget Sound. Kurt showed me where some of the other kids hung out on Pike Street which was near where I had met Lou Lou and the others the day before. It was too early for them to be out. But there were a few kids hanging around and it was on this first day of total freedom that I met my new friend. She was a petite thing with dirty blond hair longish on the sides and feathered in typical 80's fashion. Her little face reminded me of a porcelain doll. She was so pretty and soft, yet you could tell there was an edge to her. It was clear she had been around these blocks a few times.

"Hey, you are too little to be down here by yourself," she waved a motherly finger in my face.

"No, I'm not," I defended.

"I'm Roberta. I know the drill. Nothin' I say will make you go home," she stated unsurprised.

I concurred, "Nope."

I was trying not to smile but couldn't help it. I could tell she had my best interests at heart and her light adoring energy forced me to smile. The fact was once a kid makes it to this bottom of the barrel community, there is nowhere else to go.

Roberta knew this.

"You gotta have credibility if you're gonna survive on the streets. You need to be 'related' to someone," she began schooling.

"So from now on you are my little brother. People will see you and associate you with me and will look out for you when I'm not around. That's how it works down here."

"I think you should have a new name, too. You probably have warrants for your arrest for being a runaway. What do you wanna be called?" she asked.

"Do I *have* to change my name?" I asked, already challenging the new rules.

Who decided all this stuff anyway? What about these warrants for my arrest?

There was so much to take in.

"You can't really change your name - not legally until you're an adult. It's just a street name. Everybody has one. It keeps the cops confused. How about Anthony?"

"Anthony has a nice ring to it," I agreed.

"Good," she said in business mode. "Anthony Matthew Hayes. You can be called Tony for short. My nickname is Little Bit," she added.

I could see why people called her that. She was very small except her breasts. They were the size of watermelons. I could tell she was popular because every time someone talked to her their eyes would always drift down to her boobs.

With my new identity and my new street sister, I officially became one of *them*.

Roberta paraded me around like a child would a new doll. She gave me a tour of the Pike Place Market where she taught me how to panhandle money for basic necessities such as cheap food, water, and laundry money. Although her nickname fit her physical size, her street smarts and protective attitude made her seem much bigger and older than her fourteen years. I trusted her but I wasn't sure I was safe. I wondered how long her infatuation with me would last.

As the days passed, Little Bit introduced me to her street mom, Marcy, who all the kids called 'Mom'. Marcy was an old twenty-five. She had brown, greasy, frizzy home-permed hair and dark puffy bags under her hazel eyes. She wore tight jeans and a sort of patchwork looking jean jacket with big shoulder pads. She had a muffin top that hung over her tight jeans which was probably the result of too much alcohol and a terrible diet. Her face was a little swollen too, which was also from the alcohol and it seemed to droop, like gravity was working overtime making her look sad.

"He got a place to stay tonight?" she asked Roberta. Then her eyes went down to the Zippo as she lit up a cigarette.

Roberta replied, "Not yet."

"Bring him to my place till he gets his sea legs," she said as she exhaled the smoke. Her voice was low and gravelly and she smelled of liquor.

She turned toward me, coughed and stuck her lighter into one of the patches.

"Call me Mom. Everybody else does," she took a long drag on her Winston and blew it out with another loud exhale.

I was unnerved by the thought of calling this vagrant Mom. Even though my real mom chose to cave to my dad's wishes, I held her in great esteem and I really missed her. I was not about to call this woman anything but Marcy.

I would later see for myself that Marcy had a good heart. There was an entire community of young street kids in Seattle and Marcy was clearly Mother to them all. For some she was all they had. She would visit the kids who ended up in the hospital. Many of them would overdose on drugs or get stabbed or even shot in street fights.

Roberta showed me where most of the street people crashed when they needed to sleep. Some stayed at cheap motels, some slept in abandoned buildings or under a freeway called the Viaduct below the Pike Place Market.

At first I followed Little Bit around, but it didn't take me long to be on my own. I had always felt like a loner so after I learned how to beg money off people to get food, I kept mostly independent. I was the most non-threatening kid on the streets, so people let me crash with them all the time. I was fascinated to hear how the other kids ended up downtown. These narratives became my new bedtime stories. I would provide my undivided attention as I listened to their well told stories taking in all the tales of abuse. The prostitutes would tell me of their 'trick' experiences, boyfriends, pimps and family dramas. I began to feel that I was not alone. In fact, my story did not compare to what many of these children experienced in their still very short lives.

From physical and mental abuse and bullying to outright violent sexual abuse, these children were being hurt constantly and had nowhere safer to turn than these dangerous streets. We shared a unique bond and they were like me more than I would have ever imagined. Every street child had a story worthy of validating their plight and although the scale of their realities varied, they were all horrific. Yet as horrible as all could seem, everyone had light hearts and joked and played and made the best of a very difficult and sometimes heartbreaking situation.

Little Bit and I hung out almost every day and she continued to teach me the most effective ways of panhandling.

"Speak to them nicely at first and get 'em to say hello back. Then go in for the ask," she instructed.

Most people usually had a sympathetic face when they saw a little kid. Once I got them to make eye contact, I went in for the kill.

With a puppy boy, oh poor little me face, I whined, "Excuse me Mister, could you please spare some change so I can get a little something to eat? I'm really hungry."

It worked more often than not.

Roberta's new street name for me didn't stick. Most people just called me Little Justin. I didn't like the 'little' part, but got used to it.

I was happy to be away from my father's wrath and The Loft, but the feelings of being discarded were exaggerated by living on the streets. Everything was new and I knew my life was unstable. I couldn't quite deal with the sensation of being homesick while constantly wandering around aimlessly. I was hyper and had an accelerated amount of energy needing to be unleashed. I was grateful to those who did their best to protect me, but I really missed my family. I would lie in bed (or on a couch/floor/street) and wonder what my family was doing in the exact same moment of each thought. Did they think of me?

Did Nana and Baba know of my situation? Where would this road lead me?

I wondered if I was doing the right thing by being on my own, but I would look at all of the young kids who were just like me and sadly realize - I was exactly where I was suppose to be at this moment in my life.

I was just another Street Child.

∞∞∞

Over the months I built a nice little repertoire of places to sleep. The hookers were not consistent, as pimps and johns would get in the way. But there was also The Donut Shop where some of the kids would hang out during the day and at night. Gunther, the owner, took a liking to some of us and sometimes let me sleep in the basement where he kept a couple of Army cots for the kids with nowhere else to go. Gunther seemed old to us kids - at an incredible thirty-something. He had a heavier build and reminded me of the men on television that played the criminal types. He had a true kindness toward the kids and let us clean tables, do dishes, sweep and mop the floors in order to earn food. The police would come through the Donut Shop every so often and give Gunther a hard time. They believed that he was involved in illegal 'extracurricular' activities, which was exciting to me and gave him a famous credibility among the street kids.

However, my favorite place to sleep was Lou Lou and Frankie's house in the Central District - an area southeast of downtown Seattle that is predominantly African American. From the very first moment I saw Frankie I just wanted to be near him. He had this sense of smart charm that made him seem powerful. He had these soft brown eyes that always appeared to carry kindness. His dark brown skin was attractive to me and I didn't understand why my dad wasn't accepting of other races. The idea of being friends with a black boy made me feel like I was stabbing my father in the back. But that was just a bonus. I loved everything about Frankie from his cocky attitude and smile to the clothes he wore.

The first time I went to his place, he snuck me into the basement so his mom wouldn't see me. The house was large and sat at the top of a hill above the I-90 freeway. The wood siding was rotted and the light grey color faded. The house was not in good condition and was used as a Section 8 rental, a housing program subsidy for parents on welfare. Frankie often took street kids there when they had nowhere else to go.

After a few visits, we walked in and right into his mother who had seen me come up the stairs into the front door. With her fists on her ample hips and red lips pressed together, she stared at us.

She softened a little when she saw how young I was. I couldn't help but notice at how white she was. She was as light as me. She resembled Lou Lou and I could tell by her features that she was also Frankie's *real* mother. Even thought their skin color difference was drastic, there was no denying their shared features.

"Who are *you*, honey?" she asked in a tone one might use when speaking to a toddler.

"Frankie, I don't want you bringing little girls down to your room. I told you that. She's too damn young for you, anyway," she added firmly with a chuckle.

He immediately defended my boyhood, "Mama, he ain't no girl." After another once over she looked back at him almost convinced.

"Oh," she said simply. She walked back toward the living room and then blurted over her shoulder with a laugh, "Sorry, honey. Call me Mama."

I could feel the floors shaking as she walked back to her chair. Mama was a big woman and she had a healthy collection of boyfriends. She spoke with what I thought was a southern accent, but I also noticed most of my new black friends speaking that way too - yet no one was from the south.

Although Mama loved her eight kids, she was not a role model parent. She sold weed and let them run the streets. She was more interested in her men than she was of parenting and had a history of being abused in her relationships. She was usually nice and calm until one of the kids pissed her off. Then she would threaten them, and once me, with a two-by-four she dubbed the 'Board of Education'. She seemed to have control of her house, but the kids walked all over her and did what they pleased. There was not much food in the house as her food stamp allotment only came once per month, so the kids learned to survive away from home. Frankie was the youngest and had been born much later then the rest of the children who were mostly grown and leading their own dysfunctional lives in the welfare system. It seemed everyone was welcome to come to Mama's if they were hungry and she would feed them what she could – even if it was Top Ramen or maybe some cereal with water instead of milk.

After seeing me hang around and getting used to the sight of me, Mama let me stay with them for days at a time. I didn't want to wear out my welcome and would stay at other places in between, but at least I knew I had a place to crash if I didn't have anywhere else to go.

I loved the busy, big family atmosphere. We drank alcohol and smoked her pot and she wouldn't say much as long as we were cool about it. I would hang out downtown during the day where I would panhandle some cash, which helped me contribute to her very limited pantry of food and cheap snacks.

Pictured: Frankie Couch

Growing up I knew nothing about interracial children or differences. I didn't believe Lou Lou was a girl when I had first met her downtown and couldn't understand why she would let herself be perceived as and thought of - as a boy.

She had short hair, boy's clothes and a girlfriend. Her real name was Lou Ellen, which was too feminine for her persona, so everyone called her Lou Lou. All of Mama's grandkids, except one, were racially mixed like Frankie who was Caucasian and black.

Although I really liked hanging with Frankie, downtown was where it was at and was the central communication hub for all street people. Of course there were no cell phones or email, so if anybody wanted to know anything about anybody, they could just go downtown and get the information from somebody else. News always traveled fast and gossip was one of the most interesting ways to pass the time. There was also a pay phone in the middle of the block on Pike Street that accepted phone calls.

It was our house phone.

∞∞∞

I was in Gunther's Donut Shop hanging out playing video games when I noticed a familiar face walk in. For a minute I thought I was hallucinating.

"Come here you little asshole!" he barked in his fatherly language.

I stayed frozen in my spot. I couldn't move. I was terrified. I had almost forgotten the fear that came on me when I saw him angry.

"You're coming home. You are not going to do this to your mother, you little son of a bitch!" he screamed while slapping my face. All hell broke loose when everyone in the Donut Shop heard the *slap!* of his open hand.

Gunther was not about to let anyone touch any of us kids. He shot out from behind the counter, grabbed my father and threw him up against the wall. My other friends ran up to get in on it and started to 'charge' my father, aggressively rendering him useless which prevented him from harming anyone else. They robbed him of his wallet and a tape recorder he had hidden in his coat.

"Run, go!!" Marcy screamed and I followed her instruction. As I ran I saw his car parked a block away and kicked a dent in the passenger door.

I was shaken but was also relieved that my new street friends had witnessed how abusive my dad really was. Marcy witnessed the whole thing and even though I was not one of her formal wards, she was determined to protect me. I didn't know she had run out behind me and was trying hard to catch up.

"Oh my god honey, are you okay?" she comforted as she put her arm around me.

"I'm cool," I said distraught, "I guess."

She didn't believe me and I was shaking.

"Your sister Roberta just went home to my apartment. If you go now, she will be there by the time you get there," she said. She turned me in the direction to walk and shooed me off to her place about 10 blocks away. I was comforted knowing that Roberta would look after me.

When I arrived, Roberta was downstairs waiting.

"Marcy called me from the payphone. Hurry. Get in here in case anyone followed you."

She was more stressed that I was, "Come on, let's get upstairs!"

"I can't believe he did that," I complained, "He hit me in front of everyone." I was humiliated, "Why are they looking for me *now*?" It seemed like an eternity had passed since I left home and then State custody.

"Don't worry about it. You're safe now," Roberta comforted me. She was really good at it.

We talked late into the night. She gave me a few hits of weed and a whole can of beer and I fell asleep with the room spinning.

I felt like I was going to throw up, but at least I knew my family was thinking of me. It was a somewhat comforting thought.

∞∞∞∞

Drugs were everywhere and everyone was doing what they could to get away from their constant reality. It was the eighties and so the favorites were cocaine, heroin, mescaline, marijuana, Ritalin and, of course, the good Old English 800 Malt Liquor, 40-ounce bottle. Wanting to belong in this new tribe, I tried to score drugs, too. At first it wasn't so easy. I couldn't get alcohol because you needed ID, but people would let me drink out of their bottles so I could get a little buzz going. Being everyone's little brother, most of my new friends felt protective, so no one wanted me to get high. But I was determined to be a part of their world. I was persistent so it didn't take long before the joints were passed my way.

Smoking pot and drinking made life on the streets a bit nicer because everything negative or sad was forgotten or at least put on hold. I learned that keeping a buzz allowed me to feel better about the wrongness of my life. It made me a stronger person. Or so I thought.

One of the things that kept life interesting was we would always move around and hangout with different people. Whatever direction the wind was blowing, we would go. So I started hanging out with this girl Pinky who I met with Lou Lou that first day downtown. Pinky was a dark skinned black girl with pink lips. She became a good friend and I begged her to let me shoot Ritalin with her. All of my new friends did some form of drugs and I made a point to try and get in on the action. They were my new role models, so everything they did was something I wanted to do. They were modeling behaviors that could kill me but I still wanted to mimic and do what they did. I bugged her until she finally broke down and gave me a little stuff.

Ritalin is a drug used in young children with hyperactivity disorder but is lucrative on the streets - to the tune of $10.00 per pill. We would crush them up, put water on them, cook them in a spoon and draw the yellow liquid through cotton into a syringe. Once the syringe was prepped, the needle would be placed over a visible vein and inserted until a spec of blood could be seen, then the formula would be pushed inside.

"I can't believe I am giving you this," she said as she prepared to stick the needle in my vein, "Squeeze your arm at the top so the vein pops up." I didn't quite understand what she was instructing me to do, but I must have followed her directions because she put the needle near my skin. I was so nervous I shut my eyes.

I felt a sharp prick and opened my eyes to see her pull the plunger on the syringe back a little. Blood rushed into the plastic tube and she pushed the contents inside my body. Although the rush was slow and not too dramatic, the high was consistent and lasted for a long time. One hit would last for hours.

I only felt a little buzz, as she was careful not to give me much. I was amazed and was so proud to have had this happen and the initial buzz was enough for me to want more. I rolled my sleeves up and went back downtown to show everyone what I had done, proud that I had a track mark on my vein.

Proud, that I too - was a drug addict.

∞∞∞

Selling your body for money to get the drugs was also a normal way of life in my new community. Prostitution didn't really come with a moral stigma, even if you were a boy.

Hooking simply was the best and easiest way to make money. In less than an hour you would be able to make twenty to fifty dollars as compared to panhandling where you would only rake in about three or four bucks. Panhandling was okay for odds and ends or a quick bite to eat, but this more intimate line of work was a gold mine. A couple of hours could bring in a hundred dollars. That was a lot for an almost eleven year-old. I wanted in on the game. I didn't know what I was in for, but I asked my sister if she would show me how to get into the business.

"No, Justin. You are way too young," she spoke firmly.

"That's not fair. Everyone else has lots of cash and no one thinks anything about how they got it. You guys aren't so old, either. C'mon Roberta. Let me make some money, too."

She eventually realized that I would need to survive like anyone else and reluctantly agreed to discuss the matter.

I didn't even know that much about sex.

Roberta decided that she would be the best teacher if I was going to work the streets, which was a few block radius in downtown Seattle between 1st and 2nd avenues and Pike and Seneca Streets. This area was above the water and below the busy city.

"All you have to do is walk around until someone looks at you and drives slowly," she told me in educator mode. She took the prostitution game very seriously.

As we continued to walk I got my first bite.

"He's looking at you, Justin. I've seen him around before. He's cool," she assured me, "but don't do too much with him, you understand me? You are too young."

She was my oldest current role model and I listened closely like a sixth grader would when getting the low down about entering middle school. I trusted her more than anyone.

Although I was nervous at first, this was my new life and I had to do what the others did in order to survive.

The guy in a rusty looking Comet pulled over. Roberta stuck her head in the door first and spoke to him. "Hey," she said as she peeped her head up and down the street for cops.

It was an unusually warm evening for early June and the old man behind the wheel had on a dirty white T-shirt and jeans. He must have known her. "What's happenin? Roberta? Right?" he asked while stretching his neck to get a better look at me. She ignored that he mentioned her name, "You want him?" she nodded my direction. "Yeah, okay," he confirmed. I could see he didn't have all his teeth.

"Look, he's new and we are all watching out for him. No nasty stuff and *no* penetration." I got in the car and he drove to a secluded area where it would be hard for the police to see us. It was awkward at first, as I didn't know what to do. He leaned close to me and asked, "Can I kiss you?" I was sickened and began to do what Roberta told me to do.

Finally he started to tremble. I knew what we were doing was wrong. It felt and seemed naughtier than I thought it would be.

I wasn't impressed and made sure his nasty white lava didn't touch me.

"Just pay me so I can go. I'll walk back," I demanded, trying to sound professional while avoiding the perverts face. He handed me my cash and I leaped out of the car. As I walked back to Pike Street, I told myself that I was only doing what was required to survive. I was just being like everyone else which helped rationalize it in my mind. I soon found that little boys could make a lot of money. There was an underground network of pedophiles in Seattle and they all knew where to find us kids.

Soon thereafter, I was introduced to a photographer who liked to take photos of little kids – very little kids – and he paid me generously to pose for him in his studio. That money was even better and I didn't have to do anything. I just posed for him - without any clothes.

Every few weeks he would pick me up and take hundreds of pictures at different secluded locations. It was a great gig that didn't seem to have any foreseeable negative consequences.

Sometimes at night he wets his bed
As you stay playing tricks inside his head
He waits so cold, for a longer life,

There's no one here tonight…

"Little Boy Lost" – Madonna

Chapter 4

BROKED

It was September and I was about to turn eleven. I had been feeling a little melancholy missing my mom and it was longest time I had gone with seeing her or my Nana. I wasn't expecting any big to-do about my birthday, but Roberta who was now in the eighth month of her first pregnancy, told me she was going to take me clothes shopping. Her maternal instincts were probably kicking in and I was flattered by her kindness. She made me feel special. We walked up to The Bon Marche' department store and headed to the Junior Boy's section to start shopping.

"You like these pants?" she asked as she held up a pair of Britannia Jeans.

"I do like them. They look like they'll fit, too!" I replied excitedly.

She began to roll them into a little ball. "Here," she whispered, "put this under your coat and follow me out. Don't look crazy. Just be cool."

I couldn't believe it. She was making me steal my own birthday present. I had no problem turning tricks, but I didn't like the thought of getting caught by some big ass security guard who would make sure that I spent the rest of my life locked up in the other Junior Boy's section of the youth detention center.

Nonetheless, I followed her lead and we walked out of the store and up the street.

I guess the sight of an eleven-year-old boy and a 14 year-old pregnant girl looked innocent enough because we simply strolled away.

She turned to me with a big, infectious smile, "Happy Birthday!"

That was the last time I went 'shopping' with Roberta.

Six months on my own and I thought I was a little tough guy. Although I did things to make sure people knew I was a boy, some men thought I was a girl when they picked me up. I hadn't had a haircut since I left The Loft and I was still so little. All kinds of kinky men drove around itching to be with a little girl, and when they realized I was a boy, most of them just proceeded as though they wanted it. After all, I was already in the car. I suppose it didn't matter what I had in my pants. I didn't care if they mistook me for a girl anymore. It was all about the money for me, and all about the underage little child for them. Of course, there were the ones who just wanted everything and I would have to tell them no. I made it very clear that I was much too young to have that happen, and that the older kids watched closely to make sure I was okay.

After hearing all the stories of girls getting raped, I thought of myself as lucky and invincible. I was a miniature tough guy.

Even though minor crimes such as stealing, panhandling and soliciting - which is the most sacred and compromising to ones body and soul, was a normal part of survival it always felt weird. At first I was just doing what I was taught, and being naïve. I really didn't think much about all of the long-term consequences. It was a very impersonal activity for the men. To them, I wasn't much of a person. But after several months of being nothing more than a plaything for a wide range of pedophiles, it started to get to me. I wondered why those men were doing such things – then having the nerve to try negotiating our monetary value to bargain basement prices!

Is everyone so selfish when it comes to sex?

I really had no definable sexual orientation and never really had the time or a safe enough environment to contemplate my own *personal* physical and spiritual design. I was in a strange position because, though I tried not to consider solicitation as sex, I was beginning to feel dirty doing it.

October in Seattle can be cold and damp – especially at night. I was walking on Union Street with my friend Tiny when I noticed a Gold Ford Granada pull into the alley. The male driver motioned me over. "He must be looking for a boy," Tiny encouraged. I split from her and got in the car to ask the man what he was looking for.

"Are you a boy?" he asked.

"No shit," I said with a bit of an attitude.

"Why? You want a girl?" I asked, thinking that I could hook him up with Tiny and make a few bucks in the process.

"Either. It doesn't matter to me," he grinned. There was something strange about his response, but it wasn't entirely out of character for a pedophile to not care of the gender of the child. "Are you a cop?" I asked suspiciously.

"Do I look like a cop?" he shot back with a nervous smirk. I wasn't in the mood for bullshit so I started to get out of the car.

"Whoa, hold on buddy. I'm Mike. I am looking for a boy. You, actually," he replied with a warm tone to his voice.

My street instincts were activated, but I really needed the money and wanted a hot meal and to sleep in a warm motel room. I stayed in the car and continued to chat with him. We talked about sex and money and I was relieved because I knew a cop wouldn't have had that conversation with me. He drove up the street to the parking lot and I started to get nervous. "Where are we going?" I demanded.

"I just have to drop something off in this garage. It will only take a second."

He's going to kill me and drop my body off in a dumpster.

I got dizzy as we went three, four floors up the circular structure to the garage roof. As soon as the car reached the roof I saw three cop cars.

"You are under arrest for soliciting prostitution. I'm Detective Mike Murray with the Seattle VICE Unit. This is a little unusual, I must admit," he added. "I've never arrested a young boy before. I would hate to be your parents right now," he chuckled as if it was funny. The other cops were outside talking about me - the criminal they had just arrested. They seemed more amused than they did disturbed. I was the youngest male child ever to be arrested in Seattle and probably the United States though I was too young and innocent to be proud of such an achievement. I had definitely crossed an invisible line between good and bad, and I felt that there was no turning back.

I was a criminal.

I was brought to the main vice unit where my picture was taken and put on the 'wall of shame' along with other mostly female pictures. I knew most of the women on the wall, which included several Polaroid versions of Roberta. Once arrested, the vice unit knew to look for those same offenders and would put their pictures in the visors of their police cars. I was disturbed at the thought of having my picture on a wall full of hookers. Even on the streets, prostitution was not a cool crime to be arrested for.

I thought I was going to die of embarrassment.

I was transported to the Youth Detention Center. The authorities called my parents, who refused to come and get me. Of course my dad would refuse to come and get me, he hated me. And the fact that he had been strong-armed by a group of my friends at Gunther's donut shop didn't help either. Then I realized that this arrest would really hit him in the gut.

Good. I wanted him to feel the shame. Embarrassing him was the only way I felt I could get back at him for what he had done to me.

The next day the Detention staff at the youth center showed me an article that had been printed in the newspaper. On the front page read: 'Eleven year-old Boy Arrested for Prostitution'. Although my name was not mentioned, everyone on the streets knew who it was. I wondered if everyone at home would too.

I would be more careful not to get caught again.

∞∞∞

After my arrest the police who patrolled the downtown beat knew me well and looked for me. It must have bothered them that I was so young because they were kind to me more often than not. Especially Officer Cee Cee. She was well known for being a real bitch and was very tough for a little cop. She rolled solo or sometimes with her partner Officer Benson, and usually gave the older kids a hard time.

After my bust, it was like she was looking for me. She would force me into her car, un-cuffed but with the back doors locked. I didn't have any warrants so there was nothing else she could do but make me drive around with her. I knew in my heart she was trying to help me by not letting me roam the streets, but she was interrupting my cash flow. Sometimes she bought me food and while we ate she told stories of her arresting criminals. Perhaps she was trying to scare me, but I sort of liked being with her and hearing her tales. She made me feel special.

I experienced feminine nurturing from a policewoman.

∞∞∞∞

Family life continued on the streets and was unfolding as it would in a typical household. Roberta continued to work the streets until the end of her pregnancy. As her belly got larger, the dates got hotter. There were a lot of tricks that got off on having sex with a pregnant woman, or in this case, a pregnant child.

She was determined to keep her baby. I can attest that nurturing was in Little Bit's DNA. She was already in love with the little one residing in her uterus and was trying out

names on me. "What about Amber for a girl and Lonnie for a boy?"

I raised an eyebrow – not knowing if she was kidding or not, "Lonnie?"

"Yeah. Lonnie Lamont," she confirmed.

"I like it with Lamont," I told her honestly.

"Anyways, it's probably going to be a girl. I can't wait. Marcy said I can keep her with me at her place," she said.

This kind of life did not lend itself to raising a child whether you had a roof over your head or not. I wasn't sure how Roberta thought she could pull it off, but what did I know about these things? Roberta went into the hospital to have her first baby and, soon after her son Lonnie Lamont was born, she was pregnant again.

Pictured: Roberta Hayes

As well intentioned her thoughts, she wasn't able or capable of keeping any of her kids. They were remanded into foster care and eventually adopted once it was clear to the authorities that she wouldn't be demonstrating parental capabilities. It was a sore subject for her and was hard to talk about. The only time I really saw her cry was when she spoke about her babies. Life was in-session and all of this unacceptable behavior and bullshit was all becoming normal to me.

Deep inside I knew my world was turned upside down. Getting high and getting arrested was now the norm. Sitting in a warm living room with a happy family was out of the question. The only way to handle it was to up my drug and alcohol intake, which had slowly become my only available solution. The bonus was that I could hurt my family by becoming an even bigger dope fiend and I now had a lot of new role models to show me the way.

Only the young can say, they're free to fly away
Sharing the same desires, Burnin' like wildfire…

They're seein' through the promises
And all the lies they dare to tell
Is it heaven or hell?

They know very well…

"Only the Young Can Say" – Journey

Chapter 5

FRANKIE

I was panhandling during the mid afternoon, when I saw this man walk straight towards me. I flashed him the sad eyes and, instead of giving me change, he put out his hand and introduced himself, "Hi Justin. I'm Tom and I work for Youth-Care."

I shook his hand but really didn't feel like engaging with another 'professional'.

YouthCare was a non-profit agency that provided many services for homeless youth and helped the street kids out with clothes, food, outreach and emergency housing, which I really didn't need or want. He said that he had been observing me for a time and that some of the older kids were worried about me because I was so young. They thought it was too dangerous on the streets for a little kid. "Everyone is really concerned about your safety," he said overly concerned.

I appreciated his concern but was too late for me, "I am doing fine on my own. Can't you tell?" I responded in a cocky tone flashing the new clothes I had just bought with my hard earned money. Tom was in his late twenties and had a bit of a receding hairline. He wore little round glasses and looked educated. He was a gentle and persistent man and had a way about him that made a person feel comfortable.

Sometimes he'd bring big garbage bags of clothes for us kids. He and several other outreach workers were committed parental figures to us kids.

They wanted to help the helpless.

Tom hadn't intended on working as an outreach worker. He had volunteered a couple of times and couldn't believe what he saw. He wanted to make a difference and ended up taking a job for the agency he volunteered for and it turned into a career of passion for him.

Tom took me to lunch and started working on me. He wanted to help me go home to work things out. I told him it was too late for that, but he didn't believe me. They never believed me. Many of the outreach workers were nice, but it always amused me when they thought they had some kind of magical fucking powers. But I guess when you see someone so young living this kind of life you have to believe in miracles.

I may have been young, but I didn't *feel* young. After earning my own way around town for a year and a half, no one was going to tell me what to do.

Tom came around often and never gave up on me. He absolutely refused to believe that my parents didn't care about me or want me in their home.

"If you want to drive out and meet my parents, we can do it," I said giving in. Knowing well in advance what the result would be. Even though I hated the idea of going there, I let him take me to North Seattle on the condition that he brought me back downtown when his magical outreach powers didn't work.

We pulled into my parents' driveway and before we even got out of the car, my father came outside screaming, "Get the hell out of here, you assholes! Stay away from my house!"

"Mr. Early, I just want to talk to you and Mrs. Early about your son and his situation. He is living on the streets, which are very dangerous. And I thought…"

My father cut him off, "You thought wrong! He is not welcome here! That little faggot will not live in my house! He is a criminal! Get the hell out of here and take that little son of a bitch with you!"

I knew my father hated me, but sometimes forgot how much as I walked through my new life. It was good when others witnessed the sad truth of it. It was validating. When other people saw how much my dad despised me, I felt vindicated in my decision to run away. I was gloating too because I had told Tom what would happen if we went home and now he believed me. "Justin, I am so sorry. I have never experienced such hatred while doing this work. If you want, I can help get you into a good group home, one that you like," he said disappointed.

"No thanks. Just take me back downtown like you promised." I wasn't sure if Tom had noticed, but my dad had begun to pull out his gun. I saw it, but didn't want to scare an already traumatized Tom.

He drove me back to the streets and my new extended family. He made sure to tell everyone downtown what happened with my father, knowing it would give me a little more credibility with them. And he told the older ones to continue to watch over me.

I went to my favorite spot and whenever I stayed at Mama's I would sleep in Frankie's bed, as he would usually be with his girlfriend. I secretly missed him. He was bright and funny and I was developing a crush, which was foreign to me. I didn't really care to understand this attraction to my friend. If I could have made it go away, I would have. I could not.

I was already asleep when Frankie slipped into the bed with me. I felt the warmth of his body and immediately liked it. My heart began to beat when he moved in close to me. I turned over to let him know I was awake and we started talking.

"How've you been doing?" he asked touching my face.

"Things are cool," I said, not sure what I was supposed to be doing. I wanted to get closer, but my body was already pressed against his. My heart was beating fast.

"You know you can always come here," his voice drifted as he moved his face towards mine. He lips rested on mine and we finally began to kiss. His lips were full and soft. I felt a sense of relief. I needed to feel this with him. He cared about me and needed intimacy as much as I did. I admired Frankie and wanted to be close to him, emotionally and physically. But it was weird because we were friends. Hard-ass street kids shouldn't be sharing an intimate kiss either. It was all very confusing to me. If there were anything that I could have done to make this vulnerable feeling go away, it would have been done.

He confessed to me that he was bisexual and made me commit to secrecy. I didn't mind keeping this quiet 'cause I didn't want anyone knowing my secret, either. But I was comforted knowing that this was something special that Frankie and I secretly shared.

I could think of nothing else for weeks. We'd see each other and behave like everything was normal, only I felt different. It was obvious that I liked him, but I couldn't let anyone know how much. We would try to connect with each other, either with looks or a planned trip to the store where we would pull over to spend some time alone. I didn't think about having to put our relationship in a category. There was no room for gays on the streets. Anyway, we weren't gay. Frankie had a girlfriend and I was trying to find one. He accidentally became the most important presence in my life. He was sensitive to my feelings. He knew not to be intimate with anyone else in front of me. I was honored that he respected me. He was a prankster too and kept me laughing all the time.

I told him I wanted to grow faster – into, let's just say 'manliness'. I was twelve and my body was not changing fast enough. Still so inexperienced and innocent, I listened to Frankie on how to handle my urgent situation. "Blueberry yogurt. Eat lots of it. It will also make you grow body hair faster," he said as if it was well known fact and that it was my guaranteed shortcut to manhood. He kept a straight face and I believed his funny prank for some time. Trustingly, I ate as much Blueberry yogurt as I could stomach. I knew one thing above everything else, my boy Frankie cared about me.

∞∞∞

The weekends were the busiest downtown, rain or shine. All the perverts came from the outskirts of Seattle to get their little kiddies for the evening. Fridays and Saturdays were guaranteed moneymaking nights. These nights were always challenging to negotiate as the pimps and child traffickers would try to claim us, and our money. I always seemed to manage keeping to myself by remaining somewhat discreet – but I always had to watch my back. Evil was everywhere – and we all knew it.

After we would make some cash for the night, we would head up to a nightclub located on the outskirts of downtown called The Monastery. Frankie, Lou Lou, Tiny, White Junior and Little Bit would meet there and we all would hang out in the parking lot with a bunch of other kids. No one was old enough to get in, but we partied harder than the folks inside, and had a great time in the process. We medicated ourselves with drugs and alcohol, which was the only device that made us not feel the pain of the normalcy we knew we were missing in our young lives.

White Junior was always coming up with something new for us to try like MDA, an ecstasy-like designer drug. People who had cars and vans hosted lots of separate parties, so different scenes and different drugs were happening at the same time in the parking lot. The police would come through and try to disburse the crowds, but we would come right back and start where we had left off. Though I liked how the drugs made me feel numb, I did not like how I felt the next day. These poisons were clearly not easy on the human body and the only way to get past the hangover was to do some the next day – and everyday thereafter.

The club and the scene inside intrigued me. I heard it was brimming with sex, drugs, disco, fags and freaks and I wanted to see it all for myself. The building was an old church that had been renovated into a club. The main chapel was the dance floor and the steeple that rose into the sky was supposedly the bedroom of the owner, Jorge.

I had heard that Jorge was into young boys and I tried to get at him several times for money, but apparently I was a little *too* young because he never paid me any attention. After several months I made friends on the inside and it wasn't long before I got them to sneak me in the back.

I was amazed at the interior of the building. It was dark and seedy and I loved it. The booming music… Sylvester, Divine, Lime, Chaka Khan and Rick James blasted out of the speakers that were as big as the cars. The disco lights were wired to a keyboard and each key made the lights on the dance floor do something different. It was amazing to watch the process of the disco - people being uninhibited, dancing and laughing. There was an enigmatic sense of acceptance and respect in the club world. You could be anything you wanted and it was fine. You could be yourself.

In the basement of The Monastery, where the Sunday school used to be, several rows of airplane seats were set up in a theatre style viewing room where interesting clips of pornography and classic movies played. In the early morning at closing time as the sun had begun to rise, I was feeling pretty good that I had actually managed to maneuver the entire night without being seen or kicked out by Jorge. Then I noticed him walking up to me with a smile on his face.

"I tell you what," he began, "I'm obviously never going to win with you so why don't you stick around and help clean the club? I can pay you and you can earn your sneaky little ass some money - the right way." I couldn't believe he was talking to me, let alone offering me a job. He pointed me in the direction of the cleaning crew and I started helping that morning and every weekend after. He still kicked me out during the peak hours, but I didn't mind since most of my friends were in the parking lot anyway. He let me back in at closing time to clean and paid me cash. I really liked making money without compromising my personal properties.

∞∞∞∞

On one of those wild nights in the parking lot, Frankie and I were enjoying our friends, having some good laughs when I got the feeling that something more was happening between us. He was paying extra attention to me and I was taking it all in. Then our DJ friend Brad came out and offered to help us sneak into the club. We followed him through a maze of people and before we knew it we were in the main building. The club was packed tight with bodies, so it was easy for us to maneuver without getting caught. As we made it to the dance floor, I looked Frankie in the eye and pulled his face to my lips. "Don't start nothin' you can't finish," he said with a half smile on his face. He guided me upstairs where there were booths overlooking the dance floor and shut the door behind us. We were alone - not at Mama's, not with friends.

Neither of us could say any words that referred to sex.

For being so respected as a tough ass kid on the streets, Frankie was very gentle and kind.

I knew all about the stigma of gays and how they were treated. Kids on the streets made fun of them, people like my father hated them, and most of the world didn't want to understand them - now I was about to be one of them. Many times I had said things or agreed with people that had made bigoted statements even though I had never had an attraction to females. Socially, it was more acceptable to be with someone of the opposite gender, even though there would be no fulfillment. When I thought of how I would be hated if I told anyone, I decided that it would be our secret. We were doing something that I had been taught was wrong, but in a very natural and unexplainable way, it felt right.

On this night my secret love would be defined.

∞∞∞

As the year went on I fell in love with him. The way he impersonated Grand Master Flash was comical. He thought he was the flyist rapper on the west coast but couldn't remember the lyrics, so he would make up his own to replace them. He was funny and charming – and he knew it.

Our supposed one time thing became a regular affair. It was hard to find the right time and place to express ourselves and even harder to keep it a secret. When we did find the time to spend together it was special. The intimate times with Frankie were like nothing else in my world. Until Frankie, I had no idea what it felt like to be intimate with someone. The environment in which we were growing up did not provide a trusting atmosphere. I had no problem trusting Frankie and he gave me game and showed me other ways besides being naughty, to make money.

Although Frankie and I messed around, we didn't associate it with any moral stigma. We enjoyed being around each other and it felt good. Lou Lou was gay and it was fine for her. She would kick your ass if you weren't cool with it. I was taught early on that being anything other than straight (and white) was wrong. Frankie was a loving presence and respected me, how could that be wrong?

The more I was with him, the more intense my feelings became and although I never admitted much, it was obvious to Lou Lou. I was completely infatuated and she was hip to our playful script. My loyal and protective Lou Lou said nothing to rock our boat. Frankie was the most beautiful human being I had ever met and he wanted to kick it with me.

So we did.

Captured effortlessly, that's the way it was,
Happened so naturally,

I did not know it was love.

"Ain't Nobody" – Rufus/ Featuring Chaka Khan

Chapter 6

HOTEL RUNAWAY

The police presence in our downtown community was getting intense as young runaways and prostitutes were being reported missing and soon thereafter bodies were being found in a remote area outside of Seattle near the Green River. 'The Green River Killer' as the killer was dubbed, sought out and strangled young vulnerable women. Runaways were more vulnerable for this predator as they were disconnected from family and loved ones and harder to trace and identify. The detectives of this new task force were everywhere and even though they didn't want us in trouble, having them around made everyone feel anxious. They were still cops. Cops were not our friends.

Social workers and judges had tried to keep me in the group homes but I wanted no part of their institutionalization. If anything, I preferred to be locked up in detention. If I was sent somewhere without locks and bars on the windows, I rarely stayed more than two days. Every time I ran away, a warrant would be issued for my arrest and so the vicious cycle would turn.

During this period of time in the early 1980's, thanks to the Green River Serial Killer and over-zealous police protection, people were looking for reasons to get me and other children off the streets. After a while the cops figured it was easier to put me in the Youth Detention Center. I felt like a successful juvenile criminal when I went to detention, but the down side was the staff weren't as nice as the counselors from the group homes. Due to my age I was put in the 'Junior Boys' section that housed children up to thirteen-years-old.

I had no fear of this serial killer and was pretty sure he was only after women and girls since all of the bodies being found thus far were female.

The cells in detention were small like in prison. There was a metal frame bed built into the wall with a hard and a heavy fireproof mattress that was as firm as the cement floor. The sink was a tiny metal bowl with two metal push buttons, HOT on one side and

COLD on the other. Only the cold worked. It was built into the wall so no one could destroy it. The larger metal bowl that was lower to the floor with one push button was the toilet. The lighting in the cells was controlled by the guards from a master panel switch at the front security office and went off at 10:00pm sharp. Even if I was reading, they went out and a faint blue nightlight would then illuminate the cell so the guards would be able to see the young prisoners during their security checks. The doors operated by automatic locks and the guards would buzz you out when it was time to leave the cell. I noticed that several other kids had carved their names into the walls and I became inspired.

So I too carved on the wall - *'Little Justin – 1983'.*

I was bored as hell in my cell when Doug, a guard with a mean streak came walking by. "Hey, you little piece of street shit. You like it in here don't you?"

Actually I did but I wasn't going to admit it to this jerk. It was safe and they fed me. I would prefer to spend more time out of my cell but stability came with a price.

"Fuck you!" I jumped off the bed and ran up to the window. He turned on his heels and came right back to my cell.

"You're just a little prostitute faggot. A waste of time and space."

I became enraged, "Yeah? Well, you're a fucking prick!" I didn't need anyone to remind me I was a piece of shit. My dad did a pretty good job and now I was doing an even better job.

Doug called for back up and opened my door, a big mistake on his part. I darted toward him and with every ounce of available fluid in my throat and mouth I hurled a huge wad of thick spit on his face. I stepped back towards my bed and wondered what he was going to do. Without much pause, he came in and grabbed my neck in a headlock. I could see phlegm hanging from his beard. This guy was just about as crazy as me but he was supposed to be the adult, a role model.

What a bunch of bullshit.

"You little piece of shit! You need to learn how to act!" he squeezed my neck harder - choking me. "Fuck you!" I managed to squeal.

I was taken aback by his obvious hatred for me. He kept going, "You don't belong here, you piece of shit! You're going to SPU and you can rot there!" He spit on me like a maniac, several times on my face with some of it going into my mouth. By this time several other counselors were congregating around my cell and telling and even yelling at Mr. Doug to calm down. They handcuffed me and took me to The Dungeon – the Special Programs Unit (SPU). That meant total isolation. Kids slept on the concrete floor with just a blanket. I was not allowed out of the cell for any reason. Communication with staff was through a slot in the door that was intended for the meal trays. No books, no nothing.

After three days of isolation I began to feel sorry for myself. I had been wound up and ready for a good fight that night, but I was not willing to take the punishment like a man. I hated the authorities – and SPU. I knew the rules at the Youth Center, but my bad temper didn't take that into consideration once the spit fight began.

The only other human I got to see beside the detention staff at the Youth Center was Tom, my outreach worker who had a special clearance for jail facilities.

"This is no place for a human being, let alone a child," he whispered through the tiny hole in the door, "I do not agree with this punishment. I think it's cruel and everyone who knows me knows how I feel." He was a very vocal opponent of the section where I was residing.

"Can you bring me some cigarettes?" I asked. "Absolutely not! I would lose my jail clearance and my job," he laughed.

The next day he pushed a little candy bar through the door. I knew Tom cared and although I appreciated his presence, I would have never have known how valuable his work would be in the scope of my life.

While in SPU, I would plant myself on the floor near the door and listen to what people were talking about. I was pleased knowing how mad I had made Doug when I spit that huge spit wad in his beard. I had never seen a guard react like that and was rather proud for making him lose it. Every time I got put in the Youth Center, I made it my personal mission to mess with people to see if I could get them to break. The counselors that were not on my side became my target.

Doug was a job well done.

Aggression was the automatic way of coping with the feelings of abandonment that I carried. No one was available or able to teach alternative ways for me to handle unease or conflict. Honestly, street kids are not looking for a logical or peaceful way out of an argument. If anything rubbed me the wrong way, my first response was an at least seemingly violent reaction, whether it be going off on someone verbally or throwing a physical tantrum. That's just the way life was.

Or so I was being taught.

∞∞∞∞

After I got out of The Dungeon, my new parents - the judge, a probation officer and a public defender - decided that the streets were too dangerous for me. Seattle was getting a reputation for a massive population of children living on the streets. We were breeding like the Gremlins! Kids just kept coming and coming, from everywhere and there were so many new ones I could hardly keep up with their names.

There was a killer on the loose, kids were dying from overdoses and suicide and since I always managed to end up right back on Pike Street, they thought it best to send me to a Boy's Home - far away. This particular Boy's home was 300 miles from Seattle.

I was escorted to the airport by a female probation officer. I felt like a murderer riding in the State vehicle with my hands handcuffed behind my back. The probation officer soon decided I was a pretty good kid and removed the cuffs prior to my boarding the flight, which made me feel a little better. But I thought it was interesting that I was being handcuffed even though I hadn't committed any crimes. I was technically a runaway – but handcuffs?

When I arrived in Spokane, there was a man and young boy waiting to take me to my new home. The three of us stayed quiet during the first portion of the drive. I had no choice but to listen to country music, which was playing from the old trucks' raspy AM radio. I could not believe this was happening to me. I was on my way to a boy's camp in the middle of winter, where it snows and I didn't even have winter clothing.

"I don't think this is gonna work for me. I don't even have a coat. It's freezing here," I said with an attitude as if this guy was going to turn around and say, *'Ok, let's turn back...'*

"Don't worry. We have a clothing room with used clothes, and I'm sure some will fit you," explained the creepy man who I couldn't help but think was having sex with the invisible boy riding with us in the truck.

After a quiet two-hour drive, we pulled up a dirt road that was covered by snow and drove for another few miles until I saw the sign. *Boysville Youth Logging Camp.*

This was bad, *really* bad. *A logging camp, are you kidding me? God hates me.* Just when I thought it couldn't get any worse.

I like bright lights and cars and people and activity. I don't like cows and horses unless they are on TV or in a parade on big city streets. My mother was a country girl. I want nothing to do with a community of people that all look alike. I need some diversity, especially now with the people I know and the experiences I have already endured.

I already missed the streets and my friends. Frankie, Lou Lou and Roberta meant the world to me and now I'd been shipped off to some isolated youth camp in the middle of nowhere. I started planning my escape before I got out of the car.

I was led to my room and introduced to my new roommates. A heavy black boy winked at me and gave the impression he was a little too happy to meet me. I had heard what happens at these homes. Boys get raped and forced to do unspeakable things and don't get paid for it.

I was led around the camp and given the tour. It was actually a very nice facility.

As I was being shown the cabin where I would be sleeping, I noticed a package of pills in one of my roommates' cupboards. Diet Pills. Fat boy clearly needed them but my intricate plan was much more important. If he hadn't lost weight by now he probably wasn't going to.

When no one was around, I popped all the pills and threw the box on the ground so someone would find it. When I heard my roommates walking towards our room, I lay on the floor and the show began.

Curtains up!

"*Helllllllp*," I whimpered as the door opened. I was laying on the floor in a fetal position. "I can't breathe. Get help, pleeeease."

"He took my fucking diet pills!" the fat boy flustered, "Shit! I'm gonna be in so much trouble!" I was not feeling sorry for him and I knew he was up to something when he winked at me. At least now I could avoid any unwanted advances from his gay ass.

"Just let me die," my voiced drifted in award winning fashion.

Drama.

With attempted suicide they had no choice but to take me to the hospital, which was about twenty-five miles away. We left the facility but to my disappointment we headed further away from Spokane. There was not much the doctors could do for a caffeine overdose, but because I kept saying I wanted to die, they had to keep me overnight for observation. The staff from the camp had to go back to work, which was perfect. I woke up early the next morning, put on my clothes and jumped the ten-foot drop out of the hospital room window. I ran up to the main road where I started hitchhiking determined to get back to Spokane so I could start my journey back to my family in downtown Seattle. I was cold, lonely and couldn't believe that my life had come to this. What I did have, however, which had come in very handy so far, was a manipulative personality combined with an innocent-looking demeanor. This asset would help me more than I ever thought possible.

I got a couple short rides from the hospital, as people weren't traveling all the way to Spokane. The third was the charm. A young, attractive couple picked me up. Not only were they going to Spokane, they wanted to hear all about my story.

Second scene…

I reported that a mean judge put me in a boys' home, hundreds of miles from my home and I was going to go back to my poor parents.

The woman spoke softly, "Why don't we call your parents and they can get you a bus ticket?"

"My parents don't have a phone. They couldn't afford a ticket for me, anyways," I pouted. The nice lady leaned close to her husband and whispered, "Honey, maybe we could buy him the ticket to Seattle. It shouldn't cost too much." They bought my ticket, saw me onto the bus, and back I went to Seattle.

My one error was that I had told that couple my real name and the names of my parents. To my dismay they called 4-1-1 for their phone number. My stupidity resulted in my father waiting for me at the Greyhound Station in Seattle.

I saw him pacing back and forth when the bus pulled in. I had no idea what he was going to do - one minute he was screaming for me to go away, the next minute he was looking for me. I figured whatever he was doing couldn't be good, so I snuck off the bus and ran the half block distance to Marcy's house to see if Roberta was there. She wasn't - and neither was anyone else. There was no name on the buzzer and I realized that no one lived there anymore. I guess nobody stayed in one place too long.

I made the short journey downtown to see if I could find anyone I knew. The winter that year was very cold and I was surprised to see how busy it was, but no one I knew was out. Just as I was getting nervous thinking I had nowhere to go, I came around the corner at the top of 1st Avenue and saw a familiar face.

It was Roberta.

"I just went to Marcy's looking for you," I said and began to tell her the entire night-mare story of what had happened to me in the past few weeks.

We started walking the stroll, hoping to drum up some business, get a motel room out of the cold and hopefully get high - a nice bonus to end the grueling night.

Once we got on Union Street a vehicle pulled up swiftly to the curb. Roberta recog-nized the car and tried to hide in a doorway. Three men jumped out, ran up to her and started beating and kicking her. It happened so fast – the thumping sounds on her little body and then flash! They were back in the car before I could do anything. I couldn't have anyway. I was half the size of each of them.

Roberta, shaking and crying, had covered her face with her hands while they were beating her so she would have no noticeable bruises. This was important to a prostitute. To look appealing – not destroyed or beaten like their insides. I put my arm around my friend and we walked back to Pike Street where the streets were more populated.

"Who the hell were those guys?" I asked her. "The tall one wants me to work for him – to be his Ho," she explained. That was the game for many men on the streets - to get a girl or three to prostitute for them and give them all their money. They would beat or intimidate the small, young ones so they would be too frightened to stand up for them-selves. Then they would come back regularly to make sure the girls were 'working' only for them. One thing I realized was that the conduct on the streets was all learned by the actions of others. A pimp isn't born a pimp. They are taught lessons and desensitized in order to do the harmful things they do. Drugs can also play a part in lowering ones mor-als. Pimps supposedly provided protection, which was reciprocation and justification for them to take all the prostitutes money. The ones who could not protect themselves were forced to be their moneymakers. The only time it benefited the girls was when a pimp had enough respect to repel the other pimps and prostitutes – but that was rare. Boys had it easier. The pimps never gave them a hard time, at least if you knew people.

When we reached Pike Street, Lou Lou ran up to us to see why Roberta was crying. We told her the whole story. Lou Lou didn't play the violence game until an innocent person was picked on. She was always drunk and high and would easily lose control of her temper fighting fire with fire. She had a large build for a girl and wasn't afraid to fight even the largest of men, especially if they were threatening one of her innocents. Just as Roberta and I were telling her about our problems, I saw one of the guys who beat up Roberta - walking swiftly towards us.

I whispered to Lou Lou, "That's one of them." Lou Lou put her arm around Roberta, pointed toward the intruder and started speaking loudly, "Is this the guy that attacked you?" He looked smug, not caring that a girl was being aggressive.

"Yes, that's the asshole," Roberta confirmed. Before I could evaluate anyone's next move, Lou Lou lost it.

"What the fuck is wrong with you? *Punk!*" she got in his face, "Are you such a big guy that you have to beat up on little girls? Does that make you feel like a fucking *man?*" Lou Lou, in her self-appointed role as the Protector of the Innocents, was in full fighting mode. Her face, jaw jutted out, took on a manly, sinister look. Her eyes were inches away from Roberta's attacker. They looked like alley cats in a stand off the moment before they strike. Hot breath was visible in the cool air. The guy said nothing. He was trying to stare her down and intimidate her.

Lou Lou had a definitive role in our street family. We all felt a little safer knowing she was near looking out for everyone she loved and sometimes people she didn't even know. She defended the kids who were being treated as prey.

I loved the drama of it all. My adrenaline increased whenever there was a fight.

"Fuck you chump. Leave people alone. You don't scare me motherfucker. If I see you messing with any of these girls, I will kick your ass. You hear me?" she said remaining in his face. He backed away. Lou Lou was crazy when she was mad, but when her anger was combined with alcohol, she was a real force to be reckoned with.

We watched Roberta's wanna-be pimp walk away pissed off.

Lou Lou spat toward him for punctuation, as she always did when the weak impersonating the strong would cower away from her.

It was getting very late and Roberta and I decided to part ways. Lou Lou took her to Marcy's new place and just as I was trying to figure out where the hell Frankie would be on this freezing cold night, someone told me that White Junior was looking for me. This meant he probably had a gig for me. We would share our clients with each other and charge finder's fees. That way everyone would make a little cash for the transaction. I saw him come around the corner.

"What's up Junior? I heard you were looking for me."

"I met this dude. He's a preacher or something. He's a real freak, but he's got money and likes to shoot coke." Cocaine. Hmm. That's something I had been meaning to try. "He wants me to find some more boys for him. You interested?"

A warm place to sleep, some cash and a new drug?

I was very interested.

Ticket to ride, white line highway
Tell all your friends, they can go my way

Pay your toll, sell your soul
Pound for pound costs more than gold

"White Lines" – Grandmaster Flash

Chapter 7

THE NEXT LEVEL

In the words of the deceased funk king Rick James, 'cocaine is a hell of a drug'. The head rush is so powerful that the world stops as you embellish the magical intensity. When the powerful feeling dissipates, it manifests into an immediate craving, which can only be satisfied by obtaining another round. It is a repetitive cycle that is extremely hard to stop once started - easily justifying why people lose everything under its grip.

White Junior and I walked toward the bus that would take us to his new preacher friend. "This dude is a fucking freak," he warned, "and he loves to get high."

"So where does he live?" I asked.

"Dude, we can't go to his house. He has a wife. But he knows this other guy and they like to get freaky. They've been paying me to get 'em boys. But they haven't really liked any of the ones I got 'em. I don't think they were young enough."

I was two years younger than White Junior and was still one of the youngest on the streets. He was sure they would be happy with me. I hadn't disappointed a pedophile yet. We got off the bus in Ballard, which is located five miles northwest of downtown Seattle. We walked two short blocks to the two-story apartment building that was very old and not very well maintained. The front door was at an angle on the corner of the building that took up the entire one block radius. We walked up the staircase and I was once again taken aback at the foul smell of urine on the hall rug. I couldn't help but laugh to myself as I realized the smell matched the yellow paint on the outside of the building.

We walked to the end of the hallway. As soon as White Junior was done knocking, I could see the light in the peephole, which meant someone had just looked away from the little hole in the door. The door opened slowly and I could almost see the wet hot air as it made its escape into the hall. I welcomed the break from the freezing cold, but hesitated a minute because it was a little too hot.

The man who let us in was only wearing discolored underwear. He looked to be in his twenties and walked us down the short hallway into the living room, which was the only room in this ancient bachelor apartment.

I noticed spoons and syringes on the coffee table. The freak show had already begun. I had woken up that morning in a hospital, scavenged my way back to Pike, watched Roberta get clobbered by some thugs and was ready to rock and roll.

The other man walked out of the bathroom with sweat pouring down his forehead. He was high as a kite and was much older. "Can you hit yourself?" he asked me without an introduction. "I've always had other people do that for me," I said, referring to my Ritalin use with Pinky. "No problem, a nurse taught me so I can show you how to do yourself the right way. It's better you learn to do it yourself," he suggested.

He sat Junior and me down and went over all of the tricks of intravenous injecting. He explained what veins work best on your arms, how to make them bigger and how to be clean like in a hospital. I knew needles were the worst form of drug use and that cocaine was the worst drug, next to heroin. That's exactly why I wanted to use it.

We partied with the boys for the best part of the night. They were so high we didn't have sex with them. As far as I was concerned it was a free party.

But Preacher Man did ask for a rain check, convinced he wanted to see me again.

It wasn't long before we began to visit the preacher at least once a week. He was in his forties, tall, was sort of handsome with an athletic build. He took a liking to me in particular. By now my life was all about survival and I played right into the preacher's little game, although I made myself believe that I was the one in control. He had the money and the drugs. Little by little he sweetened the deal. The more I accepted his offer to meet him at a motel, the more money and things he gave me, and it wasn't long before I really *needed* the cocaine. He knew exactly what he was doing and was a very skilled and manipulative predator. I longed for that first high as it took me out of my reality. Immediately after shooting it, and precisely when I pushed the watered down version of powder into my veins, I got this taste in my mouth under my tongue through the back of my throat. That was the pleasant signal that I would be taken into another dimension. The only problem was that once I started to get high, I didn't want to stop and would do anything to get more. I trained my mind to like the Preacher, likening him to a good man.

Not the manipulative, sick child molester he really was.

∞∞∞

The large JC Penney's building on Pike Street closed down and was boarded up, so the block became more suitable for us kids. When I wasn't at a motel with the preacher man I hung out on our block where all of the street people congregated. Once we took over, the working-class people started purposely walking other routes to avoid the irritating, begging little street kids and the dope fiends that were raising us. Misfits, runaways and throwaways were all drawn to our little scene. They were usually welcomed, if they had the sense to act properly. It didn't matter what color you were, what disability you had or how you wore your hair. Everyone was welcome to the street life as long as a certain street etiquette of respect was displayed.

It was a chilly evening and Pinky and I were sitting on the cement bench getting ready to go to the YMCA Shelter, when we noticed this little dude drinking a gallon jug of wine. He was standing behind a pole and he would peak out at us now and then.

He was a sad looking little guy so we walked over to where he was standing. I decided to speak to him, "Hey, I'm Justin. What's up?" He was sipping straight from the bottle that seemed to be half his size.

"I'm a'ight, man," he slurred. "I'm jus' drinkin' some wine," he spoke embellishing his slur. We talked to him cautiously to let him know that we were nice. "What's your name?" Pinky asked.

"I'm Dewayne."

"Where are you from?" Pinky and I asked at the same time. We looked at each other with a jinx smile. "Well, I was in a receiving home (foster home), and I didn't like it, so I left. One of the kids told me where to go." I empathized with his distaste for the group home.

"My dad is in jail and he is goin' to prison. He told me I could stay with him when he gets out, though. So, I figured I'd just hang out in the streets till he gets out."

I continued, "Where is your mom?"

His face looked to the ground, "She's dead. She died when I was young."

"You're still young," I replied, trying not to sound snotty. It was obvious that he was younger than me. It reminded me of my first night on the street and how kind Lou Lou and the others were to me. It was my turn to pay it forward.

"How old are you, really?" I asked seriously.

"Fifteen."

Pinky responded first, laughing, "You ain't no fifteen. Justin is thirteen and he's way taller than you!"

"No really, I'm fifteen. I have a disease that makes me grow slower, but I'm tryin' to catch up to you all," he smiled sweetly. "Well, you can come with us to the Y. I'm sure they can give you a room to sleep in for the night, but you are gonna have to lose the jug of wine," Pinky warned.

We brought him with us to the YMCA where Tom's agency, YouthCare, had a block of Single Room Occupancy (SRO) hotel rooms for homeless kids.

We'd all sit on the cement benches, drink and smoke pot and cigarettes with Lou Lou, Pinky, Roberta and Tiny until Dewayne found his own group of friends. That's usually how it went down with fellow runaways. We looked out for little Dewayne for a little while and he soon started finding his own way with an older street couple named Kim and Steve.

Everyone socialized daily and got involved in everyone else's drama. Drama was always near. Girls and boys getting raped, tricks not paying the prostitutes, fights, more fights, stabbings, and girls gone missing. In a normal community having a serial killer threatening your serenity is a huge fear. In our community, it was just one of many things to worry about.

∞∞∞

My relationship with the preacher turned out to be a lot more than what I had planned. As I began to fall in love with the drug, the preacher wanted more and more of me. He was an oddball and liked to have his boys do strange things. I often went to the motel alone. He would be waiting for me at one of those musty, sex-scented greasy boxes located on Aurora Avenue. It was early fall and the room was very warm because he had the heat turned way up, which brought out the horrible odor of those rooms. He was only wearing a wife beater T-shirt and his boxer underwear. His teeth were on the dresser. This was the most disgusting scene I had ever been in. One look at this old bastard and my stomach turned. And if that wasn't enough, the acts he requested were repulsive and beyond anything I had heard of.

He tried to kiss me and I snapped, "What the fuck are you doin', dude? Don't put your mouth near me." Who knew what weird things this freak had been doing. My brow wrinkled in disgust and he quickly moved away from my face. He was actually scared of my large attitude. I was surprised to see I had a little control over him.

"I know it's hard to live on the streets and it's not as easy to cop your drugs - so if you stay with us, I can take care of everything," he said trying to calm me down.

Us? I knew he was talking about his wife, who he had only mentioned once or twice. I couldn't believe he included his wife in the plan and I doubted he even talked to her about it.

I sort of liked the idea of having my paycheck in one location, but the thought of living with him and his wife sounded creepy. I was hesitant, so naturally he started working - 'grooming' me. It is what pedophiles do in order to get their way with their victims. It is a long, detailed and strategic manipulative process on the part of the predator and usually happens with children that are being taken care of by a single parent or are somehow disconnected from an involved or aware family unit.

"You can come visit. I have an extra room. My wife knows everything. I don't really sleep with her anymore," he continued, "You will have a real home to come to. I'll take good care of you."

This was the perfect answer for a drug addicted street child.

The next day I went to his house for a visit, which ended up being another drug binge, only this time he let me crash in the spare bedroom.

The house was a two-story home in Ballard, a residential suburban neighborhood of Seattle. The exterior of the home fit in with the wholesome neighborhood – the perfect paint job, yellow with clean white trim. The yard was manicured, but not spectacular. The inside was bare. There was no nice furniture, just a few pieces of tacky cheap furniture. There were no pictures on the walls. No sign of warmth or a sense of pride.

The wife always left early in the morning for work. After several days of living there, I knew to stay in my room until she left. Then one afternoon as I was watching television in the living room I heard the front door opening. I started to panic - I knew she wasn't supposed to see me even though the preacher had told me she was aware of the new addition to her family. But before I could get up, turn the television off and run into the back room, she walked in - all three hundred pounds of her. She stood frozen, staring at me for several seconds with no facial expression whatsoever.

"Hello. I'm Justin," I said while staying seated on the couch. I was hoping for some kind of response to break the silence as her stare was chilling. Nothing. It was a disconcerting sight, an obese wicked witch from The Wizard of Oz with the same type of warts and growths on her chin and nose staring right at me with a disgusted look on her disfigured face. She turned away without saying a word and walked toward the staircase down the hallway.

"I know where you came from and do not want you here. Do not touch anything of mine, do not come upstairs for any reason and do not speak to me unless you are spoken to. As far as I am concerned, you are not here," she spoke without looking at me again.

I wanted to tell her to fuck off, but I had just got there and Preacher Man was my new meal ticket. I responded, "Okay. Cool."

It was odd to me that the preacher who was almost handsome and in very good physical shape was married to this huge, unattractive woman in her fifties.

What possibly could have brought these two together?

I turned the television back on and heard her go into the kitchen. Not long after, she began to slowly climb the stairs, stopping now and again to catch her breath. When she reached the top, she went into her room and shut the bedroom door, which was followed by the sound of several locks being secured, including a chain and a deadbolt.

The entire situation was very weird to me, but getting arrested frequently on the streets was the norm when I tried to remain on the streets for long periods of time. It simply seemed better to stay with a pedophile and stay somewhat hidden from police and social workers.

I didn't blame his wife for hating me. I tried to respect her wishes by staying out of sight whenever she was around, all the while manipulating her husband for more drugs and cool items I could ever want - clothes, games, music, alcohol and cigarettes. He was so pleased to have his own little boy toy to play with he was more than willing to give me anything I wanted.

One time, only, did the wife ever say anything directly to me. That was when she heard my last name.

"Is your father's name Lloyd Early?"

I was shocked when she said my dad's name, "Yes, it is."

She quickly looked at me surprised, "Well, he is a real asshole. We went to high school together." She nonchalantly walked up to her bedroom without saying another word. It really is a small world when your molester's wife and your abusive, alcoholic father shared a science class back in olden days.

Although it was nice to have a place to crash and get high, I would always end up downtown with my friends.

I preferred hanging out with normal people.

∞∞∞

It had been three years since I left home and believe it or not, I felt proud that I had become such a streetwise kid. Okay, the drug addiction, sexual solicitation and sexual abuse by a preacher bothered me, but as long as I stayed high, I felt numb to being such a loser.

LIFE Magazine had been on the streets preparing an article about all the street kids and our "disheartening" lifestyle. It wasn't too long after the article that camera crews and the photographer came back to shoot a movie. Although a little part of me wanted to be in a movie, I didn't really trust them. Frankie thought they were really cops and gave me a warning.

Pictured: Justin and Roberta - Pike St. Payphone
(Credit: Streetwise)

"I'm tellin' you, they are the FBI," Frankie told me convincingly, "Don't let them film you."

Shortly thereafter, I was hanging with Roberta when the crew walked up to us and asked us if they could film us for a while. Roberta convinced me that we could have fun with it. I put my on aviator glasses so I wouldn't be recognized. Our part was no big deal – just Little Bit and me talking and messing around in the phone booth on Pike Street. She was actually on the phone with a trick when they filmed us.

The idea that someone wanted to film us was somewhat touching.

∞∞∞∞

I stayed with the preacher when it worked out for me, but I didn't like his leering, manipulative persona. I was much more comfortable running around downtown and hustling, in various ways, to get high with my friends. Every once in a while Tom or someone would persuade me to go back to the Youth Shelters.

I was feisty and my temper sometimes got the best of me, so no matter how comfortable the bed with clean sheets seemed, I would end up back on the streets. And then one day I realized I had lost my protective status of being the little kid. The older kids stopped treating me special because I had become as bad off as they were. I had to live up to the rules of the streets, which were close to the rules at home.

Demanding to be respected, while being disrespectful.

The most important rule on the streets and in the institutions was not to show emotions or to cry – unless one of family members died. It was ok to be angry in any situation, but you always have to act like everything is fine even when we all knew quite clearly that nothing was.

However, as long as we stayed high the focus was to keep high and the rules didn't really matter.

Do you know where you're going to?
Do you like the things that life is showing you?
Where are you going to?

Do you know...?

Diana Ross – "Do You Know"

Chapter 8

JUDGE & JUDY

As I progressed into puberty and my full-blown drug addiction, I began to build on my criminal record, which I considered to be a badge of honor, sort of a street style Curriculum Vitae. After being in and out of the courts for almost four years for various criminal charges ranging from burglary to malicious mischief, I got to know one judge in particular. Judge Gary Little.

I was in court for my fifth time for running away from the youth homes, which was a criminal offense. Since this Judge had seen me a few times already I stiffened when he asked me to come into his chambers to talk to me. He sat me down alone and began speaking in a benevolent and caring way.

"It is obvious that you are a child with potential Justin. You are special. You have something I don't see in a lot of these other children," he said having sympathy for my situation. He said the best thing for me was to go into the YouthCare facility and that if I did, he would watch over me and help me. I was flattered that he had taken such an interest in me but remained guarded. He must have seen a lot of fucked up kids and I simply did not get what it was that he liked so much that he would pledge to watch over and guide me. But there was something fatherly about him that made me let down my guard a little, so I played it cool with him and tried to do the things he suggested. I stayed in the Youth Care facility for a couple weeks and true to his word, he came and took me to lunch to give me extra guidance. I liked the attention, although I couldn't shake my suspicious nature. The idea that I could trust a male authority other than Tom was hard for me to do. Tom was out there on the streets with us and he understood us. This was a judge that normally punished us. And although I felt he was really trying to help, I had heard several rumors about this Judge.

"I feel strongly that with a little guidance and support, you could get off the streets permanently and make a good life for yourself," he said in his empowering tone.

I thought about what he was telling me. I was so used to adults putting me down and wanting to lock me up that it was surprising to hear words of encouragement.

"If you get off the streets and prove yourself to me and to the court, I will personally pay for your college education when you graduate high school."

High School? Are you kidding me? I hadn't even been to Junior High! I hadn't been in school at all since sixth grade. Just the thought of trying to play catch up in a classroom full of normal kids with regular lives was daunting.

"I do want a better life. That's why I am staying at the shelter," I told him.

"I hear you are doing well there," he said impressed.

Truth is I wasn't doing that well. I wanted to get high and I was tired of living in the structured environment. I didn't have faith in any institution and I didn't like the feeling of being completely alone.

I had heard that Dewayne had gotten into some trouble and that he did not get released. He was sent up to the maximum-security youth prison, so I was considering what this judge was telling me. I did not want to fall victim to the system like Dewayne did, but it was too overwhelming to think about going to school. I felt stuck, though I pretended to go along with his idea.

Judge Little took me to a very fancy restaurant on Lake Union. As we passed Gasworks Park I had a memory of running away with Kurt from The Loft field trip, almost four years previous. Back then I never imagined this journey would lead to a lunch date with a judge. When we finished he drove me back to the shelter on Beacon Hill. I noticed his demeanor change. He said he wanted to teach me how to drive. His voice lowered to a whisper, "You can sit on my lap and steer the wheel." I didn't have a large frame but I was clearly an adolescent, so riding on an adult man's lap was peculiar.

As I kept my hands on the steering wheel, his hands began fondling my legs and thighs.

I knew it.

My suspicious radar and the rumors were accurate. He was trying to play down the obvious as he was getting off on me. I had seen and been involved with some kinkier requests so this driving thing didn't bother me. But the thought that everyone was a potential abuser was disturbing. I appreciated his offerings, but school was out of the question and I knew that if I hung around the judge any longer, I would have ended up sleeping with him.

I had grown tired of him trying to help me in ways that did not translate into immediate cash. After he dropped me off back at The Shelter, I packed what little things I owned - a couple of t-shirts and a pair of jeans, and left to go home – Downtown.

∞∞∞

Whenever I was arrested, I would be assigned various public defenders that were available for indigent children. My favorite was Judy Hightower. She was in her thirties and was a beautiful African American woman with a perfectly shaped Afro. She was confident and took a liking to me. Judy was fierce in a courtroom and could get very testy with the prosecutors and the judges. I loved her blatant compassion for the lack of resources the Seattle government had for youngsters such as myself. She didn't believe that locking me up would do any good – something they always wanted to do - and I could always trust that she would go to bat for me.

"I am going to get you into a good foster home or group home. But you have to stay this time – they are getting sick of seeing you here," she said in her motherly tone one day after court.

"Sure, I'll stay," I lied.

"If you keep running away and living on the streets, you are going to be sent up to the youth prison. You can't keep doing this, Justin."

I never stayed where they sent me, so of course I ended up back in detention. Judy was permanently assigned to represent me and we developed a warm relationship. I was the good kid that she didn't mind helping, and she was the nice lady who I wished was my mom.

I didn't have a problem listening to her and at least trying to follow her direction. Street life was becoming intolerable. And this back and forth to jail had started to grind on me, too. When I was out, I usually stayed with Preacher Man, but was getting sick and tired of being taken advantage of.

What I really wanted was to be near Frankie, but he often stayed with his girlfriend. When I was stuck in detention I missed my family. Not the family that allowed my insane father to take his anger out on me. I missed the family that loved me. That family, however, had their own problems, so I decided the best thing for me was to try to get Judy to take me in.

In detention, we were allowed five minutes of telephone time per week and I used my minutes to call her. There was no answer so I boldly left a message, "Um, hi Judy. This is Justin, and I'm calling from the Youth Center. I don't want to go to another group home, and I was wondering if I could come stay with you. If not, it's okay. I just thought I'd ask." I was nervous as I went back to my cell where I continued to wonder what I was doing with my life. I had been sucked into a judicial system I couldn't get out of. I was beginning to spin out of control.

As I lay on my cement mattress I kept thinking … *does God hate me?*

God *had* to hate me – I was such a loser.

I had enjoyed the freedom of being on my own, but now that drugs had taken center stage and I was becoming a confused, miserable, lost fourteen-year-old soul. I was terribly lonely and the gnawing feeling of emptiness made me wish for my real family. I wanted to be able to see my real brothers and have a family again, even if it just meant visiting sometime.

I needed a mom. I hoped Judy would let me slip into her life and the next day she came to see me. She looked at me with her sad face and asked, "Sweetie, I can't believe you called my house. How did you get my number?"

"The phone book," I responded obviously.

She chuckled lightly and looked away as she continued, "Look honey, I have two kids. My son is your age and my daughter is a toddler. I am raising them alone. It's hard enough for me to do what I do. I can't take on anything – or anyone else."

She knew I was disappointed and continued, "That doesn't mean that I don't care about you. I do, but I am your attorney. I'm not a foster parent." She tried to be firm but her love and compassion was notable and I knew in my heart that she would have taken me on if she had the resources.

Judy had put herself through law school while working full time as a single parent. I admired her deeply and although I was very disappointed, I understood what she was saying. I just wanted to be settled somewhere – with an adult who had a caring quality and loving presence.

The streets were wearing me down. I needed four walls and rules, but not in the form of cemented cells.

∞∞∞

I started thinking that maybe I had spent enough time on the streets. I hardly ever got to see Frankie because he was with his girlfriend, Roberta spent a lot of time going back and forth to Portland, and Lou Lou was really fucked up. Actually, we all were messed up and I was getting sick of this dysfunctional life. I decided that since four years had passed since I left home, I would try to go back.

I called my mom. She and I had talked on the phone every once in a while and every time we did, she told me that she missed me. I knew she did. She always sounded sad when we talked. I was hoping she might be ready to start over too. I think I knew deep down that it was a waste of time, but I missed my family desperately. I clung to the hope that maybe my dad would see my pain and accept me.

How does a father not love his own child? I struggled with this.

After getting Mom's excited approval to come home, I jumped on the bus for the forty-five minute bus ride to my parents. I was elated at the idea of being with my mom and my brothers.

I got off the bus and walked up the steep hills into the Sheridan Heights neighborhood of North Seattle. Feeling like a stranger, I rang the bell respectfully and waited for someone to open the door. Then I heard his voice, "Jesus fucking Christ! You know *goddamn* well I don't want him here!"

Without waiting for an even warmer response in person, I turned around and walked back to the bus stop.

Thank God for Downtown.

When I was a young boy
Tenements, slums and corner bums
Playing tag with winos,
The only way to have some fun
One thing 'bout the ghetto
You don't have to hurry
It'll be there tomorrow
So brother don't you worry…

Rick James – "Ghetto Life"

Chapter 9

STREETWISE

I arrived downtown and walked to Pike Street where I knew everyone would be. I noticed Tom the outreach man and walked up to him to say hello and check in like I usually did. He looked at me sadly. Before he spoke his eyes filled with wet heartbreak.

"I have some very sad news. Little Dewayne killed himself last night." His tears began to fall down his face, "Today would have been his seventeenth birthday."

I was stunned. People started gathering, some crying and holding on to each other.

I'd had thoughts of killing myself, but never had the balls to do it. I admired Dewayne for his follow through. "How did he do it?" I asked.

Did it hurt? Was it quick?

"He hung himself. He tied a sheet around his neck in his cell and hung himself. It was the day before he was to be released. Today is his birthday."

"And don't *you* get any ideas, you hear?" he said reading my mind.

It was unsettling to see Tom so upset. Losing Little Dewayne was hitting him hard. We've lost family members from overdosing or violent fights, but this was our first known suicide since my arrival four years ago. I guess no one can really know how much pain the others are hiding. I was touched by the fact that Tom somehow understood how truly sad I was, too. He was worried that I would do it to myself and had good reason to be concerned - I was tired and broken.

There were several outreach workers that made themselves available for us kids. They would tell me how powerless they felt and that they wished they could do more.

If they only knew how much their genuine concern meant to us kids.

∞∞∞

We were invited to go to Orion Youth Drop-In Center and attend the preview of the documentary movie that those people had been shooting. This kind of excitement was rare. Lou Lou, Roberta and I huddled on the floor to watch it together.

Lou Lou nudged me, "Ha! There's Roberta and Justin! Did you see it?"

Wow! I was in a *real* movie. My place on the streets of Seattle was legitimate. My life wasn't imaginary. Although I was a homeless street child, I felt legitimate in that moment. Though I never denied it, my world had become dreamlike and I wasn't absolutely sure what was truth anymore – not until I saw a documentary about lost children. This movie was meant to show an audience what a sad and deprived life we led, but we felt proud that night. We watched, still shocked at what had been created so eloquently. I was only in one scene because I wouldn't allow them to film more of me per Frankie's' instructions, but Roberta was threaded throughout and Lou Lou and Tiny had starring roles. We had no idea the movie was going to be so powerful. It was clear that the people who made it wanted us to have a voice and to articulate our lives for everyone to see. Many of us were flattered and very grateful. At last the world would get a glimpse of our lives on the street and maybe someone would try to help fix our problems.

We gasped when the last scene started rolling. It was Dwayne's funeral. They had finished the film prior to his suicide. We were not aware they had shot the additional footage. We wept openly when we saw our little friend - laying lifeless in his lonely coffin. Though the movie was fascinating, the ending was emotional and put us all in a funk. Lou Lou and I walked in silence in the cold rain towards downtown. We were headed to buy some forty-ounce bottles of beer.

Unidentifiable feelings needed numbing.

The film **STREETWISE** by Martin Bell, Mary Ellen Mark and Cheryl McCall was produced by country singing legend Willie Nelson and his wife Connie.

It was nominated for an Academy Award.

But don't be fooled by the radio
The TV or the magazines
They show you photographs of how your life should be
But they're just someone else's fantasy
So if you think your life is complete confusion
Because you never win the game
Just remember that it's a Grand illusion
And deep inside we're all the same.

We're all the same...

Styx – "The Grand Illusion"

Chapter 10

MASTERS DEGREE: MANIPULATION

As with death, comes new life. Frankie's girlfriend gave birth to a beautiful baby girl. Mama hated his girlfriend because she was almost her age, but she couldn't resist the thought of her littlest grandchild. I couldn't believe Frankie was a daddy.

He had barely turned fifteen. We had been intimate for almost two years, but with drugs as a number one priority for both of us, we no longer saw each other as often as we used to. I figured that was better. I loved Frankie and I hated myself for it.

I was now the one who joined in with the bigots when they confronted homosexuals screaming, "queer!" and "faggot!"

Lots of people said that being gay was a choice and that humans should not deviate from heterosexuality. Though I was sure the rules were interpreted and implemented by heterosexuals, they *were* the rules. I already chosen not to be gay – but no matter what I thought or did, I loved Frankie and I couldn't turn him off.

Not long after the birth of beautiful baby Krystle, Frankie was arrested for a serious felony and was ordered to stay locked up pending trial.

∞∞∞

I wanted to see Frankie's baby so I took the bus to Mama's on a day I knew the she would be visiting. Krystle was adorable. She was very light skinned, as her mother was white and Frankie was only half black. She had soft curly dark hair.

Lou Lou saw me staring at the baby as I sat on the couch. We both admired Frankie's precious offspring when she started talking to me, "You know he's going to prison right?" she spoke softly, "Armed Robbery is a serious crime. They are charging him as an adult too."

She told me that Frankie was being sentenced to sixty-five months in adult prison and would be transferred from the Youth Center to the Seattle Jail then off to a Washington State prison to do his time. I felt panicked and was fighting back tears. Five years and five months seemed like an eternity to me. Between the growing need for cocaine and the negligent life I embraced, I'd be dead by the time Frankie got out.

"Are you alright?" she asked quietly.

"I'll be cool." I wasn't cool. But I couldn't let it show.

She put a tender hand on my shoulder and I stiffened. The thought that she knew how I felt, and of my pain, helped. At least I wasn't completely alone. Though it was completely cool for Lou Lou to be gay, I did not have that 'I'll kick your ass' demeanor to admit it out loud. I couldn't admit it quietly. I couldn't admit it to myself.

I had to accept the fact that I would never see him again. But I couldn't even do that.

∞ ∞ ∞

People were leaving, disappearing, being sent off to prison and committing suicide.

The streets were getting tougher and were wearing me out. Not only do drugs wear the body down, I wasn't eating balanced meals that are required for young children to grow properly. I was so into drugs that I was beginning to deteriorate and had a hard time taking care of myself. I didn't even care about my appearance. What little self-respect I had started with was long gone.

By the time I was fifteen, I had blown out the veins in my arms and had to start using the ones in my hands and wrists to inject my drugs. I wore the same clothes for days, sometimes weeks, accumulating the daily dirt and the moist stench that a rain city provides. I was nasty and I simply didn't care anymore. I didn't see Roberta much because she was off in her own addictive world. She would spend a lot of her time in Portland. Without Frankie or Roberta, the loneliness was getting to me.

I decided that it was time to visit my brothers – in secret. My mom kept me informed about what they were doing. I kept in touch with her whenever I was near a phone. I would call her from time to time to catch up on family news and to let her know I was alive. I loved the sound of her voice and she always sounded happy to hear mine. She told me my oldest brother Cameron was working the graveyard shift at a grocery store in North Seattle. My other brother George was still living at home and had recently experienced a brain aneurism and almost died. Although a full recovery was predicted, the rest of the family was monitoring him until his recovery period was complete. I wanted to see for myself that he was okay.

Tired, dirty and with my growing muscles feeling like they had been beaten, I took the forty-five-minute bus ride to my parent's house. It was midmorning so I knew it was safe - my parents would be at work. However, I still walked around the property to make sure both of their cars were gone. Instead of ringing the doorbell, I walked to the back of the house and came in through the unlocked kitchen door.

71

Before the door opened all the way, our family dog Fluffy excitedly ran up to me. It warmed my heart that she remembered me. I looked through the door to the living room and saw George sleeping on the couch with the television on. Fluffy followed me in, rubbing her nose on my leg as I walked up to my brother. I touched his shoulder.

"George, wake up," I said softly. As his eyes opened he bounced off the couch.

"What are you doing here? Are you alright?" he asked as he wiped his eyes.

"I'm okay. I just wanted to say hi. I took the bus."

"Cameron's in bed, he worked last night. I'm not sure what he's going to say about you being here." We sat there talking when I heard Cameron's bedroom door open. He walked into the living room with his eyes half open and saw me.

"I thought I heard you. You look like shit. What the fuck are you doing to yourself?" he said, scrutinizing me.

"It gets tough sometimes, I guess."

"Why are you so dirty? You need to wash your clothes. You look like a fucking skid row bum," he said disgusted. Although he wasn't speaking in a nurturing tone, I knew he was concerned about me. He was frustrated.

It wasn't the emotional happy homecoming that I had wished for, but at least I was home. Cameron gave me some clothes to wear and allowed me to wash mine. We sat around and talked for hours while I got cleaned up. I hadn't eaten all day, so I was very thankful when he cooked some scrambled eggs and bacon.

"You better get going, Justin," Cameron urged, "Dad can't know that you were here and they'll be home soon." He knew what a scene it would become if my father suspected I had been in his house.

"I know, Cam. I'll get going. Thank you for the food, and for letting me get cleaned up." I gave Fluffy a big hug and realized how much I missed her. I went back downtown, refreshed and clean and started to do what I knew best: pull tricks, make money, get high, walk around, gossip and drink beer on the street in paper bags all the while trying to cover up the strange feelings that I had experienced during my visit to see my brothers. It had been a bittersweet experience.

When I saw myself through their eyes it made me see how scummy I had become.

∞ ∞ ∞

Looking for a place to stay, I went to Lisa's - another sister of Frankie and Lou Lou's. Lisa had several kids and lived in the Rainier Vista Housing Projects down by Mama's new apartment in the Holly Park Housing Projects. Lisa had taken a liking to me and allowed me to stay when I had nowhere else to go. I liked being around the busyness of little kids and they looked upon me as an uncle. They enjoyed the extra attention they received when I was there, as I always felt the need to take care of them, especially when their mom was on a crack binge.

For the next few months I followed Lou Lou around and floated between the preacher man, the streets, Lisa's and Mama's. I missed my brothers and I missed the regular dramas that being in a real family invites.

Trying to obtain some consistency, I went back to live with Preacher Man and his creepy wife. It really was the easiest thing to do. He kept me loaded with coke and I didn't have to work on the streets. I also had my own bed - most of the time.

The other thing I liked about living with the preacher was that I could get almost anything I wanted. I liked having that kind of control. Whatever I wanted, he would try to get for me.

Now that I had a place to stay per se, I couldn't get my mind off our family dog Fluffy and how happy she was to see me whenever I would try to go home. She represented my family, and the unconditional love that I yearned for. I decided that since she was technically mine, I would go get her and she could stay with me.

The preacher let me drive his car even though I was only fifteen. I put a pillow on the driver's seat and would drive all around Seattle. Preacher Man used a work truck during the day so I drove his car to my parents' and picked her up. She was so happy to see me and really loved riding in the car. My mother called, "You can't just come and take what you want. Bring her back. You are creating more problems for all of us."

I put Fluffy back in the car and drove her back to my parents. Not really wanting to remain under the radar or to help keep peace for anyone, I purposely drove the car through the circular driveway so everyone, including him, could see that I was driving.

I put the car in park and got out to let Fluffy out of the back seat. My father came outside. I was surprised when he didn't raise his voice, "Don't you ever take anything from here without permission. Do you understand me?" I was used to him attacking me verbally, but he didn't this time. By comparison I felt welcomed, even though I wasn't invited inside. My mother walked up to me and gave me hug. Dad didn't say anything about it.

"I'm sorry, Mom. I planned on bringing her back. I just wanted her to visit for a while." My father walked inside without saying another word and I talked with my mom a few minutes. I caught her up with my life, explaining that I would be staying at the preacher's house. She thought he was a good man, clueless about his drug use and pedophilia. She blessed my new living arrangement and was relieved I wasn't living on the streets anymore.

Just an urchin livin' under the street
I'm a hard case that's tough to beat
I'm your charity case
So buy me somethin' to eat
I'll pay you at another time

Take it to the end of the line

"Paradise City" – Gun's & Roses

Chapter 11

PREACHER DADDY

After getting the blessing from my mother and my caseworker for the courts, I was allowed to reside legally with Preacher Man. His wife still wouldn't speak to me but she enabled his predatory game.

It was a verbal temporary arrangement so no legal paperwork or anything in writing, but everyone was relieved that I was with an allegedly caring couple.

For the first time in years, everyone knew where I was and I had no warrants out for my arrest.

We did our drugs every night while his wife hid in her filthy room. I didn't care because by now I was pretty strung out and all I wanted was to be high. Preacher Man kept providing the drugs and so it went.

The days were endless. Once we started with Ritalin or Cocaine, everything thing took a back seat and the party was on until he was broke. Sometimes this would happen several days in a row without much, if any, sleep.

He had some seriously bizarre and disgusting fetishes and I hated to please him. But even the so-called 'normal' sexual trysts were disgusting since I knew what we were doing was wrong. If he ran out of money I would head downtown and kick it with my street family, knowing I always had a place to crash if I needed it.

Part of this arrangement required that I attend high school, which was a huge concern to me. I hadn't been to school since the sixth grade and was expected to enter back into the ninth grade. But even with my questionable past and lack of necessary education, I was accepted into Ballard High School.

I had missed so much of the basics and was horribly insecure. I was sure everyone would find out how stupid I was. I felt like I was thrown in the center of Puget Sound with weights on my ankles. It was hard to interact with kids who went to their homes to study for the algebra quiz while I went home to get loaded with my molester.

I did not fit in at all, and of course the other kids didn't understand me. I had secrets, some of which were very dark and painful. I couldn't trust anyone. I kept to myself and approached no peers for friendships.

Of course I did not do well in school. I could not apply myself to learn anything, let alone catch up on my education. All I could think about was whether or not the preacher was home yet with the goods.

My attendance was an issue from the moment I enrolled. Preacher Man made a deal that if I went to school for my morning classes, I could come home at lunch for a midday injection of cocaine. I was so addicted that it sounded like a good plan. The only problem was, that after doing the drugs I couldn't concentrate on the school curriculum and I only wanted to get high.

This arrangement would not work well.

∞∞∞

Around the time I turned sixteen, the preacher decided he needed his prey younger – the younger the better. He was my bread and butter and I did not want to become obsolete. But it wasn't long before he got what he wanted. He hooked up with another twelve-year-old and manipulated the boy to have sex with him. Only this time the boy told his parents and soon the good old Preacher Man was arrested for child molesting.

After the arrest the trial preparation lasted for months. I stayed with Lisa and her kids until I couldn't stand it. Then I went to Mama's. Soon enough I was back in the arms of my preacher. But it didn't last long. His eye was roving. His craving for little boys must have been mighty strong because even though he was awaiting trial for child molestation, he asked me to bring younger kids with me. I refused to incorporate other children into his scheme. I was used to my sick lifestyle, but I was not about to throw some other little runaway into his sinister world. Besides, I wanted all of his drugs, money and whatever else I could get and wasn't about to share them with anyone else.

During this waiting period we were getting high in his house and one day he asked me if I would testify for him in court as a character witness.

I played stupid, "Testify for what?" I didn't want to seem too eager in case he offered to pay me.

"In my trial. I need you to tell the court that you live with me and that I take care of you," he said, worried about his future as a criminal sex offender. By now I was so messed up it seemed almost reasonable.

"You also need to convince the judge that we have never had sex."

He had opted not to have a jury trial. He knew a jury would convict him on sight. He figured my convincing testimony would give him a much better chance at freedom with the judge presiding over his case. He made trips to see me downtown and brought me money or whatever else I wanted to insure I stayed inclined (bribed) enough to help him. He even came with his lawyer and they coached me for my upcoming performance.

My testimony was scheduled along with that of his wife and a couple of other character witnesses. Although his wife was not happy about the current state of their union, she stuck by him as usual. Since no children were allowed in Preacher Man's presence without another adult, I had to be picked up by the two of them. Of course, the wife said nothing to me – nor did I to her. I was only thinking of one thing – to save my golden goose from jail time. Preacher Man was like a bank to me and provided for a good portion of my habit. I would be totally reliant on streets and stealing if he went away. The thought frightened me. There was not a day that had gone by in the past several years that I didn't use some form of IV drugs. I needed them desperately.

We sat in the courtroom and waited for our names to be called. It was not what I thought it would be. I had seen big courtrooms on television when criminal trials would be covered by the news, but this courtroom seemed smaller and more intimate.

After all my coaching I felt confident that I knew what I was doing. It was my turn to testify and I was placed on the stand. I swore to the court that I would tell the truth, the whole truth and nothing but the truth.

"How do you know the defendant?" the lawyer asked. I put on my best innocent demeanor – careful not to over do it.

"He is sort of like a foster father to me. He and his wife took me in from the streets and let me stay with them 'cause I didn't have anywhere else to go."

"Would you consider Mr. King to be a credible and upstanding member of the community?"

"Yes," I answered rather effectively. The questions were easy and although I was a little nervous, I felt good about my answers. Then the prosecutor had her shot at me.

"Have you ever been arrested for prostitution?" she asked in a very bitchy tone like you see on television.

"Um, yes I have. But it was a long time ago and…" She cut me off.

"Yes or no is fine, thank you. You *are* under oath, correct?" she asked as she slowly and dramatically looked around the courtroom.

"Yes ma'am," I replied getting an attitude. She was starting to piss me off. I didn't like cops or most people of authority – and I hadn't met a prosecutor yet that I liked because either they were trying to put my friends or me away.

"So under oath, you are telling the state that you have not had any sex with this man? I find it hard to believe with your history that…" Preacher Man's lawyer interrupted, "OBJECTION, this is a child - and a child that is not on trial your Honor. What is happening here?" he pleaded.

"Objection sustained."

"No more questions Your Honor," she said knowing she had already made her point.

I figured I did pretty well, but hadn't planned on being put on the spot about my past arrests. I had planned on going in and acting like an innocent little kid. Even though I was a full-grown adolescent, I had been trying to hang on to the 'Little Justin' thing. At that moment I realized I was no longer the adorable little kid living on the streets I had been in the past. Little Justin was gone. It was disturbing. If my boyish charm had faded, then what would I do to manipulate people into giving me what I wanted? Standing just outside the courtroom I felt lost.

I'm just a common criminal. I decided not to hang around the courtroom until they finished.

As I was leaving the courtroom, I noticed a name on the door on the other side of the hallway, 'Judge Gary Little'. Judge Little had moved downtown to the adult courts. I wondered why.

∞∞∞

The trial only took a couple of days. The preacher was found Guilty as charged.

New rules were in effect now that he was convicted and no one under the age of eighteen was allowed in Preacher Man's presence, not even me and I was supposedly living with him. I had to get all of my stuff permanently out of his house.

His wife was relieved to have me gone. She made sure to smugly reiterate that my presence at her home was no longer allowable. But what she didn't know was that I made him buy me motel rooms and he would come by for visits.

After his ordeal, he became very paranoid. Every time he got high, he would peek out the windows and door holes, thinking the cops were coming to get him. I couldn't stand the way he acted. It was a lot of work being around someone who was obsessively anxious. Paranoia is contagious and I began to agree that maybe there was someone watching us. At that point I knew I had to get away from him.

His addiction to me, and my addiction to drugs made our relationship linger way past its expiration date. He couldn't afford to pay for my motels, so he picked me up and we drove to near his house. I would get out of the car and climb into the trunk so no one would see me entering his house as he violated his probation – and me.

This whole scenario didn't sit well with me. As I was crouching in the trunk of his car I thought about my relationship with him. Three years back I was the victim of a middle-aged man who called himself a preacher and used addictive drugs to lure runaways. It eventually became a convenient arrangement for me because it kept me off the streets and out of jail. And then somewhere in the middle of it all I started using him as much as he was using me. Sometimes I had the upper hand. But now, at this very point, we were equals – neither of us had the upper hand – drugs had the upper hand. And the preacher didn't really want a sixteen-year-old addict for his sexual pleasure anymore, but because he couldn't get near the younger children, he was stuck with me and I was stuck with him. Even though our relationship had run its course.

The time had come for me to part ways with the sick preacher man.

One last hit and I'm out.

The wise man said, just walk this way,
To the dawn of the light,
The wind will blow into your face,
As the years pass you by,
Hear this voice from deep inside,
It's the call of your heart,
Close your eyes and you will find,
The passage out of the dark…

"Send Me an Angel" - Scorpions

Chapter 12

DEPENDANCE

Pictured: JC Penney Wall on 2nd and Pike Streets, Seattle, WA (Credit: Bill Clarke, Reporter)

I became dependent on cheap hotels like the nine-dollar Donald Hotel located on First Avenue in a downtown neighborhood called Belltown. I wasn't thrilled with the non-profit agencies emergency housing rules and preferred to stay on my own where I made my own rules. This hotel was my least favorite but it was the easiest as they would rent to me directly and didn't require identification. The Donald Hotel was the last resort and each room was infested with rodents and cockroaches. On good days, when street life was on the upswing, I would be able to afford normal cheap motels, but it seemed they all had some sort of critters or bug infestations as well.

Sometimes I stayed with Lisa, Frankie's sister who had five children of her own. She battled a sever crack addiction, which was now very prevalent in lower income communities. When I went there I just ended up being babysitter because she would use my presence as an excuse to go smoke crack for hours, sometimes days. Lisa was on welfare and every time the check came in the mail, she would go off to do her crack dance. I would help her daughter Di Di cook for the kids and if the adults happened to be home smoking, they would share with me although I did prefer injecting.

The toughest part about Lisa's was how I witnessed her treat Diane or 'Di Di', (pronounced dye-dye). She was Lisa's only Caucasian child and was the oldest having been born when Lisa was just thirteen (Lisa was pregnant at twelve). Di Di was the rock for her four younger brothers, who all relied on her for basic necessities due to their mother's addiction. But it didn't matter how much Di Di did for the boys and the family, she was continually berated and belittled by Lisa, who seemed to hate her. Lisa treated her daughter worse than my father treated me. Oddly enough, when Lisa was high or drunk, she would be nice to Di Di. But no one ever knew what to expect or when to expect it.

Lisa was so mean it was obviously destroying little Di Di's soul. Lou Lou, Frankie and myself all had a special adoration for Di Di and wanted her know that she was loved. But I had a deep suspicion that the adoration that was being received from Lisa's male partners went beyond purity.

I think Lisa knew Di Di was being used inappropriately, which was why she hated her own daughter.

I would still frequent the Youth Detention Center whenever the cops would catch up with me, which they always seemed to do. I pretty much stayed high and sort of floated through the rest of my fifteenth year. When most teenagers were trying to find themselves, I was avoiding myself.

I continued to check in with my mother from time to time, partly to let her know I was okay, partly just to hear her voice and to get all the latest family gossip. Two young teenagers had gotten into a fight over a leather jacket and one stabbed the other in the chest with a knife. A bunch of us had gotten a kick out of flaunting ourselves on camera, a good representation of how directionless my life was.

She told me that my Nana had seen me on the news as I was running back and forth in front of the camera while they were reporting the stabbing. Then she told me the other Nana news she was clearly trying to avoid, "Your Nana passed away last night."

I paused for a moment. "When is the funeral?" I asked.

"There is not going to be one. She didn't want any services or to be buried. She is being cremated and that's it. So you don't need to worry about anything," she said sounding as if this choice was more convenient for everyone. Once more I couldn't grasp why my family was so weird. I hung up the phone overtaken by sadness. Nana was the one who always made me feel special and loved me at all times no matter what. I had started to call her and she was so happy to hear from me, but more happy to have my physical address to send cards and a little cash here and there.

Everyone has something to remember someone by, a trinket, a picture or some sort of keepsake. I had nothing from Nana that I was aware of. If I did have, my dad probably threw it away.

Nana was dead, and with no services or any type of remembrance, getting high was only way for me to deal with it.

It was now my personal solution for everything.

∞∞∞∞

I couldn't talk to anyone about my sexual or emotional desires for Frankie. By the time I was sixteen I was having more and more attractions towards men and none for women like I had hoped. I could barely think about it, but it was all I could think about.

This created a big mess in my mind. In the midst of feeling lost on so many levels, I could not begin to comprehend who I really was.

I *could* understand not living at home with a loving family and accepted my rough street life. Being drug addicted and homeless and hungry was tough, but I was able to survive.

Why did I have to be Gay?

The one thing I didn't want to be – but I couldn't turn it off or turn my attraction to girls 'on'. All I could do was begin to hate myself as many others did of such an oddly percentage of people.

I was spending more time with Lou Lou, and we were walking to get some beer. I was thinking about Frankie and how I felt.

"I like – it," I stated confidently.

"You like what?" she asked, interested in where I was going with this vague little comment. "You know," I hesitated, "men." She looked like she intended to answer, but before any word had time to get out I continued, "Not the seedy tricks. But like, Frankie. I like Frankie," I said relieved. I needed to hear the words for myself. And once I said them I knew it was much more than that. I loved him.

"No shit, Justin!" she laughed. "I always knew about you two! He likes you, too, obviously. I always noticed you two disappear and Mama told me she walked in on you two." My heart raced as I heard her words, confirming these feelings and creating some normalcy in my heart. "But he is gone. For a long time."

Forever.

"Don't let anyone make you feel like a punk, because you're not," she said with authority. "Do you think I would decide to be gay if I wasn't *already*?"

"No," I quietly answered, studying her animated moves while she talked passionately. "Shit, why would anyone *choose* to be so hated? Of course, lots of people hate me. Because

81

they don't *understand* me, they just think it's wrong to be gay, but only because *they are not*. It's easier to hate on someone than to try to understand their differences."

Her words were wiser than our times.

"Just like the racists, they're taught to be hateful. Hatred is passed down and around through families, teachers and preachers. Welcome to life baby boy."

"It's all bullshit." She flicked her cigarette onto the sidewalk. "You don't have to do anything now – just be yourself. Fuck what everybody else thinks."

Her voice got louder, "Fuck the *dumb* shit! Life is too short for this *bullshit!*"

The relief of just telling one person in turn justified my right to be real. I didn't realize it at the time, but her words were some of the wisest I would ever hear in my life. Her intentions were coming from such a pure and true sense of friendship and camaraderie. Over the years I would hear these same words (with less cussing), yet I would always remember where I heard them first.

I loved Lou Lou and her brother. She allowed me to be honest and she, at least temporarily, lifted me from my own judgment of myself. Because she was accepting of the real me, I was able to accept the *possibility* of accepting the real me. And like a true friend, she never exposed my sexual orientation publicly. I was not ready to 'come out' and didn't feel like I needed to do anything yet. I thought about Frankie and how I never had the opportunity to tell him how I felt.

I regretted keeping it a secret – for both of us.

Lou Lou introduced me to her new girlfriend, Janie, who 'dabbled' in heroin. Lou Lou was a masculine, aggressive protector and Janie was a tall gorgeous young woman, an odd couple on the outside, but their paring made perfect sense once you got to know them. At twenty-one, Lou Lou had started to lose some of her teeth. She was rough around the edges, but had one of the biggest hearts I had known.

Janie, also twenty-one, was feminine and sweet with long, perfect dirty blond hair. She had clear, soft skin with supermodel features and the kind of voluptuous body famous actresses (and porn stars) would die for.

Janie had recently moved back from Israel where she had been living with her mother. She had an exotic attitude and was sexy and confident. And knowing she was a looker, she used her looks for all they were worth. She was open and honest about being a prostitute, however she did not work the streets. She was classy. Her game was in the form of several Sugar Daddies. They paid for everything, a nice apartment, cars, clothes, cash and whatever else she desired. I was impressed by her hustle. Though I had encountered a similar deal with my former 'Preacher', she was a true hustler. She knew what she wanted and she made it happen.

She too let me stay with her sometimes when I couldn't find my digs for the night.

Lou Lou understood about my conflict about being gay. I wanted to be bi-sexual like Frankie which seemed a little more acceptable so she and Janie decided to introduce me to Janie's sister Missy, who was a younger, even more gorgeous version of their bloodline. I tried so hard to create, allow or even build an attraction to no avail. We even tried having sex.

We were in the bathroom at Janie's and started making out. I was proud that I was heading in the 'right' direction, and wasn't feeling too out of place. I didn't have an erection, but I was playin' the game pretty good (if I do say so myself). I was hoping for a boner and even started thinking about the male anatomy to help me get stimulated.

Missy whispered in her sexy voice, "Go down on me." Lou Lou had always given me various information and hypothetical lessons and had already explained the entire female anatomy. It looked a little different than she explained, but I was sure I could figure it out.

I put my face down in her special area and was proud, knowing that I was making every right-wing Republican, including my father extremely proud of my new choice.

As I began my manly duty, I took a whiff. I felt embarrassed, because whatever I was about to do didn't smell – um, fresh. I didn't want to humiliate her – so I gently got back to my feet. She knew something was wrong and commented honestly. "I'm sorry," she turned red with embarrassment, "I just got over a yeast infection."

I hadn't gotten that far in my sex classes with Lou Lou to know what a yeast infection was, but I knew I wasn't breaking (or baking) anymore of this bread. Even if it smelled like cotton candy and tasted like maple syrup – it wasn't for me. She knew that I was trying to manipulate my sexuality, and had compassion and was very understanding. I tried. She could have been summers eve fresh and I would still be gay.

Missy and I became casual friends and got high together for a short period of time until she got pregnant. She had the sense to disappear back to the real world and I heard she did well for herself.

Although Janie didn't always identify herself as a lesbian, she had no shame in living as one. And she loved Lou Lou dearly. I too loved being with Lou Lou because she made it easy to forget about missing Frankie. In some small way it was like I could be with a part of him by hanging with her.

When I was with her we could make the best out of anything especially with the help of some drugs and alcohol.

∞∞∞∞

There was one drug I had yet to conquer – heroin. Heroin was for true dope fiends. I had heard it makes people sick when they get hooked. I also heard that it is like being enveloped in soft velvet while the hardness of life evaporates. After some serious begging and showing them I already had tracks on my arms, Janie and Lou Lou finally let me use some. It was made very clear that heroin could only be played with from time to time or there would be consequences.

Thankfully I ignored their wisdom.

It was probably the best high that I had ever experienced. I had never felt so relaxed, relieved and refreshed as I did when I used heroin. It was a non-urgent high that utterly encased every inch of my body and shielded every negative emotion or thought I had about myself, or my life.

As soon as the fluid entered my veins, a mild relaxed rush would secure in my head then move slowly down my body until it covered me, protecting me from the bigots and the outside world. The transformation was like those ballpoint pens with ladies in the clear plastic shaft that, when turned upside down slowly transition to nakedness. I would become naked, shielded with protective armor.

Ultimately, I didn't give a fuck what anybody thought about me. Heroin gave me the balls to be me.

True to their word, both Lou Lou and Janie were able to gauge their usage and keep it under control. I needed more and needed it all the time. So, for the next year or so I hung out with my new love – Mr. Brownstone.

I knew this lover wouldn't leave me for a prison cell.

I used ta do a little but a little wouldn't do
So the little got more and more
I just keep tryin' ta get a little better
Said a little better than before

"Mr. Brownstone" – Guns N' Roses

Chapter 13

THANKS AND GIVING

Roberta was pregnant again and back in Seattle. It was Thanksgiving week and neither of us had been able to make any money on the streets, as traffic had been slow. Not only were we broke - we had nowhere to go. The various homeless shelters always served Thanksgiving meals, but we didn't want street food. I decided to call Preacher Man to see what he was up to, hoping that he would invite us to his house.

I didn't care what his wife would think. I just wanted to be in a warm, familiar house, with familiar surroundings and with my familiar friend and sister, Roberta. He quickly agreed, so Little Bit and I made our way out to the preacher's house for our Thanksgiving feast. Although the preacher's wife was not happy to see me again, she was very intrigued with Roberta and took a liking to her. She must have figured a pregnant teenage girl wasn't a threat, since her husband was partial to little boys. It was obvious by my post pubescent voice change that I was no longer a threat either.

"So Roberta, how far along are you?" she asked.

"I'm not sure. I haven't been counting," she replied to the stunned face of the preacher's wife.

"Oh, honey. Haven't you been to the doctor? They say that prenatal care is imperative these days."

I was shocked at how nice she was being to Roberta. I had never heard that warm tone in her voice. I enjoyed it because Roberta deserved it - prostitutes usually don't get that kind of consideration. It was also interesting seeing such an emotionally ugly woman being so fucking nice.

If there was a God, he sure had a sense of humor today.

"Well, Roberta, I am going to guess that you are about six or seven months along. You are definitely in your third trimester."

While Roberta helped the wife in the kitchen prepare the large meal, I sat in the living room and talked with the preacher. The four of us came close to looking like an eighties' version of a Norman Rockwell painting - except for the scabby track marks Roberta and I had under our shirtsleeves.

After pumpkin pie and ice cream I convinced Preacher Man to buy Roberta and me a motel room nearby on Aurora Avenue. He had some drugs stashed and I got him to give us some to take back to our motel.

The familiar wood paneled walls in the motel room reminded me of an old person's basement. Roberta clicked on the light of the glued-down, plaster lamp, then sat on the stained orange couch and lit a cigarette while I had the honor of fixin' the drugs in our respective syringes. I was getting ready to 'hit' Roberta because she didn't like needles and couldn't do herself. I didn't like needles either but loved hitting other people.

We sat under a picture of dogs playing poker and smoking cigars and talked about what a nice holiday it turned out to be. I instructed her to hold her arm and to squeeze so her veins would plump up, making the task easier for the needle.

When I looked at her face, I saw tears slipping down her cheeks.

"What's wrong?" I began to console her.

"Look at us. Our lives. We are so fucked up. I have this baby moving around inside of me. I am ruining another innocent life. I can't stop myself. I hate myself. Every goddamn year I have a baby and then I get pregnant again. And every one of them comes into this world premature and full of dope. And look at me right now, about to do it all over again. What am I doing?"

"I really want to keep this baby, Justin. I am going to try to get my life together. I'm tired of being a prostitute and living in motels and jails." I pushed the magic liquid inside her vein hurriedly so she would feel better soon. She crossed her legs Indian style, like someone would when meditating and let out a long sigh as her emotional pain dissipated. With one hand soothing the little one in her tummy, she reached up and ran the other through her long blond hair. It was parted in the middle and feathered back on each side. I was mesmerized watching her arrange a few strays back into place as the drug absorbed itself into my soul. I couldn't help notice how beautiful she was.

"I am *so* tired." She sighed in a medicated whisper.

"The old men, losing my kids, not being able to do anything about it." Tears came easily when she was pregnant but this was cutting deeper. I reached out and wiped one.

She smiled like a sad little girl.

"Can you believe we've known each other so long?" It had been seven long years since we first met on Pike Street.

"I know - and look at us. Still hangin' tight!" I said loudly with an urban drawl, trying to lift the energy of our mutually suicidal moment.

She giggled, moved a little closer, slipped her arm through mine and rested her head on my shoulder. "Sing me a song, Justin."

"I don't want to sing." It was getting late, near midnight and I didn't want to make any unnecessary noise.

"Pretty please?" I knew not to argue any more, because like a real sister, she wouldn't shut up until I did what the hell she wanted.

"Okay. What song do you want?" I was irritated. She knew how embarrassed I was when I sang. "Sing a Journey song…or a Heart song. You remember any Pat Benatar?"

"I am not singing any fucking Pat Benatar or Heart. I'm a man, Roberta."

A sixteen-year old grown ass man!

"You are trying to be a man, I will give you that." She was amused at how her innocent taunting was affecting me.

I wasn't a singer, nor had I aspired to be one. I knew at this rate I would be dead within a matter of years, so it wasn't realistic to dream - at all. But I could sing. I had a distinctive voice and hit every note perfectly.

"So now I come to you, with open arms
Nothing to hide, believe what I say
So here I am, with open arms
Hoping you'll see, what your love means to me,
open arms."

"Oh my God, Justin. That sounded so good!" she gushed.

"I think the baby liked it, too, because he - she - whatever it is, just kicked!"

She smiled and was happy that I fulfilled her request. She grabbed me and gave me a big hug, "I love you, Justin, or Anthony –whatever the fuck your name is!"

"I love you too, Turtle," I responded.

"Turtle?"

"Yea," I started to crack up before I got the joke out in true geek fashion spoiling my own jokes, "Roberta the fertile turtle!"

"You, Justin, are very goofy," she rolled her eyes.

We talked for hours about everything. Two lost souls – in limbo. Eventually we crawled in bed together and spooned as BFF's.

I went to sleep wondering how life would unfold for her with another baby; the baby that she insisted she was keeping. I didn't want to hurt her feelings by reminding her that we could barely take care of ourselves anymore. I just wanted to allow her a few moments to dream – even unrealistically. Dreams were all we had left. Hope was a distant memory. It seemed like we were just waiting for our turn to die.

If a girl walks in,
And carves her name in my heart,

I'll turn and run away.

"Send Me an Angel" – Real Life

Chapter 14

I MISS YOU

I was copping my drugs at my dealer's when in came some other friends from my downtown crew to rob them. I was in a difficult position. The one who was carrying out the robbery looked at me and said, "This has nothing to do with you, Justin. Just go sit over there." I was relieved to not be involved in being robbed, but the act of excusing me made the dealer suspect that I had something to do with setting them up. With the guns pointed at everyone but me, I walked to the other side of the room and sat on the bed.

Ernie, the robber's little brother - another friend of mine from downtown - was at the front door and had the guy who answered the door in a headlock. Before I knew what was happening, I heard the sound of firecrackers and saw sparks flying in front of me. Ernie still had the guy in a headlock. I saw him freeze with an empty stare and fall backwards to the ground. Blood quickly surrounded his head.

He was killed instantly. It was a scene out of a movie but I knew life wouldn't be the same. You don't just see a friend get shot in the head and go back to black.

The homicide was ruled self-defense and no one ever paid consequences for Ernie's shooting. Two days later the drug dealer was ambushed and shot in the head.

I needed to get out of Seattle.

∞∞∞∞

I was watching 'Dallas' while staying at Lisa's and heard a news story that got my attention as I was preparing something to eat. Breaking News. I heard the reporter saying something about "Streetwise" and went from the kitchen into the living room where the television was located. One of the players had been killed. I walked closer to see whom they were talking about. I stood frozen and waited for the whole story. Disbelief transitioned into devastation. I listened to the newscaster who I felt was speaking directly to me:

"Lou Ellen Couch had been protecting her lesbian girlfriend from four violent and taunting men. Lou Lou, as she was also known, had gained stardom for her role in Streetwise, a documentary that was nominated for an academy award last year. She was a protector to many on the streets, but lost her own battle tonight, after being stabbed in the chest while protecting yet another likely victim of the streets."

I had seen so much until this point, but this was the most horrifying. Lou Lou never backed down from violence though she never carried weapons.

When the clip of 'Streetwise' took over the TV screen and I saw my dear Lou Lou, I could not control my inside heartbreak. Pain in the form of water began to pour down my face.

This was not happening. I couldn't believe it.

∞∞∞

The following day I took a bus to Mama's where the newspapers had started to be collected. Lou Lou was in several articles, which all spelled her name wrong. This irritated everyone. It's funny how we can get caught up in something like a misspelled name and make it our business to tell everybody when what we really wanted to tell everyone was that our *whole world* was wrong.

It was rumored that in one of her final breaths, she murmured the name of the famous photographer lady, Mary Ellen Mark, who had made her and some of us known in STREETWISE.

Lou Lou died doing what she did best - protecting the vulnerable who had nowhere else to go and no one else to love them. She was a saint on the streets of Seattle, and loved everyone as long as they weren't hurting another human being. She had talked about being a counselor 'when she grew up', but little did she know that she already was one.

Lou Lou died on Thursday night around midnight, the eve of Friday the 13th. Her funeral was five days later. Frankie, still in prison, was allowed to come to the funeral of his sister and I could not wait to see him.

Many people showed up to honor our beautiful Lou Lou. There were news crews and photographers at the funeral, not to mention the entire street community. It was a madhouse and was on the front page of the Seattle Times newspaper.

After making my rounds and talking with my street friends and her family, I mustered the strength to walk up to her casket. It was hard for me to look at her.

She was wearing a white suit and was very handsome. As I looked at my precious friend, a huge, empty hole in the pit of my stomach began to grow. I kissed her cold forehead. I turned around to walk away from the casket when I saw Frankie walking across the room in handcuffs. I was so full of emotion I ran up and hugged him. I needed to feel him.

"You're not supposed to do that," he spoke with a sly grin of my hug. He was amused at my boldness in front of the armed guards.

"I miss you, man," I whispered as the deputies on each side of him escorted him to the casket to see his sister, "Are you coming to the cemetery?"

"No. They won't let me," he said disappointed. He was trying not to grin by my presence. Though the sad occasion, we couldn't help but enjoy each other.

Lou Lou would be smiling too.

Seeing Frankie made me realize how I felt for him. Every ounce of love surfaced immediately. Even though everything was wrong, the occasion, the timing and the sinful contract, it was so nice to be able to see my friend.

Reality popped into place when I realized that he wasn't even halfway through his five-plus year sentence. I looked over at Mama, her face numb with pain. I am not sure if she spoke one word. I never saw her lips move.

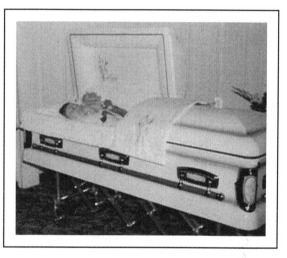

Lou Lou was put to rest at the Evergreen Cemetery. The people that made the movie, STREETWISE purchased her coffin. She never received her headstone since no one had money to pay for it.

Lou Ellen Couch. Only a little cement stone marks her grave with a lot number and her initials, L.E.C.

As we go down life's lonesome highway
Seems the hardest thing to do is to find a friend or two
A helping hand - some one who understands
That when you feel you've lost your way
You've got some one there to say,
I'll show you

Say you, say me

Say it for always, that's the way it should be

LIONEL RICHIE - 'Say You, Say Me' *
This song was played at Lou Lou's funeral on December 18, 1985...

Chapter 15

WHITE CHRISTMAS

When Christmas rolled around a few days after the funeral, I was still in pretty bad shape. I didn't go one minute without my beloved drugs to shut out the life I now hated. Melinda, one of the social workers from a Christian organization called New Horizons Ministries, seemed to be keeping a close eye on me. She invited me to go to Vancouver, Washington to her parent's house for the holiday. I first met Melinda several years before when she was working the beat downtown as an outreach worker. Though she was only four years my senior, it was crazy to me that she was light years ahead in human development. Melinda had similar features to mine, so lots of people joked that she was my sister. Except that by this time I had so neglected myself I had developed gross sores from picking at my face when I was high. My face was covered in scabby blisters, some infected and oozing puss, and some dry and scaly because they had healed while I focused on other parts of my face and arms. I think Melinda felt sorry for me so she insisted I come with her back home.

She picked me up downtown and we drove two hours to her parents' house. I wasn't sure what to expect when I arrived and was uncomfortable about sharing such a traditional family ritual with normal people. To my surprise, they were expecting me and were warm and caring – as if they really knew me.

Their house was warm and cozy with a beautiful meal with every holiday recipe from every food group - a no holds barred, spectacular meal and dessert. Christmas carols played on the stereo while we sat around the flocked tree. There were several presents under it – many wrapped and tagged with "To: Justin - from Santa Claus". They hadn't ever met me and yet these strangers took the time to buy, wrap and tag presents for me. Not just one or two, but there were several gifts, which consisted mostly of clothes, as they knew I was living on the streets. I was overwhelmed with gratitude that they would take the time to buy things that fit me. It was an amazing, emotional holiday, and hard to go back to the cold streets afterward.

I wondered if there ever would be a time that I could tap into a life like that.

I'm dreaming of a White Christmas
Just like the ones I used to know
Where the treetops glisten
And Children listen

To hear sleigh bells in the snow…

"White Christmas" – Bing Crosby

Chapter 16

LONG WAY GONE

Whenever I called home, I would get quite a hateful earful from Dad's background commentary.

"Who are you talking to, Carol? The little nigger?" he would scream loudly to disapprove of my acceptance of other races.

He had said the 'N' word a few times when I was a child, and it bothered me, but the tone he spoke in gave me a new distaste.

I listened to mostly urban music, like Michael Jackson, RUN-DMC and Chaka Khan, dressed like black folks with the little button down suits, matched in color with shoes. I talked like my father thought all blacks talked, sort of with a southern drawl and I had the capacity to speak and behave with a ghetto, socially unacceptable (at least in Caucasia) manner.

He absolutely hated much of me, but the idea of having a wannabe black son who was most likely gay would certainly be the last straw.

He would never be able to get past the gay part.

Neither would I.

Even still, I felt another urge to go home. My street family was almost nonexistent. Roberta was in and out of my life, as she was traveling back and forth to Portland. Lisa was so far gone on crack that it was too depressing to go there and see her kids living in squalor. I lost Lou Lou and Frankie. Some of my favorite hookers back on Pike Street were identified as possible victims of the Green River Killer. I was so alone and dazed and so very strung out I walked in circles for days until I called my mom in a desperate bid to get a stable life back. She agreed to let me come home – just to talk about what could be done for me.

I knew I was damaged and had seen and done unspeakable things that no one would believe, let alone understand. I felt removed and distant from everyone, yet my survival instincts motivated me to make that call to my mother – my last hope.

It was a shot in the dark, but I had to try because as attractive as death seemed, I didn't think I had the balls Dewayne did to carry it out. And deep inside I wanted to live - I just didn't want to live like this.

I took a bus from Downtown to Lake Forest Park and felt a deja vu as I knocked on the front door. My mother opened it and gave me a nervous little hug and I walked in. I figured Mom must not have prepared him for my visit when I saw my surprised father sitting in his favorite chair with a sour look on his face, which soon began expressing itself in words, "Jesus Christ! Who told him he could come here? This is my goddamn house! I don't want him here!"

"That's enough!" my mother snapped loudly, "What do you want me to do, Lloyd? He can't continue to live like this! Look at him. He is going to die. I won't allow this!" She started to cry. This was the first time I heard my mother stand up for me so force-fully.

"I don't give a damn! I don't want that little faggot in my house!"

After several years being away, his verbal assaults still tore deep into my soul. I was ready to blow. I just didn't know how to express myself. Too much had happened and I just did not have the coping mechanism to keep it all inside.

All I needed was for him to say one more thing, and I would produce the show of my life. Then he did, "You are a loser, and you're not my son!"

Curtains up.

I ran into the bathroom, locked the door and pulled a syringe out of my coat pocket. I was looking for something poisonous, like bleach or something that I could put in it and into my bloodstream. I couldn't find anything until I opened the last drawer. I figured, what the hell, rubbing alcohol would have to mess me up. I filled the syringe, while my brothers were trying to get me to come out.

I stuck the needle in my vein before I walked out of the bathroom so no one could stop me. I screamed, "You are a useless, fucking drunk and you don't have to worry about seeing me again! I fucking hate you!"

I walked across the room with the needle hanging out of my vein. I pushed the clear liquid into my arm in front of my stunned family. I pulled the needle out and threw it on the ground. It landed standing up with the needle imbedded into the carpet.

Whatever was going to happen would be quick, because that is how it works when you put liquid into your bloodstream. It is immediate. Supposedly.

A few seconds passed and I could taste alcohol in my mouth, almost like cocaine when used intravenously.

I was hoping I would at least have a seizure or heart attack.

Nothing.

The room was quiet so I had to do something quick. I had just learned the hard way that rubbing alcohol can be injected with little or no consequences.

This time, with a surge of hopelessness and vengeance, I ran back into the bathroom and grabbed a razor blade. I wasn't sure what I was going to do with it, so I walked to the front door.

"Justin, what are you doing? Why are you doing this? Please stop!" my mother yelled. Glancing towards him with my meanest face I told her, "You should make *him* stop." I dramatically showed the suicide device to my father on my way out the front door.

I began to contemplate my death. Would it hurt? How long does it take before all of the blood drains out of my body? Will I pass out quickly? I walked up the street and sat down behind the Sunshine Grocery Store, not far from my parent's house, and rolled up my sleeve. Thoughts were spinning as the razor pressed against my skin. Hyped up on adrenalin and revenge toward my father, I was embarrassed about the rubbing alcohol failure.

I was lost and alone and finally understood that this was my *only* choice. I gritted my teeth, shut my eyes and pushed the razor into my skin and up my arm from the wrist. I felt a sharp sting at first, but once the cut had started, the pain went away.

Then I did it again, and again, and again. When I looked down all I could see was bloody flesh and bones. Blood began to gush.

A sense of tranquility came over me when I realized that I was no longer scared to die. He deserved this. People would shun him.

Then my thoughts took a U-turn.

Was I going to let that asshole dictate when I would die?

I wouldn't give him the satisfaction. Jumping up I wrapped my six-inch wounds with my sweat coat and put my rain jacket over it, called a taxi and waited while applying pressure so I wouldn't bleed to death like I had originally hoped.

When the taxi picked me up, I kept my arm wrapped as tight and as discreetly as I could.

"Where are you going?" the driver asked.

"Group Health Hospital on Capital Hill."

He looked into the back seat nervously, "Everything alright back there?"

"I'm fine," I said shyly. I didn't want him too concerned. I just needed to get to the hospital. I still had coverage under my parent's health insurance policy and found it easier to manipulate their medical staff than at the free clinics.

Even with all the pressure I was applying to my wounds, my coat sleeve filled with blood. I was getting grossed out at all of the blood swishing around inside my coat, so when we stopped at traffic lights, I opened the door and poured the blood out on to the street. The most disgusting sight of purple, almost black, liquid with reddish clots poured onto the street.

The taxi man noticed what I was doing. "What happened to you young man? Are you bleeding?"

"A little," I lied, concerned at what he would do if he knew the truth, "I am fine sir. It's just a little cut. Someone is meeting me at the hospital."

"You need ambulance," he said with a thick accent.

"I said I'm fine! They are waiting for me!" I snapped back hoping to shut him up.

I had a fun time convincing the doctors and nurses that I wasn't suicidal. It was obvious my wounds were self-inflicted, but without admitting that I had done it, or that I wanted to hurt myself, they couldn't have me committed. I told them four-hundred times that I was angry at my father and put my fist through a window and kept my story straight and consistent, as they kept sending someone else in to get another version of my story trying to get me to tell, what they knew, was the truth. I was too smart for their plan.

I received sixteen stitches up my arm, and then three more rows of stitches where I had cut across.

I was back on the streets in a matter of hours.

You're a lost and lonely child
Look my way, and a smile will do
And I'll help you pull through

Lost and lonely child

"Lost and Lonely Child" – Savoy Brown

Chapter 17

GLUTTONY LOVES MISERY

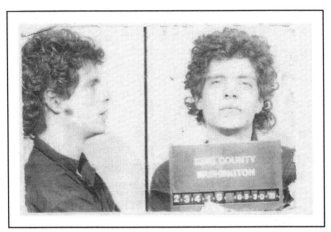

Pictured: Justin (actual mugshot), 1989

The next year went by in a murky blur. Now that I was your average strung out junkie I had no friends. I hadn't seen Roberta in a very long time and I didn't pay much attention to time or seasons unless it was cold. I slept on the streets, abandoned buildings or in jail. Kind people had run out of patience. It was only a matter of time before Frankie's release from prison but with the full blur I had going on, along with the internal despise I had for my sexual and emotional desires, I tried hard not to think about him.

While doing my day job, I was spotted getting into a car with a known criminal by the Seattle Vice Unit, who was aware that I had a warrant out for my arrest. I should have been more careful, as all the cops downtown wanted to arrest me.

I had several prescription pills on me that I had planned on selling but swallowed them all when I heard the police siren. I downed every Valium, Percocet, and Xanax I had on me. There was enough to overdose, but as long as I avoided prison, I didn't care.

I don't remember anything after getting handcuffed. I was processed in a blackout and woke up in the main jail dorm with all of my interesting roommates. The Seattle jail was fairly new and had been designed in a circular pod, with several dorms on two floors. There was a round, windowed front on each dorm so they could be viewed by the guards while they sat in the little space ship seats in between the floors. They controlled all of the doors, lights, and intercoms for all sides, upstairs and downstairs from their little UFO seats.

I was just starting to get my bearings back, when I heard the intercom.

"Inmate Early you have an interview." I jumped up off my fireproof mattress, and ran up to the glass door. The guard looked toward me, "Are you Early?" Normally I would have played around with the obvious joke, but I had no humor left in me, "Yes, I'm Early." The automatic door began to slide slowly open until I had just enough room to get out. The door closed immediately behind me.

It wasn't uncommon to have an interview. Lawyers and other social workers often called us out if they needed to talk, as they were never allowed in the dorm areas.

Usually lawyers and visitors have to conference through a thick glass window and a phone receiver. But this time I was put into an open room and was told to sit down and wait for my guest.

Still in a haze, I hardly recognized the man who used to be Officer Cee Cee's partner now Detective Benson. He looked different in plain clothes and was being unusually nice.

"I want to tighten up the information you provided to us yesterday. Oh, and I brought you this article before you saw it yourself."

"What are you talking about?" I asked defensively.

Is he trying to trick me?

I didn't remember anything. He handed me the article. It was of a child pornographer that had been arrested after a homeless informant with a criminal history provided enough additional details for his arrest.

"We really appreciate the information you gave us, it helped us to secure a search warrant for a significant pending investigation," Detective Benson stated kindly.

He wasn't like most of the cops I had interacted with. He was always considered to be a nice cop, but this was freaking me out. The more he talked the more he said stuff I had never told anyone. He was for real. I couldn't believe that I had given them all that information.

How long was I out of it?

"We found the hidden spot under the floorboards. Because of you we were able to arrest one of the largest child pornographers in the Pacific Northwest," he boasted.

This was a huge bust for his career and he wasn't denying it. While enthusiastically going over the details I supposedly provided him, he opened a file folder that he had brought with him.

"I am not suppose to show you these, but because you were so young and changed so much since the time they were taken, we need you to identify the child in these photos." I looked at them while he tried to cover the private parts of the young child in the photo – the child with no pubic hair.

Oh. My. God.

"I'm just a baby in these pictures," I said stunned in disbelief.

This man had been taking pictures of me since I had hit the streets at ten and was selling them all over the United States and the world.

When I was posing for him I thought it was no big deal. And it wasn't, compared to what else I was doing at the time. But with a little perspective, the whole thing became sickening to me.

Detective Benson continued to explain the behavior of the man who was arrested. He was a pedophile who groomed his victims and their parents. He was able to ingratiate himself into their lives and gain their guardians trust. Once he was established as a family friend he began to work on getting his victim. All were little boys who were terrified into keeping silent. My case was a little different since I was a willing runaway and was easier to manipulate, but as Benson began to educate me in the ways of the child predator, I felt more and more nauseous. I felt some relief knowing the men I had been involved with, Preacher Man included, were being targeted by the police.

Over the following weeks while I was incarcerated waiting to be sentenced for my probation violation, I provided all the information they would need to prosecute this man. I agreed to be witness for the State of Washington and was continually pulled out of my cell to meet with the police, prosecutors and the FBI. Detective Benson kept reminding me that I was making a difference in many children's lives by helping get this pedophile off the streets. As a detective, he was allowed to pull me out of the jail for business related to the case. He took me to McDonalds and then to his precinct where I met some of his detective friends, some who I knew or at least recognized.

Somewhere in the back of my mind I knew that this moment could be a turning point in my appalling life. I was ready to try to do something, anything that would be considered good.

∞∞∞∞

It was time to face my own judicial sentence. The holding cell for court was very small. They packed all of us inmates like sardines. Depending on the time of your court appearance we would sometimes have to be in a stinky room with one big toilet on the middle of the wall - for the entire day. I refused to use it, but others didn't mind. I couldn't stand it. I had been there for hours, nervously pacing, wondering what my fate would be and trying to keep my ever-present ADD in check.

Finally, I was led into the courtroom. I never bothered fighting any charges because they would usually let you out right away if you agreed with the prosecutor that you were guilty of something, even if you weren't. I was put in front of the wooden pew before the court and looked up. I almost wet my pants when I saw who was looking down at me from the bench.

It was Judy my old lawyer. Now she was Judge Judith Hightower.

She took a second look before recognizing me and then faintly smiled, which put me at ease.

"Hi Justin," she began as she turned to the prosecutor, "There is a possible conflict of interest. Mr. Early was my client for many years in the juvenile justice system."

"The state will waive the conflict, your honor, if you are willing to proceed as scheduled."

"The court will proceed," Judge Judy continued in an authoritative tone.

She directed her attention to me. And with an, 'I told you so' look on her face, she laid into me heavily and with a strong black girl attitude.

"Whatever you are doing, it's not working," she looked away in disgust and began to hand down my sentence. She gave me the maximum allowable sentence for a probation violation, which surprised me. I knew not to say anything, as she would probably find me in contempt of court.

What a bitch!

"Justin," she looked down at me now wearing her motherly face that I remembered so clearly, "you are going to have some time to think. I want you to use it constructively and to contemplate the decisions that you are making in your life. I would really like to not see you in my courtroom again."

I guess she cared about me, but I still didn't like the sentence she handed me.

"Yes ma'am," I promised.

∞∞∞

Several weeks into my six-month sentence, I noticed that I had little red spots all over my legs. I didn't pay too much attention to them at first, but then I noticed that my wrists and ankles were bruised and beginning to get swollen. Even the guard was concerned enough to call an ambulance. I was sent to Harborview Medical Center where I had to be shackled to my hospital bed with the kind of wristbands used for psych patients because regular handcuffs might cause me to bruise and bleed inside. They performed several blood tests and told me that I was not allowed to walk because a fall would probably make me bleed to death. It was 1989 and HIV in IV drug users was prevalent. They suspected that might be a possible factor for my condition, which was called idiopathic thrombocytopenic purpura (ITP). This disorder causes all of the platelets in the body to die off (platelets clot your blood). A normal human has 120,000 – 600,000 platelets. I had 1,500 and was bleeding to death internally. They performed several HIV tests and thankfully they all came back negative. But we still didn't know what was wrong. I was terrified.

Melinda from New Horizons had a relationship with the court system and was allowed to come see me at the hospital. Because I was considered incarcerated they would not let family visit. I doubt mom would have if she had the opportunity.

I told Melinda what I had done with the detective and that I was now working as an informant with the FBI.

"I'm proud of you, Justin. That is an important step if you want to change your life. I am worried about the people that you are working against but am very, very proud of you." She told me exactly what I needed to hear.

"Have you seen or heard from Roberta?" I asked.

"No, I haven't," I could tell she knew more.

"When was the last time you saw her?" I prodded.

"It's been about a two and a half years now."

I hadn't seen Roberta in almost two years. It was disappointing and gave me honest concern to worry.

"Melinda?" I asked, looking for expression on her face.

"Yes?" she answered not wanting to continue this particular line of questioning.

"She has never disappeared for this long in all these years I have known her. This isn't like her," I said clearly being overly sensitive.

The rain on the window was competing with the loud ticking of the hospital clock. With her eyes glued to the floor she began telling me what I knew she was holding back, "Justin, I am not saying this to scare you or upset you but it is quite possible that she has disappeared." I had run this scenario in my head over the past years several times.

"She is officially missing, and was reported missing by her family. The Green River Task Force was asking questions regarding her possible whereabouts."

I felt numb in this most disturbing drama. When Melinda spoke, I could hear her undertones directed at me, always reminding that there are better choices that could possibly lead to a better life. I wasn't really listening. But I heard her.

I just wanted to know where Roberta was.

∞∞∞∞

Detective Benson also came to see me in the hospital. He informed me that I wasn't the only witness in the Child Pornography case. Another child had been identified in the pictures and was willing to testify. His name was Eddie.

After a two-week vacation from jail and a blood platelet transfusion, I went back to the minimum-security facility call NeRF, the North Rehabilitation Facility. The doctors explained the meaning of "Idiopathic; *arising spontaneously or from an obscure or unknown cause,"* and told me my HIV result was negative, but were not sure what caused my platelet deficiency. However, they were confident that I would be fine as long as I monitored my blood levels periodically.

Benson made an unplanned visit to NERF and I could tell something was going on. He was quiet and was finding a hard time getting words out. He had a serious look on his face.

"I have some bad news. The other witness in the case, Eddie, has been found dead."

"What happened?" I asked surprised.

"It's been ruled a suicide, but it is suspicious. It seems he may have gone swimming at Gasworks Park, got caught in a riptide and drowned. He didn't have any shoes on and they have not been able to find them at the scene. The whole thing doesn't sit right with me."

"Detective, Gasworks Park is a lake, not the ocean," I stated referring to the lack of riptides.

He agreed.

I was not offered protective custody because Eddie's death was not ruled a homicide. But I knew that there were some angry and even more so, evil pedophiles that did not like the thought of us ruining their lucrative business.

I was not offered any form of protective custody, and wouldn't have accepted it anyway.

∞∞∞

My mom came to get me when I was released from NeRF so we could 'have a talk'. I got into her car and told her everything about the case that she had already been following in the news media.

"You have to leave Seattle. You can't be here anymore. I don't know what to do with you. You don't have any more chances - not with us and not with the court."

"I want to go to San Francisco," I quickly responded without thinking. I had been to San Francisco, but had no idea I wanted to move there until just now.

Mom bought me a bus ticket and gave me some food money. Detective Benson had gotten the FBI to give me a little money, too, so I had enough to survive for a few days.

I knew my life would need to change. I could no longer live on the streets. I needed to take this opportunity to pull things together. San Francisco seemed like a good place.

Actually, anywhere did.

All my life I've been a fool,
Who said I could do it all alone,
How many good friends have I already lost,
How many dark nights have I known?

"I Am Changing" – Jennifer Holliday

Chapter 18

CALIFORNICATION

I awoke in the final stretch of the twenty-hour bus ride as the Greyhound bus crossed the Oakland Bay Bridge with the most beautiful views I had ever witnessed in my still short life. I felt at peace as I saw the City by the Bay, the skyscrapers twinkled even in daylight, calling to me and welcoming me to my new home. It was a clear and sunny day, so I could see The Golden Gate Bridge to my right and the endless ocean between us. As the bus drove on city streets, nearing our final destination, I felt I was going to be all right even though the butterflies of the unknown were still flying in my belly. I felt a rush of adrenaline as I exited the bus depot on Market Street. I had no idea where I was or where I was going. I had no friends. I had very little money - not even enough for a hotel - and not an idea of which direction to walk. I had been in San Francisco previously, but only for a few days before I was arrested for being a young runaway. I was flown back to Seattle, courtesy of the State of Washington - handcuffed of course. But if my memory served me correctly, I knew the general direction of their streets, their very seedy streets.

Polk Street District was a stroll for male and transvestite hookers located just outside the Tenderloin District, also known as the 'T.L.'.

I knew that if I could find Polk Street, I would be fine. So I asked someone and was given the simple directions of where would become my new stomping grounds. The walk wasn't far and once I got to Geary Avenue near the bottom of Market Street, I was told it was a straight walk up to Polk Street. As I crossed Larkin I noticed a shopping cart that had been made into a camp of sorts. I peaked in discreetly and saw a tall, heavy-built, white man sticking a needle into his vein. I stopped immediately at the parking meter just beyond the little camp. Once I saw that needle, my heart raced. The fact that he was pitifully living in a shopping cart on the dirty street and the fact that I swore I was going to get my life together and never get loaded again had no power over my addiction. Without hesitation, I tried to figure out a way to talk to this guy.

I knew he could get me drugs.

I hung around for fifteen minutes when I noticed him peeking out of the covered shopping cart. I had to move quickly, yet be cautious and strategic. I had to make myself credible. I didn't want him to think I was a cop or a snitch.

"Hey man," I spoke with my street accent, "can you get me some down?"

I was hopeful he knew I meant heroin. I prayed he wouldn't blow me off because each area in the United States has there own version of street names. He crawled out of his make-shift home and walked towards me. The man had a serious case of Acne Rosacea - his face red with pustules larger than pimples, more like cysts. H was much taller than I anticipated.

His sweat smelled terrible. He had pinned eyes and was scratching himself diligently, which is obvious behavior of an opiate addict.

"How much you looking for?" he asked in a highly intoxicated tone.

"I got twenty," I replied as cool as I could.

"I got some here, man, but I won't charge you that much. I have a little extra left over from a bag I got earlier. Just give me ten," he said generously.

He was hospitable and we began to introduce ourselves. His name was Steve and he was a homeless drug-addict. I knew his type well. He was just like me. Steve invited me into his homemade shopping cart tent. The putrid stench of human funk and urine really grossed me out. Once I saw the syringe container on the cement, the smell suddenly didn't bother me anymore. He had hung sheets and blankets around the perimeter of the shop-ping cart, while using the park fence as another tie up spot, creating a manufactured home in the true sense of the term. I was impressed by his creativity. I did my hit of heroin, and the fear of being in a new city went away before the needle came out of the vein.

My unrelenting sorrow for the loss of Lou Lou, my fear of what might have happened to Roberta and the incarceration of Frankie, which were exaggerated when cold sober, became manageable.

Smooth, soothing heroin made everything - even dirty, stinky, blanket camps and shopping carts - seem fine.

I guess I was meant to get high and be a low-level dope fiend. I couldn't imagine ever passing up a hit of this wonderful stuff. Steve became a new friend and helped me get situated with dealers and needle exchanges around San Francisco. He told me that the exchanges were technically illegal, so it was all done very discreetly. The only way to find them was by word of mouth.

I began to live in the Tenderloin District at various hotels, and when all else failed, would stay near Steve on the alley street outside the park. He would hook me up with blankets and let me leave what little I owned in his shopping cart. Unlike Seattle, I didn't know anyone with housing, so surfing around for somewhere to stay in a pinch wasn't an option.

I had arrived on skid row at the young age of nineteen.

I would bring my drugs to Steve's camp and he would provide the 'works', which consisted of syringes, water and a spoon. Beyond the severe redness on Steve's face, I noticed that he also had purple birthmarks, which began to look more suspicious.

Within weeks he looked like he was deteriorating as if something was seriously wrong with him.

Finally I asked, "What are those purple spots on your face? They look like they're getting' worse." He looked at me with a dead stare and bluntly told me, "I have K.S. (Kaposi Sarcoma, a form of cancer) from AIDS." He looked back down, continued fixing his drugs, "I thought you knew."

"How the fuck was I suppose to know that?" I was freaking out.

The needle exchanges also provided bleach, but using it took extra time and when I was in a hurry to get fixed, I would easily pass on this very important step.

I had used drugs with him and shared needles with this dude, and *now* he's telling me he has AIDS? I had tested negative not long before I moved and was sure that I had been exposed at that time, so hopefully I would still be okay. But it wasn't like I really cared, anyway after I processed what just happened.

San Francisco was a harsh town compared to Seattle. I was in the same situation in a tougher city with tougher rules and more scandalous people. I was having a hard time making money. Drugs were paramount.

Basic necessities like food, housing, clothes, and water were secondary luxuries.

The city wasn't what I thought it would be and I was lonely. I thought I would meet a new crew to run with, and that the San Francisco activity would bring some kind of good fortune. At least in Seattle I had family. I couldn't stay with them or visit much, but knowing they were close made a huge difference.

After several nights of not finding a place to stay, I had a bright idea at two o'clock in the morning to steal a car and drive back to Seattle. I had been drinking, which is when I come up with most of my classic epiphanies. I knew how to hotwire cars - mainly older model American cars - but did not see any that I liked. It needed to be something that I could be seen in, too. I wasn't sure how I was going to buy gas, so whatever I stole had to have some gas, and then I could worry about getting more fuel when I ran low.

I saw a Porsche in the parking garage off Polk Street. I figured I'd look pretty good driving into Seattle in a nice, green Porsche, so I decided to hotwire it. I began manipulating the ignition, but didn't realize how difficult this foreign car would be to conquer.

The next thing I knew I was being pulled out of the driver's seat and getting the shit kicked out of me on the ground. The owner and his companion had caught me in his car and decided to give me a good beating, punching me in the head and face, and kicking me all over my body.

They called the police and I went to jail. I was almost relieved after the beating I had just endured.

∞∞∞

I was booked into the City and County of San Francisco's Hall of Justice, at 850 Bryant Street, in the South of Market area of San Francisco.

During my booking I was asked my sexual preference. I found it odd because I didn't know it was a 'preference'. I would 'prefer' to be straight, but I was not.

I was not going to disrespect any more girls trying to be what the haters wanted me to be either. Being gay for pay was still a little lie that helped me justify my sexuality. Even when people said I wouldn't have become a fag if I hadn't been a victim of the streets, I knew they were promoting their inherited beliefs.

I still wasn't really being completely honest about my sexuality.

Not even with myself. But during the intake I heard that San Francisco Jail had a Gay Tank. With my sucked-up skeletal frame, I hoped would be a safe place for me.

Everybody knows that the gays are nicer anyway, at least the ones I had met. I was beyond my old homophobic tirades, but still couldn't look deep enough inside my own soul to acknowledge I was one of 'them'. Being a dope fiend was an excellent distraction and I only loved Frankie, so maybe I wasn't really gay anyway.

Hopefully, I would be safe at the same time.

The Gay Tank was a much better venue in which to make friends while incarcerated. Although I thought I looked like shit, many of the other inmates looked worse, so I was actually one of the better looking men in the group. The tank was a family that mostly looked out for each other as long as you were respectful. It was located on the sixth floor, housed approximately forty inmates, and they were a colorful bunch to put it mildly.

There were transsexuals with silicone in their breasts and faces, which was suppose to make them look more feminine. There were gay men that liked men. There were "straight" men that liked 'chicks with dicks' (and sometimes gay men) for their personal entertainment.

Then there was me. Nobody, including me, knew what the hell I was. But since I was good looking and still had a sense of humor, I fit in and was admired quickly.

I felt at ease with my new roommates. Everyone really looked out for each other, there wasn't much violent drama going on and I made some friends who would share their tobacco and commissary food and candy with me. I had manipulated the Jail Infirmary into giving me medicine by declaring I had a sever case of depression. So I was able to get some 'happy pills' to ease the loss my body was suffering from not having any hard drugs.

These pills also helped me sleep.

I was in line to see the nurse that was distributing meds at the front of the dormitory when I felt a little shake under my feet. We were all just getting ready to watch the beginning of the World Series and the shaking, which I thought could be the medicine making me dizzy, gradually became worse – and worse.

Everyone froze and began to look at each other with complete disbelief.

Someone screamed, "EARTHQUAKE! GET UNDER YOUR BUNKS!"

The shaking got worse. I had a hard time running back to my bunk. The building swayed harder and faster and the floors were rolling and folding. The walls began cracking and the plaster and cement that separated all of the cell dorms cracked and I could see through to the next dorm through the three-foot thickness of steel and cement. The jail was rocking back and forth uncontrollably with no hint of ever being able to stop. I couldn't stand anymore as the shaking was unbearable so once I stumbled to my bunk, I tried to jump underneath my bed, which was even more difficult due to the rolling of the floors that I was sure were going to collapse.

It seemed like an eternity, but it was merely seconds as San Francisco experienced her worst catastrophe since 1906. It was dubbed the Great Quake of '89.

All of the guards and jail staff had evacuated and inmates were left in the jail alone. The power went out and we knew that it wasn't coming on any time soon. I went to the payphone and picked up the receiver, and to my surprise it was still working. I decided to call my mother and tell her what had happened.

"Mom, we just had a major earthquake!" I yelled as soon as she accepted the charges for my collect call. I was still very anxious because we were feeling aftershocks that continued to do damage to the already beaten building.

"Hold on, something is coming on the television," she told me nervously. We talked on the phone for a few minutes and she informed me that the Bay Bridge collapsed and there was a terrible fire in the Marina. I gave my report to the other inmates when my mother asked me, "Where are you?"

"I'm in jail."

Click.

All minor offenders, such as myself, were ordered released due to the overcrowding, so I hit the streets again.

Thankfully, Steve's camp was still set up and he was waiting for someone to get high with. The stores were closed, but the drug dealers were working overtime.

It wasn't long before I was back in my drugged-out routine, dying, ever so slowly, while getting used to the low level of street life that came with a very populated city.

There was no way I could live long in this environment, but at least I was out of Seattle.

I didn't want anyone to see me after all of the promises I had made.

Streets are filled with broken glass
You get buried by the past
Give me just a little taste

Lay this mess to waste

"Promises Broken" – Soul Asylum

Chapter 19

FURTHER DAMAGE

I was roaming around late at night with nowhere to go, when a large framed man came up to me and offered to get me high and off the streets. I needed to get high - the place to sleep was a pure bonus. We went back to his hotel room, which wasn't far from the Polk Street area. We partied for a while and then he made it clear that he wanted to have sex. I wasn't in the mood and told him no. He continued to make sexual advances, and was getting aggressive and then became threatening. I decided he wasn't cool at all and got up to go to the door. Before I could reach it, he jumped up and blocked my exit. He told me that I wasn't leaving until I had sex with him. His violent eyes became ablaze with anger and entitlement.

I went back and sat down and wondered how the hell I was going to get out of this. He became more agitated and was hyper aware of my every move - nervous that I would escape.

Truth be told, there was nothing for him to be worried about. He was a large man of African descent, much taller than me and very muscular. If he hadn't turned so unattractive with his demeanor, he would have been sort of handsome. But now he turned ugly - real ugly. I was very thin since my priority always was drugs, so I was easy prey. I didn't have much of a fight in me. Although I tried to look mean so people would stay away from me, I never got into fights and was quite disgusted at the sound of flesh being hit or slapped.

My legs were strong, though, from all of the walking. But they weren't going to help me now.

"Lay down," he told me pointing towards the bed. He started to disrobe, "Take off your clothes."

I was no match. There was nothing I could do to get out of this one. If had I thrown a violent fit, like I imagined myself doing in this situation, he would hurt me or maybe even kill me. The insane look in his face and eyes was unreal.

I became scared for my life.

After he had complete control of my arms, lying behind me, he started talking to me as if I was a willing participant.

"You want it don't you," his deep voice sounded like a bad villain. I did exactly as he instructed. I was trying to think myself out of this situation, out of this hotel room, but before I could figure a way out, the most excruciating pain began when he forced himself into my body. I could feel and hear the sound of flesh ripping. With the beast brutally determined to have his way, it felt as if a sword had entered my rear. I gasped loudly while inhaling in dreadful pain. He covered my mouth so no screams would come out, but my moans would not cease. I prayed for the pain to end. It did not subside as I had hoped it would. Sharp pains continued piercing through my entire mid section while I tried to hold my breath. With no other possible thought of how to stop the pain I began to breathe deeply, forcing my body to slow down by relaxing. With no more struggling, or trying to pull away, the pain started to subside. But the thought of having someone do this to me was incomprehensible. I was embarrassed and ashamed and felt helpless.

"You like it, don't you? You like that, baby boy?"

I spoke no words and only breathed as I tried to stay relaxed so the pain would stay minimized.

When it was over, he pulled his part out of me, making the pain come back momentarily. I cringed in disgust. Although I still hurt, I rolled forward and jumped off the bed and swiftly went to the bathroom. I knew I was bleeding, so I cleaned myself quickly and went to my clothes that were still strewn by the hotel door. I mechanically put them on – sickened by the thought of this man's fluid inside me. I felt him staring at me and wondered if he would stop me from exiting.

Without looking back at him, I opened the door and walked quickly out of the hotel. I needed a change of clothes and a big fat hit of dope.

I had a new problem to forget about.

My hearts at a low
I'm so much to manage
I think you should know that

I've been damaged

"Damaged" – TLC

Childhood abuse increases youths' risk for later victimization on the street. Physical abuse is associated with elevated risk of assaults for runaway and homeless youth, while sexual abuse is associated with higher risk of rape for runaway and homeless youth.

Molnar, B., Shade, S., Kral, A., Booth, R., & Watters, J. (1998). Suicidal Behavior and Sexual / Physical Abuse Among Street Youth. *Child Abuse & Neglect*. Vol. 22, NO. 3, pp. 213-222.

Chapter 20

ANOTHER IN TIME

I remained homeless often frequenting Steve's camp in Larkin Park. He had lost what little belongings I'd left with him when I went to jail. I was sure he sold them.

I would sleep during the day and roam the streets for drugs at night. I was lying on the stinky, piss smelling mattress that I had thrown on the cement inside the park when a male voice woke me from a sleep coma, "Excuse me." I opened one eye - glad to see he wasn't a cop.

"Young man," the voice continued, "you look like you need something to eat."

I was one hundred thirty pounds and I should have been one sixty.

"My name is Ken. Take this money and please get something to eat. Don't use it for drugs!" he was sort of kidding.

"I wont," I replied with my standard lie.

Drugs were paramount. I lived only for *them* now – and they existed for *me*.

I got up off my mattress and decided to actually go eat with Ken. He let me keep the money and paid for the meal, which really made me like him.

We talked for a long time and then he gave me his number.

"If you ever need help, call me. I live in Huntington Beach, down near Los Angeles."

∞∞∞

Still scheduled to testify in the case against the pedophile, I kept in contact with Detective Benson. The prosecutor's office flew me to Seattle. Special Agent Pat, whose office wasn't far from my stomping grounds in the Tenderloin District of San Francisco, made sure I made it to the airport by providing me cab fare. I had decided not to see my family once I got there because I didn't want them to see me.

I was in my hotel (courtesy of the King County Prosecutor's office) when the phone rang. It was the woman from the prosecutor's office, "Don Knutson has decided to take the plea deal that was offered to him. He will be sentenced to fifteen years in prison. You will not have to testify." I was relieved.

I checked out of my hotel in downtown Seattle and started looking for a place to crash. I called one of the only people left in my imaginary little black book. Mama was never one to get overly excited to hear from anyone, but I could tell she was happy to know I was alive, "Well, Hi honey. Where are you? Everyone was worried about you and wondering if something awful had happened."

"I'm alright. I am in Seattle and need a place to stay."

She didn't hesitate, "I'm sorry honey, you can't stay here. Have you talked to Frankie? He's been out for a while, honey. He is staying at a hotel on Aurora with his wife."

Wife?

I took the information that she gave me and made a phone call to the motel, and asked to be connected to his room.

"Hello?" spoke the familiar voice coming from the other end of the phone. I was so ecstatic I could hardly speak, "Frankie? It's Justin!"

"Hey bro! Where are you? How come nobody's heard from you?"

"Can I come see you?"

Yes, of course

His wife was at work as a stripper. It meant we would be alone. The butterflies that I had gotten used to when it came to the thought of Frankie had gone away. I now had a case of full-on elephants in my stomach. I couldn't help but think of how I was going to see my boy. I was so excited I didn't know how to direct my energy.

I walked up to the motel from the bus stop and took a deep breath. Before my fist hit the door it opened.

"Hey," I began as nonchalantly as I could muster. I'm afraid there was no hiding the intensity of my feelings. Before I could finish my sentence, Frankie grabbed me and gave me a bear hug.

"The last time we hugged I was in handcuffs," he said with a sexy smile.

I missed you.

Frankie was always sexy. But now he was beyond anything I had seen. Besides the grown up goatee that he had on his once pretty boy face, he had put on several pounds in muscle. His abs were defined and tighter than any Calvin Klein underwear model.

He was lean, muscular but his face was still soft and innocent - except for his noticeably crooked nose.

"What happened to your nose?" I asked as I rubbed my hand on his perfect head.

"Just a little altercation on the prison yard," he replied without much emotion, "it's been broken six times." I came in and sat on the chair in the motel room and we began to catch each other up about the last several years of our lives. He pulled a chair close to mine. Although it was clear he was happy to see me, he was not himself. He was quiet and more reserved than I had remembered. Prison had affected him. It didn't matter, though - I was mesmerized. Seeing him again ignited all the longing I had. It all came back tenfold. I remembered how much he meant to me and got to see again how beautiful he was. It was not just physical either.

I loved him but still couldn't say it.

As I was telling him about my gross suicide attempt, he reached out and touched my face. He knew how bad it had gotten for me. He understood how it felt to be that low.

"I'm glad you stopped yourself," he said as he leaned in to kiss me. My heart raced. I needed more and I took it. I began kissing his face and neck and without saying a word, I worked my way down his chest and abs.

We couldn't have stopped if we wanted to. I felt powerless.

We caught up for hours, became close and did what we obviously remembered how to do. It was just like riding a bike only we'd both gotten better at it.

∞∞∞∞

I was in Seattle for three months, which was about three months too long. I was saddened to learn that no one had heard from Roberta. She would have been twenty-five.

Although I was still using drugs, I wasn't using as much because money was harder to come by - so were drugs.

During this time I called my mom rather than seeing her in person. She was still disappointed in my choices and I felt uncomfortable in front of her. I mostly stayed all over Seattle with friends, at motels and with Frankie, when permitted. His wife had become suspect of our friendship and didn't like me around, but Frankie did and that's all that mattered.

I would crash at their motel, on the floor, while Frankie slept in the bed with his wife.

It was early January and my mother informed me that my brother Cameron had been having terrible headaches. He passed out at work while on his graveyard shift and was taken to the hospital and admitted indefinitely. He was diagnosed with an aggressive brain tumor and was scheduled for surgery. I stayed in Seattle a little longer as to make sure that my brother was ok before I went back to San Francisco.

It didn't take very long before I resented Frankie's wife. I was a bit jealous of his union and didn't like hanging around when they were together. I still loved him deeply, but my life in San Francisco was calling me. I told Frankie of my intention to go back after Cameron's brain surgery.

"Why don't we come, too?" he asked, "We can drive. My wife just got a car from someone."

"Really?" I questioned the thought.

"Yes, really. Why not? You say they got money down there, right? I'm sure they have strip joints for the wife to work. And we can do our usual thing."

We tied up our loose ends and drove together to San Francisco.

So when you need good lovin,' you can call on me
And I'll be there to fill your every need
No one's gonna love you
The way I do,

Nobody…

"No One's Gonna Love You" – The SOS Band

Chapter 21

BROKEN REVELATIONS

Not long after arriving in San Francisco, it was apparent that Frankie and his wife were not happy about their new location. It's difficult getting situated in a new city when someone does only what we knew how to do.

Although I still cared very much for Frankie, the bottom line was that he wasn't with me, no matter how much we hung out. I wasn't comfortable in our current situation, which was the only situation I had ever known. Drugs had become priority number one many years ago and although I tried to keep cool with some special people, like Frankie, I just didn't give a shit anymore.

We started to argue and tried to walk away from him.

"Where are you going?" he asked me accusatorily.

I shot back, "I'm just gonna go do my thing. I'll see you later." I was over it. I was over him. I was over *everything*.

"You are not gonna leave me after dragging me down here. Don't think I will let you do that," he said angrily.

"I'm out, Frankie. I'm done. Have a safe trip," I turned and began walking down Polk Street. I heard a trunk slam and then footsteps. Frankie had a screwdriver in his hand and was running up to me, angrier than I had ever seen him in the ten years that I had known him.

Please do something to make me hate you.

I stopped and faced him. With the screwdriver drawn like a knife, he held his position and stared me straight in the eyes.

I urged him, "Go ahead, Frankie. Do it! I don't give a fuck."

I wanted him to hurt me physically so I could shake the feelings that I had been holding onto for so long. I didn't want to love him anymore.

"I don't care anymore," I admitted.

He lowered the screwdriver and started walking back towards the car. I continued walking away the other direction.

"Where are you going?" he asked.

I am not doing this anymore.

Before this moment I had never had an argument with Frankie. Not one, not ever. We were both pretty easygoing when it came to our relationship, and never really rubbed one another the wrong way. I couldn't believe what had just happened. I took it to be a sign that I was ready to be back on my own. I knew that whatever it was we had, or didn't have, it was wrong.

My heart broke at the end of my friendship and affair with Frankie. Although I intended on not seeing him again, we did stick together for a few more days, hustling our way into some drugs and a hotel room.

On the second day I was giving them their space and running around on my own and had gotten some cocaine and heroin in the Tenderloin. I didn't want to share it with them, so I went to the Fish and Chips spot on Polk Street. I ordered some food and went into the bathroom to fix my stuff. There was no running water - which sucked. Left with no other options, I bent down and sucked water into the syringe from the dirty toilet. I was trying to hurry because I knew people were waiting on the bathroom. They kept knocking and I was shaky. I did my best to hit a vein in my ankle, which was the only place I had left to inject. I missed the vein, forcing all of the drugs mixed with dirty toilet water under my skin.

It became sore and agitated right away. I walked out of the restaurant, bypassing my order of food that was on the counter, and started walking down the street, angry with myself for messing up my hit.

A dope fiend's worst nightmare is missing the vein because you don't get high. That's the *worst* thing that can happen. The second worst thing that can happen is you get an infection and die. My ankle hurt fiercely and was swelling quickly.

It hurt more than almost anything I had ever experienced. The sexual assault still topped the chart. I figured I would try to get some more money to get some more drugs to self medicate the pain away.

I stayed on my own for the next few days. My ankle turned red and then purple. It was so swollen that my shoe was stuck on. As hard as I tried, I couldn't get my shoe off. If I put any pressure on my foot, I would scream. All I could do was slowly hop in short increments. Exhausted and in pain and all hopped out, I sat in an alley between Bush and Post Streets. I couldn't move another inch and my good foot was now sore from picking up the slack. I hadn't realized it, but Frankie had walked up behind me.

"We are going back to Seattle," he said bluntly before noticing my injury, "Oh my god. Are you alright?"

"Not really," I replied.

"You need an ambulance." Although we weren't on happiest of terms, it was apparent that Frankie was concerned.

"I don't want an ambulance," I told him flatly.

"Well, you need to do something," he said as helped me get back up on my good foot. He started carrying me in the direction of the car. I wasn't going to argue with him as he was in one of his serious moods. It wouldn't have done any good. Once his stubborn gene kicked in, negotiation was pointless. As he walked with me, the pain became excruciating, "Stop! Put me down! I can't do this. Let me rest," I demanded.

He put me down.

"You need to go to the hospital. I'm calling an ambulance."

I don't want a fucking ambulance.

Frankie followed the ambulance to the hospital and stayed momentarily. We both agreed that I would probably be let out that night so he stayed until my name was called.

The pain in my ankle was now in my leg, I had a fever and my entire body was fatigued. I was immediately given a nice dose of pain medication. Drug addicts usually have a hard time being properly medicated because doctors don't want to feed their addiction. But this doctor knew of the seriousness and was very generous.

With all of the pain medication, I became relaxed and the nightmare that I was living didn't seem as bad as it truly was.

I didn't have the two dollars a day for the television but was being entertained by a gay male nurse who had taken a liking to me. He would come in and joke with me when he had the chance. I was a little delirious, and high from pain meds when the phone rang.

"It's Frankie. I'm in jail."

Frankie went on to explain that the car he said was his wife's was stolen. He and his wife had been pulled over and taken to jail on criminal charges.

"Are you booked yet?" I asked.

"I'm just getting processed now. You're my one phone call," he said clearly bummed out.

I didn't blame him.

"Well, first thing is to tell them that you're gay. The gay tank is like Disneyland."

"Um, okay. I guess," he chuckled amused. I knew that Frankie wasn't worried about being in the mainline jail, because knew how to hold his own. He had already spent a third of his life in prison.

"I also have a friend, a client that is a priest in the jail. I will call him and have him come see you."

"Your trick is the jail priest?" Now he was really amused.

"Yes. Well, he's not really a priest, but he's close to being one. His name is Brother Derrick. Expect him."

"I'll try to call you and let you know what happens."

I was a little pissed that I hadn't been told about the stolen car. But then he probably didn't tell me on purpose. I would have been a paranoid wreck the entire drive.

I made the phone call to Brother Derrick and he went right over to see Frankie. He also kept me up to date with all of the details pertaining to his release.

One of the great benefits of coming to California with a criminal record from Washington is that none of it showed up in the computer. So, as far as California was concerned, Frankie was a clean man.

He would be out in a matter of days.

∞∞∞

I was staring out the window studying the architecture of the old San Francisco General Hospital when I heard someone walk into my hospital room, "Are you Justin?"

"What does it say on the door?" I responded with an attitude.

Un-phased by my rudeness he introduced himself, "My name is Scott and I am a social worker with the City of…"

I cut him off, "I'll pass. I'll be getting out soon. Thanks anyway."

I tried to brush him off as quickly as possible in case he was the type that wouldn't shut up.

"You are pretty messed up right now. I doubt you'll be getting out soon."

I had been diagnosed with Cellulitis in my leg and possible Endocarditis, which is an infection in the heart creating inflammation in the arteries. It can be deadly if not treated immediately and aggressively. I could have died if Frankie hadn't made me go to the hospital.

I figured I would try to work Scott for something, "Bring me some cigarettes and I'll talk to you." I knew that would make him go away. I was so tired of talking to all these people and having nothing happen.

Leave me alone.

"I quit smoking, but I know what it's like and will try to get you some."

His response surprised me, and I began to take an interest in why he was visiting me. I had more interest knowing that he might bring me some smokes.

"I know a little about your history and that's why I have been asked to come see you. I wanted to discuss some options, if you like."

There are no options.

∞∞∞

Frankie was released from jail and called me as soon as he was on his way to the hospital.

"Frankie?" I asked before he hung up the phone.

"Yes?" He responded suspicious of my begging tone.

"Can you bring me some dope?"

I needed a hit. Some real shit. This legal stuff was boring.

"I will try," he assured me. I knew he would come through.

Sure enough, he showed up a few hours later with a syringe full of drugs. I stuck the needle in my IV and pushed the good stuff into my bloodstream.

"I'm going back to Seattle," he told me.

"Where is your wife?"

"She already left. She got out and went straight to the airport."

This life we lead was always an interesting one.

Nothing more was ever going to happen between us. I was thankful for what we had and it opened my eyes to many things.

Frankie made me feel good and helped me get honest about some things, and although we loved each other immensely, he didn't *feel* it the same way I did. It was time for us to part ways.

"I'm staying in San Francisco," I said to him. I knew I wasn't ever going back to live in Seattle.

"Well, try to come home and keep in touch. I'll make sure Mama always knows where I am so you can get a hold of me through her."

Yea, ok.

So many tears i've cried,
So much pain inside,
But baby it ain't over 'til it's over…

"It Ain't Over 'til it's Over" – Lenny Kravitz

Chapter 22

END OF THE DEAD

Scott made a point to come visit me and continued to tell me his story. He too grew up using IV drugs and ruined his life to the point that he thought he would die. He too had *wanted* and *tried* to die. As I was being treated with high doses of antibiotics, Scott came to visit me daily and would sit and speak with me.

He brought me a package of cigarettes.

"I can get you tested for HIV. It might be a good idea," he slipped into one of our conversations.

"I just tested negative not too long ago. But thanks." I had no interest in getting tested again. I had tested so many times it was ridiculous. Why waste the money.

"You don't have to do anything. I will have the lab come here and then you can come get your results in two weeks."

"Fine," I said caving to his persistence.

I figured since he brought me cigarettes the least I could do was allow him do his job.

I rolled myself in the wheelchair to the elevator so I could go outside to smoke. My leg was wrapped and needed to remain elevated. The infection was terrible, but the good news was that I was going to keep my foot; which was a concern upon my arrival. Not being used to the wheelchair, I decided I would try to sneak a cigarette in the hallway when my favorite gay nurse caught me.

"Justin!" he screamed, "You can't smoke in here!" He wasn't being nice anymore and I became angry as my defensives kicked in.

"Fuck you!" I screamed back. I was so pissed at him yelling at me, I flicked my cigarette at him.

He turned and walked away. When I got back to my room were two security guards in my room. "Get your stuff. You have to leave."

I'm getting kicked out of a hospital?

"I have nowhere to go," I told the men.

"That's not our problem. You have been discharged."

The big gay nurse walked in before I left, "The worst thing you can do is smoke in a hospital. You could have blown us all up. There is oxygen everywhere, which is highly flammable. I have called the Social Desk and they will try to find you some emergency housing."

He was trying to be nice again but it was too late for me. He just got me kicked out the hospital.

My foot still hurt, but I was given crutches and sent on my way. I was given an emergency hotel room at a 'crack hotel' in the Mission District, along with some McDonald's food vouchers so I could eat.

I called Scott as soon as I was settled and told him what had happened. He was more amused than anything and was laughing.

"What the fuck is so funny?" I asked demandingly.

"Nothing Justin," he chuckled, "It's just a really good thing that we met. That's all."

Scott was a very gentle and kind man. He had graduated college with a degree in social work. He was in his forties, wore glasses, and was a little chubby with a goatee. He looked normal to me and didn't have any obvious scars or sores on his face. He wore slacks and a nice button down shirt. He cleaned up well, assuming he was telling me the truth about his former street life. He talked to me about his entire experience, including coming out of the closet and living with his Life Partner. The thought of being in love with someone and living a normal life never occurred to me. All I had experienced was a shady relationship with someone who really didn't want to share life with me.

Scott's honesty allowed me to look deep inside where I found I already had some hope stashed.

I just had to realize it and allow it to dream.

Hope felt good to me.

I promised him that I would go get my test results, which was located near his office on the grounds of the hospital. My ankle was healing well so I took the bus.

I sat in the chair after announcing myself with the receptionist at the clinic and waited. I had no idea what I was doing. I was contemplating what I was going to do after I got my results. Sure it was possible that the news would be bad, but probably not.

The only concern for me was my experience being raped, unprotected. I had been unsafe with needles, but it never mattered before.

A woman came out and called my name. I followed her to an office located down the hall from where we were.

"Hi. I'm Josie. You are here to receive your HIV test results today." Josie was one of the 'I-am-way-too-fucking-happy-to-be-a-social worker' types. She was irritating and I wanted to tell her, but I didn't.

She was speaking like she was a mother in a Huggie's commercial and I, or course was the toddler. Her voice went up and down and up and down and sounded like finger-nails on a chalk board; squeaky and irritating. Maybe the news was bad and she felt the need to overcompensate.

Whatever the reason, it was annoying.

She was annoying.

"After giving you your results, I will answer any questions that I am able to. I don't believe in waiting, so lets get to your results first," she said in her Julie Andrews 'Sound of Music' wanna-be voice.

She opened the envelope that I noticed had *already been opened.*

"Okay, you are positive for HIV," she said as if she was reading the results of a pregnancy test. She continued, "Now this doesn't necessarily mean a death sentence."

Yes it does you stupid bitch.

Before sweet little Josie could say another animated word, I got out of my chair and walked out of the clinic. I had nothing to say to anyone.

I had wondered what I would feel like had this ever happened, but my psychic visions did not compare to what my mind and my body where feeling when it actually happened. I couldn't cry. I couldn't speak. I couldn't *feel.*

I wondered if I had infected anyone else. I was pretty good at being safe with people that I knew, but when no one was looking, I would skimp on the bleach when it came to me.

I was never taught to care about me.

∞∞∞∞

I walked slowly through the hospital parking lot towards the bus stop, when I looked up I saw Scott walking briskly toward me.

"I know what just happened," he comforted.

Tears began to well up in my eyes with the first intelligible feeling that I had been able to muster since receiving my death sentence five minutes earlier.

I still couldn't speak as they started to leak down my cheeks. I was looking straight at Scott.

"Come up to my office. We can just sit for a while." I followed him without saying a word.

The tears wouldn't stop running as I thought of the little boy who threw his life away to hurt his father.

The boy, that only destroyed *the boy.*

Through all of my years growing up at home and on the streets, I continually dreamed of a good life. A life with a loving family like it should be. My brothers would have kids and provide nieces and nephews. Maybe I would have my own kids one day. I would dream of being called "Uncle Justin", and would be the favorite uncle of all time. I would be the best parent and my children would never be screamed at or abused by their father.

They would be loved completely and unconditionally.

I really messed everything up.

∞∞∞

The interesting thing in all these years growing up was I knew *right* from *wrong*.

There is a little alarm that goes off inside of me and I first noticed it when I heard my father display hatred towards other races.

I knew when I broke the law and when I was acting out of line. I had been taught some good things as a young child by my family and by my extended family. I was not always a bad child. I *learned* how to do bad things and then I continually perfected them. That was the only way to express my sadness and anger in a way that made people take notice.

Good kids are forgotten - they don't get as much attention. By breaking the rules, I got attention. Much needed attention that I had lacked for many years.

But now it was time to pay for my mistakes and for breaking all the rules.

Although I was going to miss my friend Frankie, I wouldn't let him know I was going to die.

Carry on my wayward son
There'll be peace when you are done
Lay your weary head to rest
Don't you cry no more.

"Carry on My Wayward Son" - Kansas

Chapter 23

WALDEN HOUSE

After several conversations with Scott, he convinced me to not return to the streets. I did not want me to give my dirty secret to anyone else, so there was some discussion of a program that was tailored to people like me - people with no more chances. The program he was telling me about was a popular topic among inmates every time I had been locked up.

Walden House (known as HealthRight 360) had a reputation as a "no bullshit" behavioral modification module and was the least favorite destination of all the inmates. It was also rumored that if residents got out of line, they would shave your head or make you wear a diaper to humiliate you in front of the other residents.

"I'm not sure if Walden House is for me," I told Scott.

"There aren't many options for you. Walden House is right for you. I can get you in right away," he nudged. "You are going to have to leave your hotel in the next day or so," he warned me.

"There are people in the program that are just like you. I think it's a good match. Trust me." I trusted him.

He picked up the phone and got me an intake interview at a facility that wasn't too far from where I was staying in the Mission District. While I was waiting for my appointment I noticed several other obvious dope fiends, and tried to figure out if anyone had the virus. Surely I wasn't the only one.

I was called into the interview room and sat down.

The woman looked like an obvious lesbian with short hair, was very pretty. She was in her late twenties with blonde short hair that had a long strand on one side hanging off her face. She was dressed very stylish, with baggy Levi's, a white t-shirt and black Doc Martin casual dress shoes.

"Hi. My name is D.K." She explained that there were many things to go over and that she would make it as painless as possible, but it may take a while.

"It is important that you are totally honest in this interview," she spoke nicely, "Do you have any warrants for your arrest? It doesn't mean you wont be admitted, I just need to know so we can take care of them if you go into the house today."

Without missing a beat I answered, "No. I don't."

The hour-long interview was uncomfortable. She wanted to know everything about my family, drug use and sexual history. I still wasn't ready to disclose my sexual orientation. I definitely wasn't checking out girls anymore, unless I absolutely had to in order to protect my secret.

"Thank you, Justin. Go have a seat in the waiting room while I finish processing your intake. I will be with you shortly," she assured.

"By the way," she continued as I turned around to look at her, "I tested positive for HIV three years ago. It may seem like the end of the world, but it's not."

I was taken aback when she disclosed her HIV status. Not that I didn't believe it, but she looked great - healthy, vibrant and there was a happiness that shined through her. There was also something in her tone that made me feel relaxed like things might be okay. Her attitude made me feel like it's not the end of the world.

I sat in the waiting room wondering what was going to happen. I was confident I did well in my interview. She came and called me back into her office, a good sign that I was accepted.

"Justin, you lied to me. You have warrants for your arrest. If you aren't ready to be honest, then you are not ready for Walden House."

Are you kidding me?

I had nowhere else to go.

"This isn't a game. It's your *life*," she told me unapologetically. She was serious.

"If you agree to turn yourself into jail and take care of your legal matters, I will make sure you are picked up from jail. But you have to prove to us and to yourself that you *want help*."

I had spent my entire life trying to run from the law and police. Now, I was just supposed to walk in and let someone lock me up?

No way. *There is just no way.* It went against everything I was taught.

The room became quiet and my mind was spinning.

How can I get out of this?

"I'll make you a deal. If you agree to do this, I will have someone drive you down to the jail to do what you need to do," she added.

She really wanted me to do the right thing. But I still couldn't believe I had to go to jail first in order to do it.

I had no other choice. I had to turn myself in and get into this program. The last ditch effort to maybe enjoy the last months or years of my drastically shortened life.

"I would appreciate a ride," I told her solemnly.

I would do what she suggested.

∞∞∞∞

Although I didn't want to disappoint my mother anymore than she already had been, it was important that I called her to tell her the truth. With everything she had recently been through with Cameron's sickness and brain surgery, she needed to know that she might, indeed, be losing a son. There were no medications to treat HIV in the early nineties and it was rampant among IV drug users. Although most of the fear was directed toward dope fiends and homosexuals throughout the nineteen-eighties, the pandemic had spread as heterosexual men and women were testing positive in high numbers. It was a progressive and fatal diagnosis. But Scott and D.K. both explained to me that "progressive" meant that there was "time" that could be spent wisely, if I chose.

I didn't feel sick. I didn't have any sores. I was pretty healthy. So I had some time on my hands to make some positive changes and go out in style.

It wouldn't be fair to not tell my mother. There had been several conversations over the years about my demise. It was expected for many years.

After I got settled in jail while waiting to go into Walden House, I called her collect.

"Hey mom. I'm in jail waiting to go into a program. I had to come here first to clear up some old warrants," I told her right off so she would know that I was trying to do something good.

"I have to tell you something serious and I don't want you to be upset."

Her voice dropped, "What is it?"

"I tested positive for HIV." The conversation became quiet and I knew she was in shock at what I had just told her.

"Oh my god. You need to get into that program and take care of yourself," she insisted. We spoke for a few minutes and near the end of another quiet moment, using her nurturing voice, she quietly said, "Justin, you are going to be okay."

"I know, Mom. I will call you from the program and let you know how I am doing."

"I love you."

It felt good having my mother be so concerned and positive about my future. It made me feel like I could talk to her.

∞∞∞

I had thought about what D.K. had told me about honesty in my interview. She said that I had to be completely honest with everyone, myself included, in order for the program to work. I knew that I wasn't always being truthful about things, especially my sexuality, so I decided that it was time to start. I decided to call my mother first. After her supportive response to my HIV report, I wanted to play it safe by trying out my new honesty on someone I could trust.

"Mom, there is something else that I need to tell you."

She was not quite sure she wanted to know anything else.

"I think I'm gay," I blurted out and held my breath awaiting her response.

"That's completely unacceptable and disgusting!" she said sounding like my father, "Don't call here anymore."

Click.

∞∞∞

Walden House picked me up from and off we went to the large facility, which was located in the Haight District of San Francisco. The building was an old convent on the west side of Buena Vista Park. There was perfect foliage around the perimeter and I noticed people walking around the facility obviously working. The building took up the entire block and was built on a large piece of bedrock situated on a hill in a triangular shape.

We got out of the car and walked towards the front door when I noticed a homemade wooden sign posted in between two beautiful rosebushes. It was engraved with the phrase:

"Today is the first day of the rest of your life."

These words struck me and my throat began to get dry as my eyes started to burn. *Could this really be considered the first day of my life?* The thought provoked my heart to skip an extra beat in excitement.

The driver had instructed me to act as a "ghost" and operate as a "monad".

He said, "That's Monad from the Greek philosophy - itself being devoid of quantity, indivisible and unchangeable. Basically, just shut the fuck up and don't talk to anyone," he added comically.

I was to lack visibility. He explained that I was to be still, was not to acknowledge anyone or activity and was to stare at the floor without looking anyone in the eyes. If I did not follow this procedure, I would be asked to leave.

I was put into a chair in the main lobby of the old convent. It looked as if it was a throne, smack in the middle of the room, only up against the wall. I felt everyone's eyes on me as I sat quietly, looking at the floor. Potential residents who come to Walden House must sit in 'The Chair' until invited into their intake interview with several other residents, who also got to decide if you stay.

The waiting period in The Chair can be anything from one hour, to three days, depending on the individual's situation. If someone had been kicked out and wanted to come back, they would most likely sit in The Chair for three days, starting at 6:00am until 10:00pm, only being allowed to get up for the bathroom and to sleep. I spent three hours in The Chair and then a man came down and told me to follow him. He instructed me to remain in this "monad" without speaking or looking at anyone. We went upstairs and I waited outside an office where I could hear people talking.

I heard the door open and an older African American man came up to me.

"Hi. I'm Reggie. Why don't you come on in and we can get started."

Reggie had a large build and was in his forties. He was very nice, which made me feel relaxed considering I had been concerned what was going to happen. Three hours is a long time to be staring at a floor.

I sat down in front of the six people in the room who were of mixed races and backgrounds. A woman started asking me questions. I figured she must have been a staff member, as she seemed to be running things.

"Why are you here?" she asked without telling me her name.

"I was just brought here from San Bruno jail," I responded.

"That's not what I asked you," she countered sharply.

"*WHY* are you here?" she asked again, frustrated but barely raising her voice.

I was starting to feel uncomfortable and wanted to jump up and run out the building.

"I was diagnosed HIV positive and don't want to live on the streets anymore. I can't stop doing drugs. I have been doing them since I was ten and I cannot stop. I have nowhere else to go," I replied desperately. I could feel my tear ducts activating, but made sure nothing came out.

Yet.

They all pondered my answer, looking at each other and then fixing their eyes back on me. It was Reggie's turn.

"What will you do in order to get into Walden House?"

"I will do anything. I have nowhere else to go and I am dying. I just want to live the rest of my life in peace." They looked at me suspect when I spoke of my inevitable death. They probably didn't want me either.

I wouldn't do it anymore. If they didn't accept me I was going to kill myself.

I wasn't going to be able to do anything bloody, but I started thinking about preparing a large hit of drugs, heroin and cocaine, and go out with a bang, like John Belushi did not too many years before.

I had no idea I was going to have such a hard time convincing them. After a few more questions, Reggie looked at me with his hand on his face in deep thought.

"Please have a seat outside so we can make our decision."

I can't even get into a drug program?

I waited outside the little office for a couple of minutes when Reggie came out and invited me back inside where I took my seat. It didn't look good. They looked sad for me, like they were going to have to tell me to leave. They just kept looking at me and shaking their heads so I figured it was time to start heading for the door. As I postured to get out of my chair, Reggie spoke.

"Listen Justin," he said very serious.

"Yes, sir," I replied.

Before I could know what was happening, they all jumped up out of their chairs, "Welcome to Walden House!"

Thank you.

As I suspected, the woman in the interview was a staff member. She, too, gave me a quick welcome hug and introduced herself, "Hi. I am Shannon and I am the Program Coordinator. Reggie is going to be your Big Brother. You won't need much from staff until you get out of orientation period, so anything you need you can get from Reggie.

"How long is orientation?" I asked innocently.

"Thirty days. Maybe sixty. It depends on you."

Thirty days? That is forever! There is no way!

"I will help you get adjusted and learn the rules. There are many." Reggie handed me a rulebook that must have been two hundred pages.

"None may be broken or you may be asked to leave. Any questions you have, you ask me. I am your contact. Understood?"

"Understood," I told him.

"How long is this program anyway?" I had no idea and had never asked. I was suspecting it to be around thirty days, so that seemed like a long time for an orientation period.

"Eighteen months," he answered.

Thankfully I didn't have any food in my stomach, as it would have definitely exited my body.

∞∞∞∞

Reggie escorted me into the dining room for my first meal since my jail breakfast earlier that morning. The dining room was located downstairs and had many large tables scattered with several chairs at each. The food was prepared by the residents working in the house, and was surprisingly good. There were planned menus with instructions that cooks had to follow, so if anything got messed up there was hell to pay because it meant someone wasn't following the chef's directions. After dinner he introduced me to several of the one hundred-twenty other residents as we walked towards the largest room in the convent. It was beautiful with cathedral ceilings and was called, Harvey Hall - named in memory of Harvey Milk who was the first openly gay Supervisor in the City of San Francisco. He was murdered and his life was portrayed in the documentary, *The Life and Times of Harvey Milk*. I remembered his story clearly because it was nominated for an Academy Award along with *STREETWISE*. Harvey Milk won the Oscar.

These people named an entire room after a gay man? There was not a high population of gays and lesbians in Walden House, but it there was a required respect for all communities of people.

Instead of rows of pews, there were chairs around the entire perimeter to accommodate all of the residents for meetings.

This would be my first meeting. The senior residents began reviewing all types of business including chores for the evening.

As I sat overwhelmed by the people and activities happening, my eyes wandered to the original stained glass windows in the cathedral. The character of the building was historically stunning.

The gentleman standing at the podium asked if there were any announcements. Reggie, who was sitting next to me, raised his hand.

"Good Evening family. I would like everyone to meet their new brother, Justin, who just came from jail this morning." Before he finished his announcement, everyone jumped out of their chairs and began clapping while looking at me. They continued to clap until all going into a "sync" of clapping. It was an overwhelming welcome.

I just may fit in somewhere other than the streets.

Now if I could just get through this thirty-day thing.

∞∞∞∞

I spent my days in group therapy when not working in the cleaning crew with all the other newer residents. D.K. was a respected counselor and worked under Shannon, the tough gal in my interview. They both introduced me to some people they felt would help me get grounded in this structured environment.

The groups were intense and it wasn't long before people started putting the focus on me. One minute they would be talking (yelling, screaming) at someone in the group and then in the next they would be talking (yelling, screaming) at me.

They called it "seeing yourself, through the eyes and hearts of others".

I hated the things that they would say to me.

"You are a selfish, ungrateful asshole!"

"But my family is fucked up and my dad is an asshole!" I would tell them.

"Your daddy isn't sitting in a fucking drug program! It's time to look at *yourself!*"

Although it was hard to hear this at first, it was true. I was a liar, a thief and an asshole. I made bad choices and did bad things. I was selfish. With their help I could finally see that I had taken a wrong turn in my own childhood. I began to understand that there were many issues pertaining to the journey that I was traveling, but I had the ultimate authority to make the necessary changes.

I now had a chance to do just that.

I clearly remembered my interview when Shannon informed me of "some good news, and some bad news."

The good news was that I only had to change *one* thing.

The bad news was that it was *everything*.

∞∞∞

Although I was intimidated by all the rules, I quickly began to make friends in the house and became a respected member of the family. I watched as other people would be kicked out or would leave on their own accord. This happened almost every day, so there was a high turnover rate.

I did not want to go back to the streets. I decided to be honest about everything including my sexual identity. As much as I hated to admit it, I was only attracted to men and I had to be completely honest about everything.

I was sitting outside smoking when a resident who I had been friendly with came up to talk to me. His name was Barry and he was a bit of a clown. He spoke with a Long Island accent and reminded me of a used car salesman. He had a curly mop on the top of his head and a great big smile. His face was sickly, as he had been ill and wasn't doing too well.

"What's up little faggot?" he asked.

What the hell did he say to me? I was shocked. This was not the way we were supposed to speak to each other.

"It's okay man. You are not the first faggot I ever met," he said with a grin.

I couldn't help but laugh. Barry was in some of my daily group sessions because he had AIDS. His wife had recently passed away (they were IV drug users) and he came to Walden House on the same premise as I did; to try to make the best of what remained of our lives. I was estranged from my family and he was estranged from his children. They were grieving the loss of their mother and were blaming her death on Barry. We became very close and he helped me learn to lighten up about my sexuality. Usually gays would surround themselves with their likeness but it was the heterosexuals who encouraged me to be myself.

They believed in me.

Walden House had an internal school for people who were eligible to get their GED's and, although everyone else was allowed the choice, I was forced by all of the staff and fellow residents to attend.

I was very blessed by substantial friendships and caring peers as well as a wonderful staff and counselors. Although I had some tough times while dealing with many pent-up issues from childhood and living on the streets, they carried me through and walked with me during some of the darkest times. Some of the groups were endless and emotional and lasted twelve hours or more. That's when we would talk about our deepest traumas and turn our anger onto a pillow with a baseball bat. It reminded me of The Loft, but with a structured output, as to put things to rest and move on.

After three months I was allowed to make phone calls. The first person I called was my mother.

"Where are you?" she asked before wanting to converse.

"I'm still in the program. I've been here for months," I bragged.

She was proud of me and didn't mention the last conversation we had. I figured I would just let it go.

I wasn't allowed to speak to Frankie or any of my other friends that I had lived with on the streets. They were from a period in my life that was now to be forgotten. Not many of them were left, anyway.

I never told anyone about Frankie. I followed the guidance of Walden House, but never forgot him and all of the years that we shared as friends and discreet intimate partners. I hoped I could reach out to him one day, but I had to focus on my life – and what I wanted to be when I grew up. There were so many options now.

I began to see things and understand things about myself that would help me be a better man and possibly live a good life. In the beginning my peers cursed, yelled and screamed at me for all of the things I had done to others, as well as myself. Then as time went on, I understood these new principles and was able to help and support the new idiots that came in the program after me. "Why are you killing yourself?" I would ask. "You have an opportunity to have an amazing life!"

My spirit was renewed and I knew it as true.

Some times in our lives,
We all have pain. We all have sorrow.
But, if we are wise, we know that there's always tomorrow.
Lean on me,
When you're not strong,
I'll be your friend. I'll help you carry on.
For it won't be long, 'till I'm gonna need somebody to lean on.

"Lean on Me" – Bill Withers

Chapter 24

NEW BEGINNING

Scott, my friend from the hospital, knew other young people in my situation and suggested I meet them. I reluctantly attended a support group that Scott was facilitating and was pleasantly surprised by my experience. All kinds of young people, from all types of backgrounds, came together in camaraderie to talk about our common predicament. It was a lifesaver for me. I found comfort in knowing we all came from the same place of fear and, although our stories were different, I could relate to the feelings.

I made some great friends in that group and we did community outreach work together. We did public speaking to try to stop the spread of HIV, particularly among youth. My new friends were well aware of my background and history and came to my rescue while I adjusted to the new environments that I was experiencing.

We decided to incorporate our group into an agency to provide professional peer-based support to other youth in our communities. Our goal was to combat the HIV infection rates that were increasing among young people at alarming rates, especially among young women and African Americans. We felt empowered by our mission, which gave purpose to our lives as we faced the inevitable truth that we were possibly going to die from our mistakes.

Faith and hope came to life into my consciousness. Since childhood I was trained to think that anything religious or spiritual was a crock of shit. Their views of me were disempowering to my spirit. I just want to be loved and to love one person in a healthy way. I would have been heterosexual if I had a choice in the matter, just so people would approve of me.

When I came to know a higher source, or God, my life began to change. Once I committed to clean up and give back, God became the only source of power that could help me. There were no medications. There was no guru to relieve my obsession for drugs, the streets and self-destruction. Not one person could help me the way I needed help. Thankfully, I had discovered one option that worked, a loving concept of God, without all the disempowering bullshit and oppressive bureaucracy.

And my new friends supported my beliefs. No matter whether they were straight or gay. That was what our support group was about. It didn't matter who you were, what you were or how you got there.

You belonged to the group – a very exclusive group who's motto was, "We're not dead yet".

My new friends created a Board of Directors and incorporated the name of our new agency, Bay Area Young Positives (BAY Positives). We were recognized by the San Francisco Mayors office and were invited to serve on a special youth commission for the San Francisco Board of Supervisors.

Scott and his co-worker, Julie, were our mentors as we wrote the grants generating the necessary funding for our program. We then found an office space, bought office furniture and computers and opened for business. The Board of Directors decided to hire an original founding member, Antigone, who was twenty-four at the time, as the Executive Director – and so went history.

∞∞∞∞

It was nice to have a life outside of Walden House. I wanted to know what was going on in the world and this group was my venue to learn, grow and get ready to be on my own. I was getting tired of my treatment experience due to my stay being extended. The staff wanted to make sure I was ready. But it was frustrating watching all of my peers, and some residents that entered after me, moving on to the advanced phases with more freedom and planetary perks.

Shannon was promoted to run the re-entry program, which I was still waiting to get into. She had been a paramount source of support during the first nine months of my stay and I relied on her knowledge and advice. She had gone through Walden House many years before me and had come directly from prison. Our stories were similar and she willingly gave of herself to guide me.

I heard Shannon's voice over the intercom system, paging me to her office. Due to the size of the program, there were intercom speakers in every ceiling corner on every floor, so whenever the paging system was used, the voice would reverberate throughout the entire City of San Francisco. Being paged could be a reason to be concerned because sometimes it meant that one could be in trouble. But I knew that Shannon liked to check in on me from time to time, so I walked up to the main floor to see what she wanted without stressing.

"You're late," she said.

"Late?" I was dumbfounded.

I hated being late or forgetting things. I had turned into an anal-retentive Virgo. Mistakes were not an option for me and I didn't like getting into trouble, which happens in these therapeutic communities when you are late.

Punishment; in the form of 'learning experiences' - as they kindly referred to them - was usually in the form of scrubbing toilets or writing trillion-word essays on topics as educationally advanced as "Why I Was Late" or "Why I Am So Special The World Should Wait On Me".

"You are late for... Are you ready to get a job?"

She wanted to surprise me.

"Have you thought about what you want to do?"

I had no clue. I had been awarded my High School Equivalency Diploma, but had not received any training other than various job functions in the house.

I decided to call Sean, one of my new friends from the support group. Sean and I got along well. He provided crucial information - sometimes as simple as how to order gourmet pizza. But at this point in my development all new information was important. Sean was African American and very handsome. He wore glasses that made him look like a bookworm and had an independent persona that made him hip. Most of my friends, white or black or latin, were either ghetto or trailer trash; so I was grateful to have a friend that was so well rounded and willing to teach me things.

"Have you thought about being a waiter?" he asked.

"I've never done anything like that." I couldn't even picture myself doing something so difficult.

"All you do write down what they want to eat, give them their food when they're done, hand them a check with a big fat smile and you got it made!" he assured me that waiting tables would be a good experience. Sean was in food service and had been trained as a chef and pastry chef.

"I know someone at a restaurant in the Marina. I want you to call him."

I made the call, went to the interview and was hired on the spot to start work the next day. I shared the good news with Shannon, who was thrilled.

I had no idea what went into Food Service. There were so many things that I had to explain to the customers and I wasn't allowed to write it down on a piece of paper. I had to study the menu and the ingredients, and remember everything for when I was giving information and taking orders.

After completing my training, I started to wait tables on my own and although I was nervous, did fairly well.

I was helping an interesting couple when the elder lady asked me a question.

"What does the grilled chicken come with young man?" She must have been in her nineties and was sitting with a younger man who was probably in his fifties.

"You have three options, ma'am. Mashed potatoes, a delicious seasoned brown rice or placenta," I explained efficiently.

The man had a confused look on his face. He looked at her and then at me. It made me feel uncomfortable.

"Placenta?" the lady asked sweetly.

"Yes, ma'am. It's delicious." I said with confidence. "I tasted it in the kitchen and it's *very* good." I smiled at her encouraging her to make a decision.

She looked at her male friend with a smile. Now amused, he gladly chimed in.

"Do you mean *polenta*?"

"Oh." I said seriously, "Yes, I do," trying not to acknowledge that I just offered someone afterbirth to go with their chicken.

What an idiot. I started to panic inside, but remained somewhat calm.

"Excuse me, please," I said as I walked away. I couldn't finish their order. I walked to my station where the manager was standing observing my performance. I told him what happened and he started laughing uncontrollably at my mistake.

As soon as he calmed himself down he walked directly to their table to clean up my mess. He waved for me to come over.

"Darling," the old lady said nicely, "we are allowed to make mistakes. I'm so old a little placenta might do me a bit of good. There is a little too much 'sag' in the old 'bag'." she said as she rubbed her aging face, "its almost time for a date with Dr. Wonderful."

With the ice broken and everyone laughing so hard we had wet spots in our underwear, I completed their order. When they were done eating, they left me a one hundred dollar tip and insisted that I call them. She wanted to invite me over for tea.

That is how I started my relationship with one of San Francisco's elite socialites, Marjorie and her caretaker, Gregory.

∞∞∞∞

I continued to work as a waiter and enjoyed my new friendship with Marjorie and Gregory. Their interest in me deepened after learning a bit of my history. They wanted to support me and encourage me to continue the good life. They taught me everything from how to sit and eat properly to how to dress for events. One wrong word out my mouth and Marjorie would make me sit with her while she explained the entire English language and the importance of presenting well in order to win friends and influence people. Marjorie knew everything and loved sharing her information. After our nice visits, she would walk over to the piano and play beautifully for long periods of time. They taught me the things I never would have learned at Walden House.

Marjorie decided that she was going to throw me a birthday party at her penthouse, which overlooked the San Francisco Wharf. The building had several luxury apartments that where stacked at an angle on a large hill on Bay Street. The top floor was Marjorie's penthouse and was three stories. There was a miniature trolley that ran on tracks at the same slant as the building. It would transport guests and residents to their respective destinations in the spectacular residence. As the trolley traveled up the slanted hill, the view of the water and Alcatraz would stunningly appear as you reached the top.

It was my twenty-third birthday and they had invited my dear friends from Walden House, including Shannon. When I walked into the penthouse, I noticed a large sign hung perfectly across the large ceiling near the windows looking out to the Bay Bridge that said, "Justin E. is 23!"

Barry approached me while I was outside on the deck enjoying the view of the San Francisco bay. "I want to talk to you about something." He was looking a bit serious which was out of character for him so we sat down.

"If you hadn't noticed, I am not getting any better."

I noticed. His AIDS was full blown and he was deteriorating rapidly. There were still no medications for people with AIDS. Hope was a fallacy.

"I am going to have fun with this," he told me.

"Fun with what?" I asked confused.

"My demise. You know I got AIDS right?" He charmed with his '*I have a 1970 Ford Pinto for sale*' accent.

"I am going to plan my memorial and I want everybody to do exactly what I say. I am working on the music right now. Wait until you hear the song I picked. There won't be a dry eye in the house!" he said immaturely. He *was* going to have fun with his death. He was too much.

"What song did you pick?" I asked him.

"I can't tell you! I have to make sure you attend the memorial. I need people to show up," he joked. We continued to share how appreciative we were for each other's support during the past two years. Barry kept me smiling and enjoyed looking out for me and watching me grow. It was sad to see what the future held for him. I couldn't think about it much.

"That's enough of this mushy bullshit!" he said.

"Why don't you go get me some food before I waste away."

∞∞∞∞∞

A few of us had been introduced to a physician, Dr. Janet Shalwitz, who wanted to start another program for other youth affected by HIV and I was welcomed to participate in that venture, as well. I was asked to contribute to the HIV/DRUG and GANG prevention program. I was a good fit because I still had a rough exterior that many of the urban youth could relate to.

Walden House had saved my life, but my new friends, that were unexpectedly so much like me, *gave* me life. All different, we shared amazing similarities.

Whatever differences we had, we celebrated. It was the opposite of anything I had ever been taught at home. Sean was one of the writers of the new grant, and asked if he could write me into the project with a position created just for me.

"You would be great. You already do public education work. Why not get paid for it?"

The opportunity was perfect for me. I could develop some solid professional skills and learn on the job. There were so many aspects to learn in order to perform my duties, the thought was overwhelming, but I agreed. Sean and I had done several public speaking engagements together and were good friends.

Around the same time that we started our new agency, I was ready to leave the nest at Walden House and live on my own. I wasn't quite ready for my own apartment, so Sean offered to rent me a room in his large apartment. He enjoyed teaching me little life things.

I had no idea that coffee came from beans!

∞∞∞∞

It took months to get situated in our new agency, but things began to settle down and I was enjoying my new career in Human Services. The pay was good enough for me to live on my own, so I moved out and into my own apartment. Then I bought a new car.

Life was good.

While working on the agency newsletter the receptionist made me aware of an important phone call from a police detective. I was a bit nervous at first, thinking I forgot to take care of something from my past and that it had caught up with me. I picked up the phone to a pleasant voice on the other end.

"Hi Justin, my name is Detective Thomas Jenson," he spoke softly, "I am with the King County Police Green River Task Force in Seattle."

Shit. My heart started to pound. I quickly shut my door so no one could hear my conversation.

"What can I do for you, sir?" I asked respectfully.

"Melinda gave me your number. I know you were close with Roberta. I am calling to notify you that we have positively identified her remains through dental records. I am so sorry to be the bearer of such bad news."

I sat there for a minute or thirty and thought about my precious friend.

Roberta was dead.

When I'm tired and thinking cold,
I hide in my music, forget the day,
and dream of a girl, I used to know.
I closed my eyes and she slipped away.

"More than a Feeling" – Boston

Chapter 25

THE BIG REVEAL

Though I had come clean on a lot of things during my stay at Walden House, once I graduated I mostly kept my past, quietly in the past. I had an air of denial when it came to some of the things I went through and the friends I had known and lost along the way.

I was ashamed of my history and the players.

Melinda called me and gave me the information regarding Roberta's memorial. I did not want to attend. I didn't want to review and reveal that part of my life. As much as I loved Roberta, I had left that world behind me.

Melinda sent me the program that was created for her memorial. It had a beautiful picture of Roberta, smiling brightly on the front.

As I opened it and read its contents, I had a moment of clarity.

There is nothing to be ashamed of.

I wasn't going to run from it anymore. I couldn't. Roberta, Lou Lou, Frankie and countless others were part of *me*. I realized that I needed to acknowledge all of them and everything. Not that I was going to run down the street naked screaming what lying, thieving drug addict I used to be. Nor would I mention it casually or professionally. But at this point, I needed to embrace and forgive my past, even if it made someone else uncomfortable.

Looking at Roberta's sweet smile, I recognized that I had to hold my head high and accept my own upbringing – my street child story.

∞∞∞

Walden House recommended that I not contact anyone from my past. Their program was set up so we would not be tempted by past behaviors. Once people began to get their lives together it was natural to want to brag about it, but once integrated back in their old surroundings, temptation was looming to take them down again. Walden House was adamant about this. I agreed with their philosophy pertaining to avoiding old friends and behaviors.

I respected their suggestions, but why was it okay for me to speak and see my brothers? It seemed hypocritical because George was still using drugs and Cameron was drinking heavily. I could not understand why I was not able to reach out to Frankie. Frankie was more my family, in a twisted little way, than my brothers were. We had a lifetime of friendship and intimacy.

Okay, so my feelings were romantic. I never told anyone – including him. In fact, I would tell people he was my brother to get as far away from suspicion as humanly possible. It was comical - a white boy telling people a black boy was his brother. I guess it wasn't too far fetched considering his family tree.

There was something about knowing that Roberta was dead that made me want to see Frankie again. I secretly wanted him to know that I loved him, but I also really wanted him to know that there was another life available to us, if he wanted it.

I'd think about the intimate times we shared and realized that he was the only one I had let in completely. As messed up as we were, there was no one else I had ever given my heart or loyalty to.

I missed my boy Frankie.

I reached out to Shannon to get her advice. I was completely honest about our history, my feelings and my intentions. She agreed that I was ready to handle the reunion and told me to be careful. I needed to be validated and was assured that what I was doing was right. I also talked to Gregory about it. Gregory and Marjorie were wonderful influences in my new life. Gregory guided me in ways that my father was never going to. He empowered me with wisdom that only a deeply spiritual person could, and I appreciated the time he and Marjorie had invested in me. Gregory was the first older gay man that didn't want to exploit me sexually. He only wanted to be a friend and I needed that dynamic desperately.

When he agreed that I should go see Frankie again, I felt supported.

∞∞∞

As I dialed the phone to call Mama, I felt nervous and scared that Frankie wouldn't want to talk to me. The phone picked up and my heart began to beat faster.

"The number you have reached has been disconnected," the soft-spoken disappointing robotic bitch told me in the recorded message.

I picked up the phone again and called 4-1-1.

He wasn't listed, which meant he didn't have a phone, but his brother, Mike, had a listing in North Seattle near my parents. I wrote the number down and thought about what I was doing. Can I really handle continuing in this fantasy? What if he doesn't want to speak to me? There were many items to think about. I had good intentions surely, but I also had a few ulterior motives that were selfish.

I picked up the phone and dialed the number. I felt like I was going to puke.

"Hello?" the spooky familiar voice greeted. The voice was a combination of Lou Lou and Frankie, which bugged me out, so I knew it was definitely his brother.

"Mikey, it's Justin," I began.

"Bustin Justin! What's up little buddy? Everyone thought you were dead!"

"I'm doing well, man. I miss you guys." Mikey and his wife, Janie, had looked out for me when Lou Lou passed away. Mike married Lou Lou's ex-girlfriend, Janie and they had a child together after her death.

How is that for reality drama?

"I need to get in touch with Frankie," I said bluntly.

"I bet you do," he joked. Mike knew how I felt about his brother. I never said anything out loud, but that's why he started calling me Bustin Justin. He would always tease me about Frankie, since Lou Lou told him about us one night when she was drunk.

"Frankie is in prison."

He gave me an address so I could write Frankie.

I wrote a short letter and placed it in the mail. I didn't know who would read his mail so I didn't say much.

But I said enough.

Wake up my sweet child
There's something I've got to say to you tonight
It's time you took a look at me
Cause there's so much more to me
Than meets the eye...

"Love's a Hard Game to Play" – Stevie Nicks

Chapter 26

A NEW LOVE

Although I tried to enjoy my life and keep my head up, I was obsessively checking the mail every day hoping to hear from Frankie.

I needed something else to keep me busy. I had been going out to nightclubs and was still amazed at the scene of the disco. I really liked how the DJs played music and made the people dance.

I reached out to a woman that was a popular DJ in San Francisco, and told her what I wanted to do. Her name was Mixtress Page Hodel and she told me that I should go for it. She took me under her wing, taught me how to mix records and then allowed me to "open" for her and mix records the beginning of each night at her club The Box, with two other DJ's, Lily Tran and DJ Pause.

My new love was just what the doctor ordered. I took my new hobby seriously and began to gain credibility in San Francisco, playing little gigs all over the city. I made friends with several other DJs, including one of the biggest radio DJ's at the time, DJ Pete Avila. Pete and I became inseparable and he inspired me to continue with my new dream of working in the music industry. He gave me records, taught me new techniques and showed me the ropes while introducing me to every DJ in the United States at the Billboard conference, which was taking place in San Francisco.

Music was back.

∞∞∞

Finally, the letter came. Frankie said he missed talking to me and wanted me visit if I was ever in town.

I filled out the visitor application and began coordinating my trip to Seattle. My parents weren't going to be in town, but they would be back in Washington for a family reunion toward the end of my stay. Cameron wanted me to go to the reunion with him, or he refused to go. My parents, who were traveling in their motor home, would meet us up in Northern Washington the day of the reunion. I hadn't yet spoken to my father, but he hadn't been actively trying to keep me from talking to my mother anymore, so I must have been on his version of good graces.

Gregory said he could drive with me to Seattle. We had become close friends and he wanted to support me on my first trip home.

I received a letter from the Washington State Corrections Department - a response to my request to visit Frankie.

Your request has been denied due to your prior criminal record.

I wasn't taking this lying down. I became a resource whore and approached everyone I knew who had credibility, including a woman I knew from the San Francisco Board of Supervisors who was running for Mayor of San Francisco, the President of Walden House and several other politically active people with attractive titles and letterheads. Every single person that I asked to do a letter of reference did so without reservation. I compiled the letters and wrote my own letter to the warden. I told him that if anyone was to see Frankie, it *should* be me because I have taken great steps to change my life. I stated that I only wanted to show my dear friend in person that he had someone who was living the good life that cared about him.

Within a matter of days I received a kind letter from the warden, who was impressed with my diligence.

The denial was reversed.

If you want something…

Gregory and I planned our trip to Seattle.

> *You can't always get what you want,*
> *You can't always get what you want,*
> *But if you try real hard,*
>
> *You'll get what you need.*

"You Can't Always Get what You Want" - The Rolling Stones

Chapter 27

SEATTLE BACK

Once we got to Seattle, Gregory insisted that I take his car and handle all of my affairs. He had a good friend that we were staying with and they would keep each other company. I felt excited as I pulled into the circular driveway of my parent's red brick rambler home in Lake Forest Park. Cameron was looking out the window came right outside to greet me.

"Hey bro!" he yelled as he ran up to the car to hug me.

"Dang, you look great!"

This was the first time Cameron had seen me healthy since our childhood. This was also the first time I saw the big scar on his head from his brain surgery. It went from one ear to the other, all the way up and around his forehead. He couldn't miss the look of wonder on my face. It had been almost three years since his brain surgery. My mother played down the seriousness of it all – probably because I was trying to recover at Walden House.

I wasn't prepared for what I was seeing.

"Pretty *sick* huh?" he said rubbing his head.

"You have a cancer head," I joked, knowing Cam appreciated warped humor that I most likely got from him anyway.

"It's been pretty crazy. But at least I am back at work now."

Cameron assured me that his recovery was successful and that life was to continue for him as planned, almost at one hundred percent.

"So, are we going to the reunion?" I asked him.

"I told Mom I'll go if you go," he said un-thrilled.

Mom wanted us to come and represent the family at the reunion. She hadn't seen her brothers and sisters in years and wanted to show off her boy since I was no longer an embarrassment. Cameron was still getting headaches periodically and wasn't comfortable driving long distances. So much for him being 100% recovered.

"What about George?"

"He isn't doing well. He is heavy on drugs and living downtown where you used to be." My stomach sank.

"I don't understand what you guys see down there."

He never would unless he lived it for himself.

"Mom and Dad will be in the motor home, so we can always hide there if they get on one of their Jesus kicks," Cameron joked, referring to my mother's right-winged, Dutch Reformed Catholic family. This side of the family didn't know much about me or my problems or my recovery. I didn't want to answer any questions or get stares.

But to have my father at this reunion made me very nervous. I hadn't seen or talked to him since entering and completing Walden House. He had picked up the phone a few times when I called, but never spoke to me. I'd ask for my mother and he would just set the phone down without speaking to me. He would notify Mom or Cameron that I was on the phone. I would hear him say, "Carol, *your* son is on the phone." Not *his* son or *our* son. He still wouldn't use my first name.

With my parents always gone in their motor home, Cameron was a little lonely in the house that we, or *they*, grew up in. I was glad I could stay the night and keep him company. We hung out, ate pizza and talked about our lives. He told me more about the tumor and the experience of cancer surgery and recovery. I was still shocked at what he had been through. I told him about Gregory and Marjorie and some of what I had been through. This is what I had been longing for when I was on the streets. I felt relaxed with him. I had a big brother again.

He suggested that I sleep in my old room, which was still furnished as it had been before my exit into foster care, but I respectfully declined and opted to sleep on the couch. Sleeping in that old room would have haunted me.

The reunion was the next day, so we woke up, had breakfast and hit the road. Thanks to Gregory loaning me his luxury car, we rode in comfort for the two-hour drive north to Lynden, WA, near the Canadian border. We used the time to strategize a plan for the reunion. We would stay close to each other and deflect questions with questions. We didn't want to have to answer things like, "are you married", "what college are you in or planning on going to?"

Then Cameron, in typical big brother fashion, provided his philosophy pertaining to my father, "He's fucked up, Justin. We may have done some things that weren't right, but Dad is not normal. He has been sick since his car accident."

"C'mon Cam," I argued, "Dad was drunk when he had the accident. That's how it happened."

I had heard from my grandmother, Nana that my father had been in a car accident as a teenager and had suffered a serious brain injury. He had been drinking.

"You're right," he agreed, "but it messed up his brain. He is still on medication for seizures and they don't mix with well with alcohol." He went on to warn me that my father was never going to change. He pointed out that even though he and Dad now got along, my father still wasn't very nice to him either.

"That's just the way he is. He's not nice to anyone. Just get over it," Cameron advised. We arrived at the fairgrounds where we were to meet our parents and began walking through all of the rows of motor homes. Cameron spotted their vehicle and we walked up to it. I could see my mother through the window. She jumped up excitedly when she noticed us walking together towards her.

"Well, hello!" she cooed as she opened the door. She carefully stepped down the little portable stair and ran up to give us hugs.

"It's so nice to see you!" she said overly excited.

"That's enough, Mom," Cameron joked.

"Come in, come in," she instructed.

I was nervous as we prepared to walk into their motor home. Would he speak? Be nice? Understand? Would he see how I had changed? I had been doing well now for a long period of time and maybe that would have an influence. Maybe he wouldn't have any reason to reject me. Maybe he would even be proud that his son was doing good things, and trying to make a difference in the world. As much of an asshole as my dad was, he was my dad. I really wanted him to love me, and I really wanted to love him.

I wasn't sure what to expect, but Cameron had warned me properly. I hoped for the best but expected the worst.

He was sitting on the couch looking up at us through his glasses.

His judgmental eyes went up and down the entire length of my body. He hadn't seen me in years and I guess he was curious what I looked like.

"Hello," I said to his stone face.

No response. He looked down as if he didn't hear me. Cameron nudged me to forget about it. He had warned me – and yet the rejection was still as cutting - the silence painful. He didn't even need to say epithets anymore. They were still programmed into my brain. I did my best to take Cameron's advice and focused all of my attention on my mother and brother.

∞∞∞∞

The reunion was what we thought it would be and we tried to stay out of the right-wing conspiracy happening outside. Cameron and I did our best to be social, but strategically hid in the motor home from time to time to take a breather. My mom was beside herself that her two sons were in her presence. I guess that made the trip worth taking. It was getting late so we respectfully made our way around and hugged our aunts and uncles. Mom was disappointed that we were leaving, but she reminded herself and all the relatives how easily tired Cameron got since having his surgery. We said our goodbyes and made our way back to the freeway.

We didn't talk much on the way back. We were listening to the radio (rock of course, disco still sucked) and enjoying the scenery of the beautiful trees and hills that spread across Washington State.

Cameron decided to ruin the healthy silence, "Is it true you called Mom and told her you were a fag?" This was a subject I hadn't planned on discussing ever again.

"Yes," I answered strongly.

He stayed quiet in thought for several moments.

"Well, I don't care what you are. But do me a favor, don't tell any of my friends that you are a booty bandit." he said serious and trying to be funny at the same time. I found his humor offensive even though he was letting me know that he was accepting my personal design.

"We don't ever need to talk about this again," he said, ending the conversation.

"Fine with me."

I didn't want to talk about it in the first place.

∞∞∞

My visit to the prison was scheduled for the next day. I dropped Cameron off at home and made my way back to see Gregory and update him on the last two days of events. He was excited and proud, and reminded me where I lacked a father, I made up in good friends.

"Justin, you are an amazing young man and you have come a long way. Your father is missing out."

Yes he was.

I woke up the next morning with the nervous energy I always had when it came to seeing Frankie and not knowing what to expect. I hopped in the car and began another two-hour drive, alone, to the fire-camp where he was serving the remainder of his sentence. This place was very difficult to find, but nothing was going to stop me from my task. Although the facility was low security, it still had a fence with barbed wire surrounding the perimeter. I walked up to the guard who was in a booth and announced myself. I was on a list of approved visitors, so was allowed inside where I was searched prior to seeing Frankie. Although everything had been done the right way, and I knew that I didn't have any warrants for my arrest, I was anxious in this environment. I guess the memories and concerns of the past never go away fully.

All the hard work I did in order to give myself a new life was reflective as I visualized these drab surroundings of what once was familiar. I was hoping that my feelings would smooth over once I saw him again and then I would be able to continue my life without the constant craving. Maybe when I saw him I would snap back into reality. I was waiting in the visitor's area when I heard the page. *"Frankie D., you have a visitor."* Moments later, he walked toward me. He had an Afro. He was wearing a white t-shirt, jeans and a state-issued blue shirt. Everything was pressed and he looked sharp and extremely handsome.

Damn Frankie looked good. He was perfect.

He was Frankie.

The feelings I hoped to deny or hide were present and I was almost disappointed to be so conscious of how much I truly loved this man.

He walked up to me and gave me a nice bear hug.

"Hey boy," he whispered.

I felt goofy and childish as my crush re-surfaced. The happiness that emanated from his demeanor didn't minimize the situation.

He was the same funny, sexy and beautiful Frankie that I had met all those years ago. He was happy to see me, but we kept it toned down. This was a prison and he had unspoken rules to live up to. I didn't want to disrespect or jeopardize his reputation. But I loved getting that vibe from him. I looked at him in awe, wondering how someone so beautiful could be so messed up. It was almost like looking in a mirror. We were good people. We had just gotten lost along the way and lacked direction in our lives.

We were sitting on the picnic table catching up about our families when another inmate walked up to us, "You guys want pictures?" he asked.

Frankie explained, "That's his thing. He sells Polaroid pictures." We both thought it was funny, but I really wanted to have a picture of us. Growing up on the streets we never had pictures taken, so it was time to at least have a memory on paper.

We took two and each kept one.

"I want you to call me when you get out. I think you should come to California, at least for a visit." I really wanted to take him with me, but then I would go to prison, too.

"I would like that," he said with a smile, "I get out in a little over a year."

His eyes met mine and he gave me the look that I had lived

for since I was young and my attraction began. He looked through me, his eyes cut like diamonds.

I couldn't tear away from his gaze, and I allowed myself to be vulnerable. We connected for what must have been a minute, or even two, until I finally broke the stand off.

I gave him a hug and walked back through to get my things and start my drive back to Seattle. Mission accomplished.

As much as I enjoyed seeing my brother and mother, I felt a tinge of guilt when I realized that my visit with Frankie was the highlight of the trip, and maybe of my life.

Now these are not the only words I say to you.
From the moment you entered my love, it was a dream come true.
To have said how much I cared, would never be enough, oh no.
I lived for you each day my love,

But I loved you much too much.

"And I Loved You" – Arnold Jarvis

Chapter 28

REFLECTIONS

I woke up early so we could get started on the long drive back to California. I had one more item of business that I needed to take care of. I asked Gregory if I could borrow his car for an hour and drove to North Seattle to visit another old friend.

I parked the car on the one lane road that provided access to the large access road. I walked around for several minutes maneuvering between headstones. Her grave still didn't have one and with nine years of grass and weed growth, the little four-inch cement stone was impossible to find. I stuck my fingers into the grass hoping to find my friend's location. After several frustrating attempts, I looked towards the parked car and recognized a tree that was standing a quarter of a mile away. I remembered staring at that tree when she was buried. It was raining and everyone was unusually quiet as they transported the coffin from the hearse to the gravesite.

I walked down to where I believed the angle would have been. I saw a series of empty plots and again started putting my fingers into the soil. On the third try, I felt a hardened substance. I dug around it, clearing the dirt and grass that had completely grown over the tiny cement stone marked "L.E.C.".

I cleaned it up and sat down on the grass facing the stone. I fixed my eyes on her initials and listened to the cars passing the cemetery at a distance as I verged on the state of meditation.

Honoring Lou Ellen "Lou Lou" Couch for all she had done for me as a child, and for being such a good friend.

I miss her deeply.

I looked to the sky and thanked God and the universe, which saved my life and blessed me with another second chance.

So show me how
To do things your way,
don't let me make the same mistakes,

Over and over again…

"I Open My Heart" – Yolanda Adams

Chapter 29

REAL VACATION

I had created a nice little life in San Francisco and was reveling in homesickness from my trip to Seattle. I missed the new puppy I had just gotten. Her name was Honeychild and was being taken care of by a kind neighbor. Gregory was dying to hear about everything that had happened and I was ready for some good advice. I explained about my feelings for Frankie, most of which he already knew, but I emphasized how I felt when I visited. I needed to talk to him because, as much as I liked feeling happy and fuzzy about my crush and all that came with it, and there were several aspects to create a happy ending that were missing. One was Frankie as he was in prison.

Gregory was very quick to try to get me to see these aspects.

"You have feelings for him and there is nothing wrong with that," he started with the part that was easy to hear.

"You've known him your whole life, which isn't that long, I might add. But as wonderful as Frankie may be, he has not gone through the process that you have gone through." I couldn't stand what he was telling me.

"Has he ever told you that he loves you?"

I didn't even have to think about this.

"No."

He could tell I was getting upset, which wasn't a good thing because I was driving. But I reminded myself that my moments with Frankie were not only sexual. There were feelings. The way he kissed my neck, my face and body. The way he looked at me and smiled. He was kind and sensual.

He never told me he loved me and I never told him either. I don't think we ever had to.

"I am not telling you this to upset you. But Frankie may not be the one for you," Gregory warned.

"Then why is it impossible to feel this way for someone other than Frankie? Why can't I shake this? It's been fourteen years now. It's never gone away," I defended.

"Love is a gift of God. Cherish it and honor it. If you feel as strongly as you suggest go for it."

I was happy to have the car quiet again. I did not like having this conversation. I felt stupid and humiliated. Not that Frankie did anything, he didn't. I knew we cared about each other. But I was ready to head my life in a direction that would be feasible for me to share certain aspects with a partner. I had longed for a normal, loving relationship. I wanted to share a life and simple things such as dinner or a movie on the couch. While living on the streets, it was hard to admit that I had a romantic fantasy. As much as I wanted it to be with Frankie - and never met anyone else that I would even consider this to be possible with - it wasn't a good bet.

This love thing was very disappointing.

I wouldn't put money on us.

∞∞∞∞

As soon as we got home I discovered that my good friend Barry from Walden House had passed away. I was impressed at how well they took care of him through his illness. Everyone would go to see him and bring him food or laughs. Everyone - except me.

I was too busy in my new life and now felt selfish for not visiting him in his final days. Barry would have preferred me be busy than tend to him, but friends show up for each other and I didn't show up much for him.

Maybe I purposely stayed busy so I wouldn't have to see my own future. Barry had been sick for a while and had gotten bad. He was emaciated and all of the flesh and muscle on his body had begun to disappear even before he was bedridden. I had seen some others get sick and deteriorate, including a few peers in Walden House, but wasn't in a hurry to see it up close again.

As much as I didn't like memorials, I decided I would attend his since it was being held at Walden House. I walked in to the treatment center that saved my life and saw faces of people I did not know. There were new ones who, like me, were now being given another chance. Seeing them gave me goose bumps as I contemplated the beautiful life they had in store for them, if they chose to change that 'one thing'. I am sure I was emotional because I was about to say good-bye to a good friend, but it was warming to know that there were others following the path that I had traveled.

I felt excited for them.

Barry had planned much of his own memorial and I was happy to see that the photos that he had chosen were put out on the table for the public to view. There were family pictures and photographs of he and his wife, obviously before drugs were a problem. They were a handsome family of upper middle class. This shouldn't have happened to them.

This shouldn't happen to anyone.

It was almost a reunion of sorts. I saw old peers and staff that I hadn't seen in months, some in a couple years. We caught up and enjoyed much small talk and stories about our friend, Barry. The facilitator announced that she was going to play a song that Barry requested to start his memorial service. When the music began, everyone hushed and paid close attention to the words of loss and spiritual transition.

There wasn't a dry eye in the house.

∞∞∞∞

I was ready for my first real vacation. I was going to a city that I had never been before and was excited. New York City. As much as I enjoyed my new life, I was tired and emotionally drained. Working in the field of Human Services was intense.

I had been dating a bit but the thought of opening myself up to someone else made me feel dirty.

HIV had impacted in my life.

∞∞∞∞

I had been DJing in San Francisco and once I was in Manhattan I wanted to see some nightclubs and famous DJs there. So the trip had some networking value, as well. I did some research and found a couple of clubs that I wanted to check out. The one that seemed important was called Sound Factory Bar. I took a disco nap at the hotel and ventured out to the club at one in the morning, as true New Yorkers do.

I felt so independent. I was in New York. I had money in my pocket. I was going out, by myself. I paid the cover charge and entered the club.

I walked immediately to the dance floor and was shocked at how amazing the music sounded on the humongous sound system. The music was so loud I thought I was in heaven. I needed this distraction. I went to the dance floor and began dancing alone for what must have been hours. I just moved to the music and watched the lights and enjoyed myself.

I decided to take a break and walked over to the bar near the DJ booth so I could spy and see who was DJ'ing and what the booth looked like. I was standing there checking it all out when I felt someone staring and then approaching me. He was a tall man and was racially mixed. My guess was Puerto Rican and Black. Whatever his genes were mixed with, it was working. He was beautiful. I didn't say anything even though he perched himself right next to me. I tried not to look at him, but he towered close and continued to stare at me. A little annoyed but more curious, I turned my head and looked at him. Without missing a beat he smiled, stuck out his hand like a gentleman and introduced himself.

"Hi, I'm Michael," he spoke loudly over the music. I told him my name and felt a little uncomfortable. I wasn't used to getting hit on.

"You are very handsome," he yelled out.

"Thanks. So are you," I screamed back. I didn't know what else to say.

He spoke loudly, "What did you say? I can't hear you."

I screamed, "I said, you, too." He smiled and I realized he had heard me the first time.

He had the most amazing and perfectly white teeth. His head was shaved and he was in very good shape. He was taller than me at about six-foot-two. He had a scar on his cheek, but it didn't take away from anything. He looked like a prince. His facial features were defined and his skin was soft and he glowed masculine beauty.

"You want to get something to eat?" he asked.

∞∞∞

We were both in New York to celebrate the 25th anniversary of the Stonewall riots. Michael and I walked from the club and went to get a slice of New York pizza, where we sat and talked for hours. Michael was from Los Angeles and was very excited to know that I lived in the same state as he. He had just "came out" himself and had never had a boyfriend. He had also never hit on anyone before.

He had never had sex with a man either.

"Do you want to hang out tomorrow? I am here with my two friends, who are in a relationship and you know how that goes."

"That would be cool." I was excited to have an attraction to someone other than Frankie.

It was a big relief, actually.

He called me the next morning and we went to breakfast where we talked more. I was worried that at some point I would have to disclose my HIV status. I had thought about what I would do if he wanted to have sex and decided that I would disclose, just as I recommended others to do.

We decide to go to his room so we could be alone. His friends would be out all day. He was sharing an upscale hotel room in midtown and was staying on one of the higher floors. I stood at the window and looked out at the city, amazed at where I was and whom I was with. Michael sat next to me and placed his hand on my leg. I had dated outside of Walden House, so this wasn't the first time. What was different was Michael's intensity. There was definitely a charge of special energy between us that was very unique. Aesthetically he was more beautiful than Frankie. But he wasn't.

He stood up and began taking his clothes off. I had been working out trying to take care of my body, but I was enamored when I saw his chest.

His body was of an Adonis. He had perfect ripples down his stomach, a six-pack that was lean and tight. Just looking at him made me nervous.

What I was about to tell him made it even worse.

Then I just bit the bullet and disclosed my HIV status to him.

"Really?" He was surprised. "I appreciate you telling me. I still really want to be with you, though." I felt relieved and had a new admiration for him. I wasn't sure what I would do if the tables were reversed. I figured he must really dig me. He was obviously educated about it.

We discussed safe sex, which would of course be the only option for us.

As soon as we finished, the door of the hotel opened. His friends walked into the hotel, saw us both naked and started giggling uncontrollably.

"I guess Michael 'came out' while we were out on the town," one said to the other. *Yes he did.*

I never believed in love, I was deceived by love
I never had much luck with lovers before
And I couldn't compete
I seemed Just part of the street
To be walked on by everyone

But then, then I found a very special love in you...

"Very Special Love" – Maureen McGover

Chapter 30

TORN RELEASE

My trip to New York was beyond anything I thought it would be. I was in love with New York and I felt at home there. It felt as if I had lived there my entire life. Michael and I started dating long distance and he took my mind off Frankie. He came up to see me in San Francisco and we enjoyed each other's company. Michael worked in the music industry in Los Angeles and had mentioned that he wanted to move to New York. We talked about it about it for a while, and then finally I told him I wanted to move, too. We decided that we would move separately, but continue dating and then if everything worked out, we would move in together. I felt a tinge of guilt because I had always remained loyal to Frankie, god knows why. I wasn't even sure he would call.

And then of course, he did.

He wanted to come to California. I wanted to and booked him a ticket without addressing my preliminary relationship with Michael.

Frankie still had priority, no matter what. He had gotten out of prison to learn that his mother had moved to Florida and he had nowhere to go.

I wasn't sure how I was going to handle this situation. I still had intense feelings for Frankie. But a lot had happened since that last visit we had and I now knew I needed more than I had ever received.

And Michael was the nicest person I had ever met.

∞∞∞

Frankie arrived and I was so nervous when I went to pick him up from the airport. I wasn't sure what the moment would be like. But I was not about to let my hopes and worries get in the way of a nice visit. Once I saw him all the feelings I've ever had for him were unleashed. There was an uncontrollable connection.

We talked and hung out and he was amazed at what had transpired in my life.

"I am so proud of you, Justin," he told me, "You are a beautiful man. Thank you for bringing me here." He was grateful of the time we were spending together. I was sure there would be no sex since I was seeing Michael and I had no idea who Frankie was seeing or if he was still married. I didn't even want to know.

After running around San Francisco and taking him on a partial tour of The City, we came back to my house for the evening and were getting ready to get some sleep. I set him up on the couch and he was noticeably unhappy about the arrangement.

"How come I can't sleep with you?" he asked, trying to smile.

I had gone over this scenario in my head a thousand times since he had arrived. There was no way I could do this. I had been introducing Frankie as my "brother" to all my friends, trying to run from my feelings inside, hoping that avoiding the truth would push us apart. I still felt goofy and my heart starting beating faster again as I prepared to tell him why he couldn't sleep with me.

I thought of what I would say that would support the notion that it wasn't a good idea. *Frankie, you're married and I'm seeing someone. No. Frankie, I'm HIV positive – not a good idea. No. Frankie, we don't have what we used to have anymore.*

NO FRANKIE.

"Ok, you can sleep with me," I caved.

"That's more like it," he replied with an entitled demeanor. I disclosed my status to him pertaining to my health, although I had a feeling he already knew. Maybe that would stop this train. He said nothing as I explained it all to him. He just looked at me lovingly. When I finished he kissed me and didn't speak a word.

We lay in the bed and slowly began to get closer. I felt my flesh resting upon his and was purposely trying to connect against his body. I felt calm, as we remained close, slowly becoming intimate. Just as I thought we couldn't get any closer, I felt his leg wrap over me intertwining our bodies together. We were in awe of each other.

Although I was in temporary heaven, the good feeling began to dissipate when I realized I had to move forward without him.

I'm all out of faith, this is how I feel
I'm cold and I am shamed lying naked on the floor
Illusion never changed, into something real
I'm wide awake and I can see the perfect sky is torn

You're a little late, I'm already torn…

"Torn" – Natalie Imbruglia

Chapter 31

DISCONNECTION

Frankie's visit was more than I had anticipated. We connected deeply and I could tell that he wanted me openly. I took him with me everywhere and introduced him to all of my friends who all thought he was amazing. They could see his admiration toward me and though it was everything that I had ever dreamed of I had already begun letting go.

I sat him down and explained that I needed to send him to Florida to stay with his mother. Before I could finish speaking, a tear developed in his eye, though he tried to remain stoic and appear unaffected.

I was breaking his heart. I was breaking my heart.

"Are you sure about this?" he asked confused.

"I think it would be best. I will keep in touch from New York. Your mom needs you now, anyway," I said trying to make the situation seem noble. I didn't know what else to do.

I had waited my entire life for this moment, this incredible situation and I was throwing it away. I knew it, too. I had never had such feelings for anyone. But at this point in my life I needed to run away again. It was too much for my head to wrap around.

And still, I knew I was making the biggest mistake of my life.

I still think about you everyday,
Maybe two or three times, when I get carried away.
I could never push rewind and erase, but at least I know now that it wasn't a phase.
You're everything I want, and you have been all along,
But oh, it's too much.

Too much will never be enough.
Whenever we touch, it happens every time,

I have to turn around and run…

"Too Much" – L.P.

Chapter 32

I HAUL, U HAUL

Although it hurt terribly to see Frankie go away, I was relieved because I had started getting honest feedback from friends that I should move on. Trying to suppress the emptiness, I kept telling myself that we just weren't meant to be. Michael was a good dude and I looked forward to hopefully spending more time with him.

My mother called and told me that my brother George had tested positive for HIV and had been arrested for drug possession in Seattle. She said he was noticeably sick and was living on the streets and doing drugs when arrested. He went to jail and was sentenced to three years in prison for his petty crimes.

"He won't live three years," my mother told me desperately. I wanted to console her, but this was a tough one. I had tried to get him to go into Walden House a few months before, but he did not want help. Programs like Walden House are not equipped to help people who are not ready for it.

I tried to give her hope, but we both knew what was happening. I had been sending notes to my brother and heard through Cameron that he was grateful for my communication.

That was all I could do for him, though it didn't seem like enough.

∞∞∞∞

The five-day drive to New York was hideous. I thought the trip to Seattle was long, but this was deadly. My nerves were on edge most of the way and I still couldn't believe what I had done.

New York City? Will I be able to survive? I had no idea how I would begin my music career. I was not very educated. I had a couple of jobs in non-profit, but not in music except as a DJ. This was a huge leap for me and even a bigger risk. Somehow I knew it was the right one.

I was so happy when I finally drove into Manhattan, via the George Washington Bridge from New Jersey. It was already midnight and the city was lit up beautifully. The streets in New York were different than any other city I had been in. I was still in awe at all the traffic as late as it was. This city didn't sleep and I didn't want to either. I felt high when I saw the magic of New York City.

Michael had told me to go to the Sound Factory Bar if I made it into town in time. I wanted to surprise him even though I was going to stay with him and his friend for a night or two.

I had trouble finding parking for my big U-Haul, but finally did and made my way to the bar. I was tired and felt a little gross from driving all day, but went inside and immediately grabbed a cocktail. I had started drinking after I graduated Walden House, with their permission, of course. Their philosophy was that dope fiends could drink socially if they didn't have an alcoholic history. I definitely had an alcoholic history, but I downplayed it enough to get the Executive's Permission to drink. I had been able to maintain my drinking and was proud of myself for being able to drink without doing drugs.

I really wanted to fit in and be normal.

I ordered a Rum and Coke and began making my way around the bi-level club. I was walking up the stairs to the second floor when I felt someone grab and kiss my face. It was Michael wearing a big fat smile. I was so relieved to know someone and to be doted upon. Thank god for Michael. He made me feel so welcome, as if he was waiting for me.

"I'm so glad you made it," he said still smiling.

He wouldn't stop staring at me and I was getting a little self-conscious. I wondered if I should ever tell him about Frankie, but decided that I needed to keep that subject to myself. I never told anyone else, why start now? Plus Michael had a tendency to get jealous.

Frankie was history and would now remain there.

We walked towards the DJ booth.

"Come with me, I want to introduce you to Frankie Knuckles." I knew Michael was pretty connected in the music industry but Frankie Knuckles was the biggest DJ in the world and was a musical hero. He invented 'house' music, and was dubbed the Godfather of his own Genre. This was huge and we hung out with Frankie for a few minutes. We walked out of the booth and back into the main club when Michael whispered in my ear.

"I missed you."

Michael and I enjoyed each other for a couple of days as I looked through the papers for an affordable apartment. There was no such thing in Manhattan and I didn't do my research prior to my arrival. In fact, there wasn't an affordable *anything* within a fifty-mile radius. I was flipping out. I really didn't want to impose much longer on Michael and his roommate.

"Why don't you get a roommate?" Michael asked as I stressed through the newspaper. *Why didn't I think of that?*

∞ ∞ ∞

I couldn't find an affordable share in Manhattan either, but finally found one in Brooklyn. I felt a sense of relief as I moved into my new home, a four-story walk up. The pre-war building was located in the Park Slope section of Brooklyn, on Seventh Avenue. The neighborhood was beautiful and I was made breathless by all of the architecture and history that was all around me.

Brooklyn was just as fascinating as Manhattan.

My bedroom had a small view of Manhattan and a full view of the Brooklyn Bridge and the canal that stretches from the Verrazano Bridge to the Hudson River. Since we were on the top floor we had full access to the roof, which had a full view of Manhattan.

Michael had started working for a record label and was doing very well for himself. I was having a hard time. I didn't have many contacts in the industry, so I decided to take Michael up on his offer to use his office to prepare my resume.

He made a few calls on my behalf and by the end of the day I had an internship at a small independent record label. It was non-paid gig but it would get my foot in the door. Two days after I started my new internship, the label manager quit and before I knew what was happening, I was running a small record label. It was almost comical. I had no clue about anything. There were so many elements involved with music from promotion and marketing to publishing and distribution. It was overwhelming and, thank god, Michael came to my rescue…again.

"Justin, you are smart and can do this. I know enough about you. I can help answer any questions when confusing issues come up. You have an opportunity to prove yourself and to become a serious player in the music industry. Show them what you got."

Michael was amazing and he was perfect. He was loving and kind and empowering. The more we saw each other, the more I let him know about my past, and to my amazement, it made him love me more.

Even though he liked to bicker about my questionable decision making process (I can be a bit hardheaded at times) he was the sweetest person I had ever met.

But he wasn't you-know-who, (whose name I am no longer speaking).

My job was stressful but stimulating. I began to learn so many things I needed to know to be successful. But there was a price to pay – my relationship with Michael. I was too busy to see anyone socially. After many months, Michael became frustrated, so when I finally made the time to see him, it wasn't a pleasant visit.

"Where have you been?" he asked, clearly annoyed that we hadn't seen each other in weeks. It had gotten so busy we were only able to have a few short telephone conversations.

"It seems now that you are here, you don't want to be with me. I can feel you pushing me away." He knew what I was doing, even if I didn't realize I was doing it.

"It doesn't feel right," I told him honestly. There was no sense pushing something that I wasn't ready for. By this time, I was really good at making romantic mistakes.

Michael and I would remain good friends.

Like a clown I've been smiling
Whenever people were around
But when the curtain comes down
And the circus is through
No one is left but me – you - and all my Tears.

So many Tears...

"Tears" – Robert Owens

Chapter 33

BROTHERS WHERE ART THOU

Time sure flies when you're having fun. I had begun to DJ at some of the coolest nightclubs, was enjoying my new job and was extremely busy in my New York state of mind. Christmas time had rolled around and things had leveled out. Maybe I was not the loser my father thought I was. I had been calling my mother regularly and had stayed in touch with Cameron, too. I missed them but was exactly where I needed to be.

The day before Christmas, Cameron called and was distressed.

"He's not doing well," he said referring to George, "he is in and out of consciousness. Mom and Dad are in their motor home in Arizona. The nurse told me to tell them to come home immediately."

I had sent George a money order around Thanksgiving. I knew he was getting sick and wanted him to know that I loved him and was thinking about him. The thought that he was dying in prison around people he didn't know killed me.

I put on my winter coat and took the train into Manhattan where I decided to hit some clubs and go drinking. I needed to get buzzed. Actually, I needed to get totally wasted that night.

∞∞∞

I woke up the next morning with a terrible hangover. Combined with the memory of the phone call, I wasn't doing too well. I called my mother to check on her.

"Did Cam tell you to go home?" I asked trying to start the conversation.

"Yes, he did," she answered quickly.

"When are you leaving?" I figured she was packing and would leave soon and that was why she was being so brisk.

"We're not. You're father refuses to go."

"Mom, you are the only ones that they will allow to visit George," I said irritated. Where they really going to let my brother die with no one but prison guards around him?

I could tell she had been fighting with my father.

"Mom, you need to get home. You need to be there for George. No one else is allowed to..." I heard him scream in the background.

"Get off the god damn phone, Carol! We are not going to see anyone! He is a fucking loser! They're all losers!"

"You need to go home," I spoke sharply like a parent Scolding their child. Without waiting for a reaction, I slammed the phone down.

Through the next couple of weeks I kept in close contact with Cameron and then was allowed to speak with the prison hospice nurses. They kept me updated and told me my brother, who wasn't able to speak on the phone said hello. I wanted him to know that his little brother was trying to look out for him.

That he was loved and more importantly, that he wasn't alone.

∞∞∞

I felt the need to get out of the house. It was late on a weekend night so I figured I would go to a popular club in Manhattan ironically called The Shelter. By this time I had developed a little drinking problem, but for some reason that night I did not have any alcohol. I didn't need it. I danced to the music and was enjoying myself when an amazing feeling came over me.

It was a peaceful feeling that gave me the sensation that everything was fine. The feeling of calm and peace continued to flow through me and I became a little concerned that someone had slipped something into my water, since I was not used to feeling so spiritual, especially at five o'clock in the morning.

I had a strong sensation that I was in the right place – that everything was as it was suppose to be. I was comforted by this keen sense of wellbeing. I went home, fell asleep and was jarred awake by my phone ringing. I answered it to hear Cameron's voice, "He's gone. He passed away at 2:00am."

I remembered the beautiful experience I had on the dance floor. I was astonished when I realized that due to the time difference, this experience happened at the exact same time my brother passed.

The connection was undeniable.

My mother had finally convinced Dad to go home to see George. They were only half way home when my brother passed away. My mother expressed guilt and was crying to me. I couldn't say anything that would comfort her.

"What are we doing for a memorial?" I asked, trying to prepare for my trip home.

"We're not going to have one. He is being cremated and that's it," she said coarsely, "there is no need for you to come home." Sweep it under the carpet. AIDS, prisoner, drug addict.

He doesn't warrant remembrance.

I wasn't going to argue with anyone and I wasn't the one who could legally make decisions. They were going to do what they were going to do and I had no control. I didn't care how messed up George was, he was my brother and had a beautiful soul.

He would be missed and most importantly, remembered.

∞∞∞∞

One way to avoid dealing with sorrow is to become extremely busy with work. I took on a special project that required me to travel to London for a few weeks and was excited to leave the United States for the first time. I couldn't stop thinking about the death of my brother and had to keep reminding myself that he was in a better place. I was no stranger to loss but it never really gets easier.

I traveled to England with a singer to supervise her mini-tour. I did a lot of thinking while we traveled by cars and trains all around the beautiful country. It was healing for me. I thought about my British grandfather and researched cemeteries where my ancestors were buried in South London.

After two weeks on the road, we finally settled into a little flat we rented near Piccadilly Circus, a busy section in Westminster, London's West End. It had been exactly a month to the day since George died so I decided that I would call home to the United States to check on my mother.

She answered the phone and sounded hysterical. I felt bad as I realized she was surely crying at the thought of George's passing.

"It's your brother, Cameron. He is having a terrible seizure and won't wake up." The ambulance was transporting him to the hospital.

I was stunned.

"His tumor is back," she sobbed into the phone. There was nothing I could do to calm my mother.

"I am leaving London tomorrow for New York. I will call you when I get there." Click.

∞∞∞∞

Much had been determined by the time I got to New York. Cameron's brain tumor had returned and was very aggressive. He could have surgery, but they said it would only extend his life for one to two years. Without it, he may live six to twelve months. He hadn't decided what course to take.

I wanted to speak to my brother.

"Do you know what you want to do?" I asked him.

"I don't know," he began, "the headaches are so bad I don't think I can last six months. I have to opt for the surgery."

"My last surgery was hell. The recovery. I don't know if I want to go through it again." He was finally honest about how hard of a time he had gone through. He never had admitted it before and had always braved through like a soldier.

Cameron made his decision and went into surgery a few days later on Friday afternoon. Thankfully, his second brain surgery was successful.

"There will be brain swelling and so the doctors will put him into a coma to combat pain," my mother explained the entire process to me on the phone. I was glad she was there to hold Cameron's hand as he went through this traumatic event again.

"He woke up for a moment and said 'Hi Mom', and I fed him Popsicle," she added excitedly. Things were looking up and I had a comforting sense of relief. I wasn't prepared to lose another brother.

"Do you want me to come home?" I asked.

"No, he is going to be fine," she told me assured. I checked in with Mom throughout the weekend. He was doing well in his medically induced coma.

On Monday morning I was getting ready for work when my Mom called with an update, "You need to come home." She spoke somberly.

I was scared to ask, "What is going on?"

She started to cry, "He suffered a massive stroke in the middle of the night." It was surreal. I could not believe what was happening.

Was I suppose to go to work and act like everything was normal? I was losing my only other surviving brother and I felt like I was losing my mind. I felt sick and empty as I dialed the phone. Michael was very quiet while I told him what had happened. He didn't even know what to say to comfort me, which validated the intensity of my situation.

"I am flying you to Seattle. You need to go home and be with your family." His directive was the guidance I needed because I had no idea what to do.

I flew to Seattle, rented a car and drove straight to the hospital. I went to the floor where my brother was located and saw my father in the waiting room. He looked up at me and gave me an evil stare just as my mother walked into the waiting room.

"What the hell are you doing here?" he snarled.

He was angry and hurt and somebody was going to pay. I guess it was going to be me as usual.

My mother exploded, "If you can't act right, leave! I have had enough of you!" She screamed at him like I had never heard before. "He flew all the way from New York to be with us!"

"I don't need his help," he mumbled. She shot him a look and he turned away.

We were called into a meeting with the doctor. I had expected to hear something hopeful as in a possible recovery.

"There is no miracle that will help your brother. He is brain dead."

He would be removed from life support. I think it was the first time we all agreed on one single thing. Cameron continued to breath on his own as we waited for his body to shut down. It would be days, maybe weeks.

I stayed the evening and tried to console my mother. There was no comfort to be had for any of us. I didn't want to leave, but I had to get back to New York.

As I drove down the freeway to catch my red-eye flight, I decided to make the stop to see Cameron for the last time. He was going to be moved into a hospice facility, but was still in the hospital, which was right off the freeway exit.

I sat next to his bed and looked at him. He had a bandage on his head, where they had cut over his old scar. He looked peaceful.

This had to be the saddest day of my life.

Cameron David Early passed away on April 7, 1996 - Easter Sunday.

There was no memorial service.

Chapter 34

MR. BROWNSTONE

Though I would try not to think about it, all I did was think. I would be reminded daily, hourly and sometimes by the minute, that both of my brothers were dead.

Even something checking the mailbox proved difficult and reminded me of them. While going through my daily mail delivery, I noticed a familiar letter. It was addressed to my brother George with a stamp next to his name, RETURN TO SENDER. There was another stamp in red, DECEASED. The money order I had sent him never made it to him.

I went back to work and tried to live normally, but the thought of them swirled around in my head everyday - as did the thought of Frankie. I wanted to reach out so badly. With my brothers gone and loneliness pervading my being, it was time I tried to call my boy. I needed to at least hear him. I dug out Mama's phone number and dialed her number in Florida.

"Hello?" She sounded a bit depressed. "Mama, it's Justin."

"Oh, hi baby." She perked up a little. "Where are you?"

"I'm in New York. Have you heard from Frankie?"

"I haven't seen him in months. I don't know where he is."

To disappear in our world meant too many things. I gave her my phone number and address to pass along.

"Please have him call me right away if you see him. It's urgent."

But with Internet access just in its beginning phases, Facebook or online social media invented yet, finding someone was nearly impossible.

∞∞∞

The only thing I could do to avoid the thoughts of my loss was to work hard. The music industry was a great field for that. And the bonus was that once the daytime duties were done, there were plenty of nightclubs and concerts to go to. I had been hired at a major record label and was doing relatively well. The status of working for a known label brought about many perks, such as traveling to several conferences and artist's gigs around the country. I stayed very busy and very buzzed. I tried to keep it together but noticed that I was getting a little more intoxicated than I should. I had gone dancing at a club called Twilo in Manhattan when I went to the bathroom to relieve my bladder. I was standing at the urinal overly buzzed from the alcohol when someone asked me an odd question. "Hey, you wanna bump?" I had no idea what he was talking about.

He raised his hand towards my face and I noticed round little mountain of white powder on his fist. His hand lingered right in front of my nostril.

Without thinking twice, I sniffed the pile of white magic. I didn't know what it was until the taste hit the back of my throat. My sweet ex-lover wanted me back, and I was in too much emotional pain to tell Cocaine anything but yes.

At the time, it seemed this was the answer to my past and developing problems.

∞∞∞

I had made many friends in New York and was pretty well linked into the music scene, but I hadn't met anyone I would hang tight with until the night I was out at my neighborhood bar in Brooklyn. There was a little lesbian joint on Seventh Avenue about three blocks up from my apartment. I always felt an affinity toward lesbians with Lou Lou having been one of my closest friends.

After downing a few drinks, I was feeling pretty buzzed when I noticed a short Italian girl with pretty, long, wavy hair walk into the bar. She had a little dog under her arm - a white Maltese named Ralphie. I could hear her talking to the bartender in her little Brooklyn/Italian east coast accent. She was adorable. She had overheard a conversation that I was having with another patron regarding a DJ gig I had coming up in Manhattan and walked up to me.

"How yew dewin'?" she said in her cute little Brooklyn accent. She was so adorable. She was petite at about five foot two. Her hair was long and perfect and I could smell the Aveda products. She had a little tomboy vibe that attracted me to her like a magnet. "I'm good. How yoo doo-in?" I responded in my pathetic New Yawk accent.

She looked at me with a stone face when she realized I was impersonating her accent. Then she smiled. "Let me buy you a drink so you can work on your accent. Hey bartender, give this man a drink on me," she instructed while reaching out her hand. "I'm the owner, Lisa."

"You are a very cute lesbian."

"I know, I am." She replied in her little girly voice. As we laughed she snorted out loud like Fran Drescher, and that sealed the deal.

∞∞∞

Lisa and I became inseparable. She owned another lesbian bar in Manhattan called Henrietta Hudson's and we split our time between their and Brooklyn. We partied and we laughed and we partied some more.

I had decided to start my own promotion business and was able to work from my new loft apartment not far from where I had lived previously in Park Slope. Life was good and I was so happy to have a close friend. Lisa and I shared our deepest, darkest secrets and she knew everything about my past, my family and the death of my dear brothers. She supported me and encouraged me with Frankie, saying that I would see him again - although I knew in my heart I never would. I had tried to call Mama's number again and it was disconnected. But I had my new Lisa and everyone thought we were turning straight and getting married. We cuddled on the couch and watched South Park and Absolutely Fabulous and ate meals together almost daily.

On Holidays, I would be invited to the Cannistraci family dinners on Staten Island, where I became one of her parents' other 'kids'. There were three girls, and her mom Genevieve would joke that she finally had a son. I was welcomed into this wonderful family and little did they know that they had saved my spirit from a very deep and dark sadness. I hadn't wanted to go on much longer after my brothers passed and now my life had new meaning. My sadness was put on the back burner because of wonderful friends that loved me unconditionally.

I was still DJ'ing frequently on various nights and worked during the day from my house in Brooklyn. I had started to use more and more drugs, which helped take the messy effect from all of the alcohol that I was constantly drinking. But unfortunately drugs were pricey, and I was running low on cash. Lisa offered me to bartend at her bar up the street from me to help me get back in the black financially. It was perfect. My cocaine dealer came in every night so I knew I would be hooked up regularly and I was bringing in the extra dough I needed to pay bills (and buy coke). I rationalized my cocaine usage because I was snorting it - I wasn't like those IV drug users, or crack-heads - like I *used* to be. Besides, I was a professional in the music business and many of us used socially. I was not going to be one of those addicts again.

Saturday night my dealer came through the bar as I'd hoped. I told him I wanted a couple of bindles of cocaine and he informed me that he didn't have any. "What do you have?" I asked.

"I got some down," he said. 'Down' is slang for heroin - my savior from childhood.

I swore off heroin when I went into Walden House and knew that I would never do it again. It had been seven years and was the last accomplishment I was hanging onto that I could still be proud of.

"Give me two," I said immediately without contemplating or even thinking of the consequences.

There was a phenomenon of craving. I say that because I didn't crave it. But there was a voice inside of me telling me that I would be fine.

I felt reassured by this sweet voice that I could do just a little bit of heroin and things wouldn't get bad. Besides, it had been years right? A *little* heroin never hurt anybody.

I went into the bathroom, opened up the first bindle and snorted the tan powder. I felt the protective shield slowly cover my being as if I was a Transforming super hero. I walked back out to finish my shift in my imaginary full body armor.

Mr. Brownstone (heroin), my real daddy, was ruling my life with just one little snort.

I don't ever wanna feel
Like I did that day
Take me to the place I love

Take me all the way

Red Hot Chili Peppers – "Under The Bridge

Chapter 35

TWO FAR GONE

In true drug addict fashion, I lost everything within two years. All my friends eventually became exhausted and burnt out with me. I had sucked every bit of trust, patience and money from as many people that I could. Even Lisa was through with me. I had come to her bar a disgusting mess and when she refused to give me money, I threw an ashtray at her brick wall in frustration.

Nothing, but dope, mattered again.

With nowhere else to go, and having lost my apartment for not paying rent, I walked into the welfare office on Eighth Avenue in New York, homeless.

I was so humiliated and couldn't stand the thought of running into someone I knew from the club scene or the music industry. I was truly at bottom. I had no money, no food and no shelter. My only possession was a plastic shopping bag with a few items of clothing.

The City of New York put me up in a hotel that was turned into a homeless shelter on 155th Street and St. Nicholas in the newly redeveloping area of Harlem. Everyone at the Hotel was a drug addict and in no time I made many friends and continued my downward spiral, while living in a stinky dirty room - with a terrible rat and mouse problem.

I was receiving welfare from the State of New York and would get a small sum of money twice per month, as well as some food stamps once per month. It was definitely not enough to feed my voracious habit, so I took the advice of one of my neighbors and went down to the Kaleidoscope Methadone Clinic on 125th Street in Harlem. That stuff was no joke and kept me good and medicated. Then when my welfare money came, I would blow it on cocaine and beer and lie down again until the next "issue" of money came through.

This went on for over a year and a half. My day consisted of getting up in the morning, getting my methadone from the clinic and returning to the hotel where I would go hide in my room and lie back down. I would drink beer and eat cheap packaged donuts and cookies from the bodega up the street. Little Debbie, who manufactured these tasty little treats, fed me for months.

I lived off cheap food. Sometimes I would get someone to wire me money and then I would actually eat something healthy.

I had made friends with a young girl named "Slim". She and I would get high together. Slim was tall and very skinny. She had kinky long hair and bad teeth, chipped and stained. She was mixed - Caucasian and Black. Where I was living, it was hard for white people to get serviced by dealers because they thought we were all cops, so I had to use Slim to score most of my drugs. She was one of the only trustworthy dope fiends in New York and would always return with the goods, or my money and remained loyal, as she knew I would always share with her.

I was disgusted with where I had come back to. I had another moment of clarity when my friend "Slim" disappeared for a few days and came back to the hotel. I had wondered what happened to her and went up to her room to see where she had been.

I knocked on her door. "Damn, where have you been?" I asked concerned.

I figured she had been in jail, but wanted to hear the juicy details from her.

"I just got outta the hospital." She had a sad look on her face and was keeping eye contact with me, like she really wanted to tell me why.

"What happened? Are you alright?" I prodded.

"I had the baby," she confessed.

Baby? We had been getting high for months and I never noticed any lump in her stomach. But then again it was wintertime and she always had a big coat on. I didn't know what to say.

Congratulations? I'm sorry? What the hell were you thinking?

We hung out for a little while, and then I took my near obese deteriorating body back to my room to lie down and watch talk shows. The form of methadone that I was on had a small side effect – weight gain. I had blown up to almost 200lbs. from 160.

My looks, which were important to my ego, were gone. I was never drop dead sexy or even close – but I wasn't horrific either.

I looked frightening and knew that I would never be able to do well again. I was too far-gone. I would never be able to get out of this death game – this cycle of suffering.

My mother had learned of my fate and didn't have much of anything to say. I had my chance and I blew it. As far as my parents were concerned - and as far as my father was always concerned - all of their children were dead.

What a loser I allowed myself to become.

∞∞∞

I had fallen asleep in my welfare bed watching a Forensic Files marathon. When I awoke, I could only open my eyes. As I tried to move my hands and feet I could not. I was completely paralyzed.

I lay there momentarily, thinking that my body needed time to catch up to my mind, but all I could move were my eyes and eyelids. I was propped up on the two pillows I usually lay on when I watch television and could see around the room. But I couldn't move. I began to panic. I was powerless and lifeless. Just as I was about to try to scream, I felt the left side of my bed move. As though someone had sat on the corner of my bed, my body leaned to the left slightly. I focused my eyes on the side of the bed and noticed another dent in the mattress.

There is a fucking ghost in my welfare hotel. This is crazy.

I couldn't believe what I was seeing and was about to try to scream again. As I watched in awe, a dent began to appear in the top pillow, as if a head was laying on it. There was a fucking entity lying next to me!

I am not the most spiritual person in the world. I had always told God, *"If you are real, then give me a sign. But I ain't believing until I get a clear sign."* All of the spiritual tools that learned in Walden House were gone. Especially after Cam and George died.

The sense of panic began to dissipate as I realized that there were angels, or some form of invisible spirits in my room - comforting me during the most horrible time in my thirty-two year life.

This incident was as real as the tracks on my neck veins.

As I lay there frozen, the sense of comfort increased. After a moment, the dents disappeared and I slowly regained my physical function. I sat up on the bed and couldn't believe what had happened. Being paralyzed momentarily didn't surprise me, knowing how much I had already put my body through, but witnessing the movement on my bed was bizarre – and undeniable.

I was coherent and had an identifiable spiritual experience that I knew I should probably keep to myself, so no one would think I was a total freak.

I cared what people thought of me yet I hadn't washed my underwear in six months.

I wasn't as alone as I thought – a wake up call in the truest sense. Was it my brothers or maybe Roberta or Lou Lou? I guess it didn't matter who or what it was. Something was in my room and was trying to tell me something.

Everyone, including me, had given up on me.

It was time for the Angel's to intervene.

You are pulled from the wreckage,
Of your silent reverie,
You're in the arms of the angels,

May you find some comfort here…

"Angel" – Sarah Maclaughlan

Chapter 36

GLORIOUS SADNESS

I had the number of my old friend Ken – the man that woke me up in Larkin Park in San Francisco to give me money. He lived in Huntington Beach, CA, roughly thirty-five miles south of Los Angeles. We had kept in touch and he was the only person I could think of to call that I knew would speak to me while I was in full addict mode. He always told me that I could call him if I was ever in a 'pinch'. I was in a pinch and I needed to get out of New York as soon as possible.

I went to the pay phone in front on the hotel and called him collect (for those of you who know what that means). "Hey Ken," I began, "I need help. I am in big trouble."

"What's new? You're always in trouble." He said unsurprised.

Yes, I was always in trouble when I called him and I always made sure it was bad trouble. Thankfully he still had a little patience left for me because no one else did.

He continued with a bit of an attitude, "I am not an idiot. It's obvious you are on drugs again. I can hear it in your voice."

I began to explain my predicament when he cut me off.

"I will buy you a one-way ticket to California. You can stay with me until you detox off that strange stuff you're on. But then you have to get a job and pay rent or find your own place." His invitation was nothing short of a miracle. I had to do something drastic to get out of the daily routine I was now almost being forced to endure. Methadone is no joke.

I went to the methadone clinic in Harlem and took my final dose of their highly addictive medication. I knew I would have hell to pay for trying to do this alone, without medical assistance but I didn't have any other choice. I wouldn't be able to get off the stuff if I didn't go all the way across the country. I saw the people that were on methadone, and many had been on for years.

It's not something you just stop on your own.

I hopped on a plane, went to California and began my endless, sickening and unexplainable experience of kicking methadone. I had been on a particularly high dose and was sweating profusely and throwing up regularly. When nothing was left to throw up, I would heave and heave until a nasty yellow liquid mixed with phlegm would finally come out of my angry intestines. Somehow that substance was endless. To make matters worse, sleeping was almost impossible when in withdrawal. I was in hell.

And I deserved every minute of it.

It took five weeks before I began to feel better. I started making my way to the pier in Huntington Beach, which was just three blocks away. Ken was the only friend speaking to me, but I was feeling better and knew that I could do something with my life again if I put my mind to it.

I would listen and watch the waves crash into the pillars on the pier, and I would think of my brothers and the other players in my life story. I thought of Frankie, whom I finally started to realize I would not see again. I wasn't going to waste time and effort to try and contact him, even though the Internet was gaining popularity and becoming a popular route for reunions. He would remain in my heart and although I didn't know what happened to him, I vowed to always cherish his memory.

The sense of loss that I had tried to cover up with drugs and alcohol, were back. Only now I had to deal with them.

Above all these thoughts and feelings, I remained grateful for I had been given a **third**, second chance.

∞∞∞∞

I put feelers out in the music world, but the Internet boom and digital delivery methods for music made it a very volatile industry. I needed to find something else – something urgently.

I was searching on the Internet for available jobs when I noticed an interesting heading - *'Gay Couple in Beverly Hills Seek Personal Assistant'*.

I sent my resume and fudged the employment dates on it, so there wouldn't be an obvious gap in employment. Nothing about my recent past would help me get a job, so I took my chances with the lie. After a few days of a focused job-search, I was frustrated and had not received any calls or emails for interviews.   Finally the phone rang from a potential employer. It was the gay couple from the ad. One was a doctor in Beverly Hills and they invited me for an interview. I was to come to his house and meet with him and his partner. Although I still had a little 'street' vibe and wasn't the most articulate, it was mostly from lack of education and acclimation. I am a good actor. I put on the nicest clothes I had. I drove up to Beverly Hills, where I had never been, and parked in front of their house. I nervously walked up to the front door and rang the doorbell. It was one of those loud obnoxious doorbells. I felt like I was intruding when it went off. I could hear footsteps coming down stairs, towards the door, and the door opened. A man with dark skin, my guess was Puerto Rican or Middle Eastern, opened the door and welcomed me in.

"Please have a seat in the living room," he instructed. "My partner is on his way down."

I went in to the living room and was amazed at all of the artwork on the walls. The furniture was antique and I didn't want to sit my dirty ass on any of it. I looked around the room, which reminded me a bit like Harvey Hall at Walden House. It was large and had vaulted ceilings and a large fancy fireplace. I could see the signatures on the paintings that were on the walls –Andy Warhol. These gays - I mean guys - were not playing around.

There was no way they were going to hire my ghetto self! They walked into the living room while I was still admiring the paintings and art that was hanging perfectly throughout the amazing sitting room.

The now obvious Puerto Rican introduced himself again. "I'm the Doctor, but you can call me Doc," he said nicely. He was a chubby man, about my height. His hair was obviously dyed but was styled very nicely. He had on very expensive clothes. Not quite a suit, but fancy enough and pressed tight. He had a large gold ring on his wedding finger. I noticed it was a college ring, probably from Medical School. They both had the same Shoes: Prada. And Shirts: Brooks Brothers.

"This is my partner, Marion." I shook the white man's hand.

"Hello Justin," he said with a British accent. Not sure if it was the accent or his demeanor that made him sound so gay. The fact that he sounded so feminine and had a girls name almost gave me the giggles, but I controlled myself. Barely.

"Please have a seat," the funny sounding man instructed.

The Gays were very serious with what they were looking for and the more questions they asked, the further I got from getting the job. The interview lasted over an hour and I was exhausted and ready to leave when it was over. Though neither of them seemed thrilled about me, they were appreciative that I met with them.

I drove back to Huntington Beach and immediately started sending out more resumes.

Even though I knew I wouldn't be considered for the job, I thought it would be proper etiquette to send The Gays a thank you note, even though the interview was – not great. They were fairly nice and I was glad to have had the experience interviewing with them regardless.

Before the confirmation from the fax printed telling me it went through successfully, my phone rang.

"Hi Justin. This is Doc and Marion." They were both on the phone.

"We appreciate your fax and would like to offer you the job."

Huh?

"We have interviewed over twenty candidates and you were the only one that sent a thank you note. You are what we are looking for. We need someone to think like us – and it seems you know how to think things through."

I was hired as a Personal Assistant.

∞∞∞∞

On my first day I was assigned to assist Marion and was to work with him in a Medical Office, of which they had several. We were driving together having small talk. "How old are you?" I asked innocently. "I'm twenty-nine," he said seriously.

"Ha-ha!" I laughed. I was thirty-two and he was obviously older than me. "You are not twenty-nine." I was still laughing because I really thought he was pulling my leg. He wasn't laughing. In fact, he shot me a bitchy look and then looked back at the road. We drove in silence the rest of the way to the office. Once there, he stayed very quiet. I worked until the end of the day and we drove back to their house in mostly silence. This guy wasn't twenty-nine and I didn't care how fucking Beverly Hills he was; I wasn't going to buy into his bullshit. I figured I would just start looking for another job. We walked into the house and up to the home office where the doctor was working at his desk. "How did it go?" he asked Marion. "It was fine," Marion said in a bitchy tone and a pout on his face. He was clearly pissed that I didn't kiss his ass about the age thing. The Doctor eyes got larger as he realized his lover was upset. He looked at me and smirked.

"See you tomorrow?" Doc asked me, still amused that his partner was acting like a two-year-old. "Um, I guess," I responded unsure of what their conversation would consist of once I left the building. No one called to fire me so I woke up the next morning and headed to work.

I rang the doorbell and was greeted by the housekeeper, who instructed me to go upstairs to the office. The doctor was sitting in his chair in his underwear and a t-shirt.

"It looks like you are working for me now," he told me, "which is good. I needed you more, anyway." He opened the drawer to his desk and pulled out a wad of one hundred dollar bills.

He unraveled a few and handed them to me. "Why don't you go buy some new clothes, you can't dress like that and work for me." He noticed I had on yesterday's work clothes.

I was so embarrassed and humiliated. Part of my job would be traveling around to his many medical offices, with one very important office located in the heart of Beverly Hills near Rodeo Drive. I had to look professional.

I enjoyed working for the doctor, and Marion soon began warming back up to me. The days were long, but I was learning a lot about medical administration and as a bonus, got to help take care of their many animals, including two Doberman guard dogs that loved me immensely. My dog Honeychild was being taken care of by some friends in San Francisco - I had shipped her there when I first relapsed. I knew I wouldn't be able to take care of her in my addiction.

I eventually saved enough money to move into a dog friendly apartment in Hollywood. I drove to San Francisco and picked up my beloved Honeychild. The Gay's wanted me closer in order to be at their beck and call.

Life wasn't perfect, but things were looking up.

Take this time to listen and grow,
Take the time to know.
Immerse yourself in your own goodness,
And a beautiful flower will grow...

Chapter 37

ON POINT

Doc had to deal with some business in New York and would be gone for a few days, which was good because I had DJ gigs lined up and would need to sleep-in later on those days.

I had gotten off work at four in the morning and went home. I put my little cell phone on its charger in the kitchen - like I normally do - and went to bed and immediately fell asleep.

The ringer on this smaller than usual phone was set to a quiet "chirp", so I was surprised when I was awaken by it's barely audible noise at five-thirty in the morning. It wasn't like me to hear it when it was turned up let alone be able to wake up to the sound of it. I got up and went to the kitchen to see who was calling me. It was Doc and I had just missed his call. He didn't have a problem calling me at all hours of the day; evenings and on weekends so I wasn't surprised by the early call. But something struck me about this call. He wouldn't call this early unless it was urgent.

In a daze, I picked up the phone and hit redial. The phone picked up, be he didn't say anything. "Hello?" I asked, trying to ascertain if he could hear me.

"Yeth!" It was his voice, but he sounded funny.

"Doc? Are you drunk?" He could have gone out drinking, but that would have been highly unusual for him since he doesn't enjoy alcohol. Whatever was going on, he was slurring badly.

"NO DUNK!" he screamed.

"Where are you?" I asked getting frustrated at not being able to understand him.

"*Floooooor*!" he mumbled, when I heard the desperation in his voice.

"What the hell are you doing on the floor?" I was starting to wake up but was still confused what was happening.

"*TROKE*!" He still wasn't speaking clearly. But I knew something was wrong.

"Are you having a *stroke?*"

"YETH! HELPH ME!" He needed help – and I only had one phone.

"I have to get off the phone to call someone for you."

"NO!!" He started to cry not wanting to hang up.

I immediately dialed the doorman of his Penthouse apartment building in New York and told him what was happening. I knew if it was a stroke, we couldn't waste any time. He needed to get to the hospital. The doorman had a spare key and dialed 9-1-1 from another line before rushing up to the apartment.

I called Doc back on his cell phone and he picked up without speaking.

"The doorman is on his way up," I assured him.

"Otay," he slurred. I heard the apartment door opening in the background.

The ambulance came, and just as I had suspected, Doc had suffered a massive stroke. It was a tender subject for me because that's what killed my brother. Marion was unable to fly to New York immediately, so I booked a ticket for the first flight and went directly to the hospital where Doc was being treated. I took a deep breath as I approached his room and entered with my game face on. He looked at me with tears welling up at the sight of me. One side of his body was paralyzed and his face was drooping.

I didn't know what to say. "God Damn! You look like a messssss!" I spoke with a flamboyant accent, like a stereotypical gay would sound.

He looked at me and half of his face smiled back.

"Fuck you!" He muttered, as he laughed at my joke. He couldn't speak much, but cuss words apparently were available from his now limited vocabulary.

"I'm scurred," he whispered.

"I know. I know," I comforted him. "You are going to be fine. You better be, I just flew all the way from L.A. to make sure you were."

He smiled again. It seemed easier this time. Marion arrived a couple of days after I did and I was relieved of my Hospital duties and returned to California.

"I need you to make sure the offices run smoothly." Marion told me.

He continued, "You are in charge of everything business and personal and I am holding you accountable," he dramatically ordered in his bitchy 'I wish I was born with a vagina' attitude.

I returned to California and did as requested. It was a great opportunity to prove myself even though I had been doing a little of everything and knew my way around their business. After a long day at work, and The Gays still in New York while my boss recovered from his stroke, I decided to treat myself to a Twelve Step meeting, since it was the only thing keeping me out of trouble. I knew of a meeting on Melrose Avenue and went alone. The meeting had already started so I snuck in quietly. There was a row in the back with several empty chairs and I sat down in one.

I was getting myself situated and listening to the readings that they do at the beginning of the meetings, when I felt someone looking at me. It was to my left and whoever it was kept staring. I was a little nervous and annoyed at their rude persistence. As I turned my head I noticed a handsome dark skinned man with a salt and pepper goatee looking back at me.

Frankie was smiling sunshine and brightened the entire room.

Chapter 38

LAST CALL

We jumped up and hugged. The meeting was still going on so we both had to sit back down and not make a scene. I couldn't believe it. I had told myself that I was not going to even try to find him, and then God or the Universe or whatever, brought him to me and placed in on my lap. It was miraculous!

We exchanged cell phone numbers and he promised to call after he dropped his friend off. He called and came to my apartment. I gave him another hug as he walked in and noticed him flinch. "We have to talk," he said with no trace of a smile. "I am in a relationship. My lover and I live together and I want you to know that before we say anything else to each other." I was disappointed, but happy to know he was alive and well. We sat on the couch for two hours catching up about our families and lives. We had an awkward good-bye, careful not touch each other improperly.

And that was our reunion.

∞∞∞∞

I forced myself to step up and accept this new person in Frankie's life. I tried my best to be friends to them and succeeded, but it was difficult. It was weird having someone who had been such a part of my life be so close to someone else. I had thought he was gone forever and had gotten used to that idea. Now that he was living with his love a few miles away from me. It stirred up feelings again. The feeling of being alone was now exaggerated.

At this point, I needed him in my life and I didn't care at what level. Though I couldn't just fall 'out of love' - I would try.

∞∞∞∞

Doc began a miraculous recovery and their company was running smoothly. They were very entertained when they found out that I had fired a problem employee that had been giving everyone a hard time during their absence. That was the icing on the cake. They celebrated by giving me a promotion and a substantial raise along with additional job duties, which turned out to be the perfect answer to getting my mind off Frankie being with someone else. Actually, I found it easier to be angry at the situation. I tried to do social activities together with the happy couple, but it was always awkward. But it wasn't about me, or us anymore.

∞∞∞∞

Months had passed and I was finally being lifted from the emotional pain that I couldn't stand to experience. I was used to not being with him and thoughts of wanting to be subsided. Then just when I was almost in the clear, I received his call.

"I need a place to stay. I am having some problems at home."

"Of course you can stay with me." Ulterior motives began flying through my sneaky little head.

He stayed for a few days and slept on the couch. We would have long talks and were warming up to each other. I was getting to know him again.

We were standing in the kitchen one night and he was looking at me too much. I felt that familiar tension of unacknowledged bond building between us. I didn't plan on saying anything. I didn't want to say anything. But the words had to come out or I would die with them inside of me.

"I love you Frankie, I never stopped loving you." my voice was shaking.

Though over the years my actions said it loud and clear, I had never actually said it out loud. The look on his face told me that I was not alone in my feelings. He began to move closer which was a queue to a kiss. His silence turned into a sexy smirk. We began to do what we knew best with a kiss that was better then the first kiss a quarter of a century before.

It was just like riding a bike, only we'd both gotten better at it.

I must have rehearsed my lines,
A thousand times,
Until I had them memorized,
But when I get up the nerve to tell you,
The words just never seem to come out right...

"If Only You Knew" – Patti LaBelle

Chapter 39

LET THEM FLY

We spent the next few days close together and I felt the kind of love that I had craved for so long but had been too hardheaded and embarrassed to admit. It was truly the most beautiful quality time that we had spent together. And we actually started to break the ice and discuss our past, something we rarely brought up.

"I really care about you, Frankie." I started humbly. "The moment I laid eyes on you... I fell in love." He seemed a bit stunned, which surprised me. Rather than letting me see his raw emotion, he turned away as he spoke.

"I know you do, but my situation is complicated." Yes it was.

"What are you trying to say?" I already knew, but for some reason needed to hear it aloud.

"Why did you wait all this time to tell me how you feel?" he asked. "All these months – years - you have said nothing. I always imagined you to be the type to 'claim' something you wanted."

Why would I need to claim something that is mine?

"I really care about you," he said. He looked me deep in the eyes and a piece of me died when his eyes started welling up with tears.

He left and went back to his New - old life.

∞∞∞

I was surprised a few months later when my phone rang and I saw his name come up on my caller ID. "We are moving to Seattle," he said. He was angry that I had decided to not speak to him anymore. I had also said some "not so nice" things behind his back and that didn't help our situation. Acting like a two-year-old was the only thing that made me feel better and then only for a moment.

"Have a nice life, Frankie. I don't think we should be speaking to each other anymore. We had a good run. Let's just leave it at that." Hurt feelings and pride were controlling my responses. My ego wouldn't allow me to say what I really felt – how hurt I was inside – so being an asshole was the best way for me to get it all out without feeling vulnerable. The pain of knowing we had our last dance was tormenting.

∞∞∞

There have been few people that have broken through the cement around my feelings. Frankie filled a noticeable void. The thought of him guided me for years. Knowing he did not love me, or loved someone else was torturous. The only relief I got was when I was participating in spiritual activities and lectures. So I went to the Agape International Spiritual Center in Los Angeles and was spellbound when I heard the reverend speak of a loving God. He joked that some of us might be used to "another God, a God who needs anger management".

I just started laughing at this mans conceptualization of such a loving presence. I could relate and I wanted to be closer to this source.

He said, "We decide of the God we allow into our lives."

It made sense that I had an extraordinary love for Frankie. Given the male influences in my younger years, he was at times, my hero. He brought out a kind tenderness in me that no other person could. I decided to accept some of this truth and move forward in my life knowing that Frankie's roll was as perfect as a Christmas song in winter.

Though I still wished he would have believed in me.

I'll be something like the rebirth of love, with a twist,
It started with a simple kiss,

What could be more precious then the rebirth of love?

"Believe" – Raheem DeVaughn

Chapter 40

VICTIM HONORS

I moved through my disappointment of Frankie by remaining a workaholic. We weren't speaking anymore but there was a lot going on in my life to keep my mind off the drama. I had recently bought a condominium and had been able to keep myself busy with minor renovations, some of which I was doing myself. Combined with furniture shopping and the potential purchase of a new car, I remained busy. Retail therapy is a sure fire way to feel better. It's only temporary, but it helps. The car I really didn't need but I had seen a really cool BMW commercial. It inspired me enough to go have a look and then a test drive. I had been working hard on my condo on Sunday evening when I saw an ad on television for an upcoming special. I put on my pajama sweats, laid on my new king size bed and waited for the commercials to finish so we could get down to business. This was my first TV night in a long time and I was looking forward to nesting in my new kingdom. I was getting settled into a comfortable position when the announcer spoke of this evening's episode.

"To catch a serial killer; The Capture of the Green River Killer..."

My attention postured towards the television. My heart pounded nervously as I wondered what they would talk about. The man who killed forty-nine women? The man who I knew killed Roberta?

I had heard they'd caught someone. I saw on the Internet that they had arrested a suspect but I purposely avoided reading the article in detail. They had arrested suspects before - to no avail. I wasn't hopeful and didn't put much thought into it. I had only known a mystery killer for twenty-five years.

They flashed a mug shot of a skivvy little overweight white man. He was married. He had a mustache and brown hair that was combed over to the side covering an obvious balding head. He had beady little eyes and was described to have below average intelligence. I balked at his IQ relevance. He killed forty-nine plus women and went uncaught for twenty something years.

He can't be *too* stupid.

They quoted him, "I killed so many women I have a hard time keeping them straight." He admitted that murdering women became his career, "Choking them is what I did and I was pretty good at it."

I watched dumbfounded as they went through the evidence and how they finally matched his DNA to some of the victims in the case. My heart never slowed to a normal pace as I waited to hear of Roberta. I watched the entire show waiting for them to memorialize the girl I knew but they showed pictures of everyone but her. During the ending credits, they listed the names of all of the victims that were killed. I watched attentively scared to blink, waiting for Roberta's name. I just needed to see someone acknowledge her. The show ended without one mention of her existence.

I was furious and could not sleep. I got out of my bed and went to my computer. I pulled up the website for the King County Police and found the link for the special Task Force assigned to the killer and I wrote an email thanking them for breaking the case while expressing my extreme disappointment that Roberta wasn't honored in the television special they helped produce. I went back to bed only to toss and turn all night.

A few days later, I received this response:

Mr. Early,

Thanks for your kind email. I was the one who contacted you in 1993 upon identifying Roberta's remains. I am glad that you managed to survive the streets of Seattle. Too many kids didn't. Roberta's case was very pivotal in the investigation of Gary Ridgeway. She disappeared significantly after the last "official" Green River case, which was in 1984. She was not really an 11th hour addition. I had long suspected that the Green River Killer was responsible for her death, as well as a number of others. But money and politics being what they are, I was never going to convince those in charge that the killings did not stop in 1984. While her name never appeared on any of the lists, she was never forgotten. When Gary Ridgeway agreed to clear up all of the murders that he had committed over the years, he was very firm at first that he had not killed after 1984. Fortunately, one of the traits that made him seem like such a cold blooded SOB, exposed this as a lie early on in the interrogations and opened up our investigation to large number of additional cases. On one of our field trips where Ridgeway was to lead us to places that he had dumped the victim's bodies, he took us directly to the site where he left Roberta's remains. I knew we were in the exact spot. By his own admission in court later, he "killed so many that he couldn't keep them straight". That was certainly the case here because we knew that Roberta did not disappear until sometime in 1987. We were able to use this case against him to break him of his claims of stopping in 1984 and we were eventually able to clear several more cases and bring some resolution to a few more families.

So, her case turned out to be important in the overall scheme of things – just a little tid-bit that does not show up in the newspapers and TV specials.

Thanks again for taking the time to write,

S.O. Tom Jensen

Roberta Joseph has been dead for over 25 years. She will never be forgotten.

Chapter 41

AMEND ME

I had started to learn some lessons in forgiveness. What I heard is that when we forgive we receive life-changing relief. For my lifetime, it had all sounded like a bunch of crap - but I thought I would try it with one ultimate test. I went to the computer and typed Frankie a simple email:

"I am sorry that I was such an asshole. Can we forgive?"

I made my morning coffee and took Honeychild for a walk. When I got back there was an email: *"Justin. Of course. Love, Frankie."*

I jumped into my daily routine with a gentle sense of release. Although it was Saturday, I decided I would go into the office to catch up on some work.

Living with you in my life,
Is like feeling the whole world's on my side,
Putting a smile in the place,
Where a tear used to run down my face

"Stay This Way" – The Brand New Heavies

Chapter Zero

Continued...

PART II

Chapter 42

MOTHER, FATHER

I still couldn't believe my father hit me in the face. As I drove on the freeway towards the Seattle airport, I thought of what had just happened. It didn't matter how much personal work I had done, something cracked when my father hit me and for a moment I wanted to kill him. I had learned to be a good man and this went against everything I was trying to represent. It made me realize how easy it was to jump back on that old train of anger. I needed to be more careful, especially when I was angry. But I also needed to stand taller when dealing with this very sick man. Little Justin has grown up and things work out better when he *stays* grown.

The reward of revenge faded as fast as it came. I realized and admitted to myself how inappropriate my actions were. I didn't want to be stuck on my Los Angeles plane angry and surrendered to calling my mother before boarding my flight.

"Mom, I am so sorry. I don't know how to tell you," I began.

"You don't have to apologize. You've been through enough."

"It won't happen again." I promised. I continued home to Los Angeles, to my life, my dogs and my friends.

I started to resolve myself to the idea that I would not see my father again before he died. I have found that when I open my mind and listen to what is happening around me, I usually hear whatever it is that I need to hear. I was in a cautious place and had run this situation by several friends, family members and had evaluated their feedback. I decided to attend a spiritual service at the Agape place when I heard something that was in line with what people were telling me.

"It's not about what others do for you, but what you do for them and for the world that will define you, your life and your happiness. You owe your life, life does not owe you."

My father was an abusive, alcoholic, asshole who did nothing to advance me on this planet, as a parent should. He did none of this because he couldn't. It was time for me to act like an adult and be the role model for him and be what he wasn't. With this new consideration I would step up and be a good son to define who *I am* as a person.

The integrity and definition of my character is my responsibility. I write my own story. I had felt freedom when I was able to step all the way up to the top of that stubborn mountain of resentments - and forgive. This was the Everest of mountains, but I needed to do it for myself, and for my father.

We both needed this freedom.

"Hey mom, I want to fly you and dad down to Los Angeles for a visit. Come see my new condo." My offer was greeted with silence.

"I have to ask your father, hold on," she said as she put the phone down.

I heard her speak to him and then she got back on the phone surprised, "He said yes."

"How is he doing, anyway?" I asked concerned.

"He is not well. He is coughing up blood. He has all but stopped eating and is deteriorating." The trip had to happen soon. "I'll book your tickets. You should probably start packing."

My mother laughed and was excited about the possibilities.

∞∞∞∞

I picked my parents up from the airport and began the short drive to my home in Inglewood. My mother was very talkative. My father didn't say anything - to me. I viewed him like he was a patient in a hospital, and didn't get angry with him. It was tough as my pride and ego were on the line – but I gritted my teeth and proceeded as a good man. I decided to surprise both of them by inviting Lisa from New York. Years ago my parents had taken a trip and had met Lisa, whom they fell in love with. My father actually adored her. I had never seen him smile so much as when he was around her. As we pulled into my complex, Lisa walked out of my condo. My father's face lit up and my mother started giggling.

"Oh, you shouldn't have!" my mother said to her shyly.

"I wouldn't have missed this for the world," Lisa said hugging them both at the same time. My father kissed Lisa her on the cheek. "It's nice to see you. Thank you."

He ignored me.

We made dinner plans at the nicest restaurants. Lisa and myself acted as hosts to the lucky couple. My father and I didn't speak much, but I did ask him if he needed anything a few times and he responded respectfully. We definitely weren't going to have a moment, or hug or anything like that, but it became comfortable and tolerable.

My father was out of breath most of the time and I could tell he didn't have much time left. He managed to smile several times.

I was at ease the whole week and just wanted to be of service to my parents. Lisa was amazing with my father and helped keep him under control. I had to remind myself that I didn't bring my father to my house with the intention of changing him. I brought him down with the intention of changing *me*. My behavior. My attitude. My perception.

The visit went rather fast and they were ready to go home after all of the busy activities we had planned for them. My mother asked to speak to me before I drove them to the airport.

"Thank you Justin. I know he appreciates it. I can't say enough how proud we are." She had tears in her eyes as I hugged her. I was proud of her too.

∞∞∞∞

My mother called when they arrived back home and informed me that my dad went straight to his bed and was experiencing miserable pain in his back and legs. They went to the doctor and he was diagnosed with secondary bone cancer. It was recommended that he stay in bed until he transitioned, though no one said the word. Mom talked as if he was going to get out of bed someday. I figured with the trip going as well as it did, and with my mother being completely alone taking care of my father, I would fly up on the weekends and help as much as I could.

The first trip he was not doing well at all. He had lost weight and was clearly in pain. I just hung out with mom and helped cook for her. He ate nothing. He was cranky with me but tolerant and appreciative of my presence.

Mom would try to put protein shakes down his throat, but that only lasted for so long. He asked her to put Bourbon in them.

It was time for hospice, but mom would have nothing to do with it.

"Mom, you are too old to be changing linens everyday. He can hardly move now. It's time for some outside help," I demanded kindly. My father agreed with me. For the first time, ever.

I fed him shakes and he reluctantly allowed me to put pills into his mouth. He would always give me his, 'what the hell are you giving me' look, like I was going to poison him or something. I smiled and asked nicely if he needed anything and he finally started responding in kind adding "could you please" and "would you mind..." to his sentences. I was surprised he was able to be so polite.

I was sitting in their spare bedroom resting and noticed an old dresser that I had grown up with in early years. I decided to see what was in it. I opened the first drawer that contained old pictures. Some I had never seen of my brothers and me.

I opened the second drawer and froze. There were two plastic containers with tags on them. They had my brother's names on them. It was their ashes. I figured their remains had been somewhere in the house. My mother would always tease, "Well, at least now I know where they are." And now so did I.

I shut the drawer.

∞∞∞∞

I had continued to travel the three-hour plane ride to my parents' every weekend.

"He is starting to go," mom admitted, "he hasn't eating anything or had any water in a week." I went up to my father, who was now in a hospital bed in the middle of the living room. He seemed coherent and looked up at me. I saw his eyes look over me just like he did in the motor home at the family reunion. I waited for him to say something mean or give me a nasty look but this time his eyes looked boldly into mine. He kept looking into me, almost into my soul.

Then he smiled. A smile so big his eyes slowly wrinkled. He couldn't speak but his smile just kept getting bigger as he stared me in the face. A moment of clarity overtook me.

Everything bad slipped away. Love and forgiveness replaced the oxygen and joined with the angels in the room. It was as if someone took a broom and swept away every negative thought from my memory.

Dad and I were forgiven - our traumatic relationship healed. In an instant - we became family. I bent down and grabbed his hand as he continued to proudly stare at his son. His smile widened.

I enjoyed the moment of the loving presence with my dad until he slowly drifted back into his nap. The weekend had come to an end and I needed to get ready to go back to Los Angeles. I walked out of the house from an interaction had changed me forever.

I sense of freedom came over me.

∞∞∞∞

I wasn't home two days when I got the call from my mother. "He is getting worse. His breathing is labored. You should come now."

I booked a flight and left immediately to Seattle. I decided to fly the connecting propeller flight to Bellingham after landing in Seattle so it would get me there sooner.

When I got to Seattle everything went wrong. My flight was delayed and then cancelled. The next available flight was full. I walked to the rental car station and called my mother to tell her that I would be longer than anticipated.

"He's gone," she said quietly. "He just took his last breath."

I pulled into the driveway at my parents' and noticed my mother sitting in her chair - staring into the sky.

She sits alone, an empty stare,
a mother's face she wears.

"Mother, Father" – Journey

Chapter 43

THE AWAKENING

By the time I walked into the house, my mother had seen my rental car and was up and out of her chair to greet me.

"Forty-four years," she whispered as she dove into my arms.

"I know, Mom. I know."

After releasing my mom, I walked into the room where my father's body still lay. I went up to his lifeless body and closed his eyelids. My mother came next to me and grabbed his arm, which was starting to get stiff. It had been three hours since his passing. She was kissing his arm and rubbing his hand.

"Mom, you're grossing me out," I said. She started to giggle and continued to sob.

"You know, if you want, I can carry him into the bedroom and you two can have one for the road. His rigor mortis is kicking in." I said referring to the rumor that men get erections when they die. "Shut up!" She laughed into tears as we said good-bye to the old man for the last time. We sat down at the kitchen table and talked as we waited for the funeral home to come pick up his body. I looked back in the living room and noticed his eyes were open again. I closed them again.

"I would really like to have a memorial," I told my mother as I sat back down.

"For your father? That's fine," she said excited.

"For all of them, Cam and George, too. We could charter a boat and spread their ashes out on the Puget Sound." I had thought about this for a long time. "Oh, that's a great idea!" I hadn't seen her animated in years when discussing my brothers. We started discussing the details immediately and whom we would invite. She wanted her sisters and brothers and I would invite my cousins Debbi, Diana, Greg and their spouses and children.

We sat in the kitchen and looked through pictures as we discussed the possible memorial. "Mom?" I said to her trying to be serious.

"Yes?" She looked up at me.

"His eyes are open again."

The van finally pulled up and one little, tiny short man got out and came to the front door. I thought it was a joke. There was no way this little guy was going to be able to get my old man in the van without dropping his body in front of my mother. As he pulled the gurney with the velvet body bag up to the hospital bed where my father was getting stiffer by the second. I walked up and offered my services.

"No, its alright young man. I can get this."

"I insist." I replied strongly.

We carried the gurney down the stairs and across the gravel to the waiting van and placed it into the back of the vehicle.

I walked back inside where my mother was standing at the window.

"I will never forget how you helped carry your father's body," she said through her tears.

"Thank you."

I know I'm prayin' for much too much,
But could you send back the only man she loved?
I know you don't do it usually.

But Lord, she's dyin' to dance with my father again…

"Dance With My Father" – Luther Vandross

Chapter 44

I RELEASE...

We decided that we would take our time coordinating the memorial service. When my father was ill I had started to call my mother daily. I continued to do so everyday since his passing. We would have nothing to talk about, but I would call her anyway just to say nothing and hear her laugh at the ridiculous silence.

"Mom, what are you doing now?"

"The same thing I was doing two hours ago when you called."

"I promised I would take care of you. So enjoy my calls, I will call you in an hour."

Laughing she told me, "I am not a child!"

"Well, I had a Nanny Cam installed so you don't get in trouble."

The laughter we experienced contributed to the healing of our losses. I was developing the strongest relationship with my mother that we had ever shared. I had decided to fly her down again so she wouldn't be alone before the memorial. She stayed with me and watched the dogs while I worked. The Gays decided that they wanted to take her out for a nice meal at a fancy restaurant, so we got dressed up - me in a tie, reluctantly - and went to The Palm in West Hollywood.

We were eating and my mother was having the time of her life joking around with my bosses and drinking a few too many glasses of wine when she said to them, "I would really like to have you both come to the memorial. Lloyd adored both of you." The Gays were flattered and accepted the invitation graciously. It was interesting that my mother mentioned how my Right-Wing father adored them and yet it was no secret that they were gay. Yet my father loved them. My father loved Lisa and he knew she was a lesbian.

It seemed fitting they attend. I was happy to have the support. I sent my mother back to Seattle and began to research vessels that we could charter for this event. Mom, who barely knows how to use the Internet says she has to "go on the line" while referring to email going on the Internet. She found a beautiful sixty-five foot sail boat that was docked in Bellingham, about forty-five minutes south of her house. I called them and we booked it. The boat was secured with a deposit and my bosses purchased catered food for the floating memorial.

I found a Minister through my church, a woman who had just moved to Seattle and was willing to facilitate the memorial celebration. I picked out some songs to play through my iPod and created memorial books with pictures and inspiring quotes.

I remembered my mother once saying that she had a letter that my brother had written while in prison. I asked her to get it out for me and read it to me over the phone. "Do you mind reading it to me?" I had to hear what it said. With a disclaimer provided, she read me the letter that my brother George wrote to God, weeks before he died.

I had been worried about how the memorial details would work out since so much time had passed. I had a conversation with my church friend Rob who said something very meaningful to me.

"Justin, you are on an amazing journey and have become a good man. You trusted in yourself and have done things to advance your relationship with God and your family." .

"Everything will work out perfectly. *Allow* it to happen perfectly."

He was right.

By doing some work in my life and by helping others my obsession to shoot dope has been removed. I am no longer a homeless drug-addicted, lying, thieving scumbag with sores all over my face. God (Allah, Buddha, Spirit) saved me. *Nobody and nothing else could* they all wanted to – the judges, the agencies, the outreach workers, my family my friends - but couldn't. Only I could - with assistance of something unseen by the human eye. Many did help me by being there for me – but I had to have faith.

Then I had to act upon that faith and change one thing. Everything.

I get down on my knees daily, and I pray to the universe, thanking the power that saved me, for a 'second, third, and fourth second chance', and for blessing me with unlimited happiness, a home, a family and amazing friends.

Including Frankie.

∞∞∞

With everything almost together for the memorial, I called my mother to tell her about the booklet I had designed and printed. We were going over the guest list when my mother asked me, "What about your friend?"

She knew more than I had ever told her.

"He was the first person I called."

When I was lost
I saw you pointing towards the sun
I know I'm not the only one standing here
And in the darkness
I was walking through the night

I could see your guiding light very clear

"The Journey" – DOLORES O'RIORDAN

Chapter 45

...AND I LET GO

The memorial was on Sunday so The Gays and I flew to Seattle Friday. They had never been there and decided to see the sights as tourists. We flew into Seattle relatively late, so I stayed the night in a hotel and got busy first thing in the morning. I stopped at Starbucks for some coffee and decided to visit Frankie and his family quickly before I hit the road.

"How are you doing?" He asked. "I think I am okay. I am just trying to get everything together." His look was intense.

"I want you to call me if you need anything, or if you need to talk. We can't ever do this again."

"Do what?" I asked. "Lose contact or not speak over petty garbage. I need you in my life," he said sincerely. "I will always be in your life," I promised my friend.

The fact that we had this conversation was huge. In fact, we had a bit of a hard time thinking of things to say and knowing how to act around each other in this new version of our relationship. The dynamic of our relationship had changed. We were learning how to be healthy friends.

I hugged Frankie and began the drive to my mothers.

∞∞∞∞

With everything ready and the car packed with the memorial books and flowers, Mom and I headed toward the pier where our boat was to launch. The day turned out to be spectacular and sunny. A bonus considering the weather is unpredictable in the Pacific Northwest. It was warm and the skies were clear and blue. I could see the Olympic Mountains across the Puget Sound - the rolling hills and totality of greenness. It was an absolutely stunning and perfect day and the views defined beauty.

As we parked I could see the guests arriving. My mother's siblings arrived first. My cousin Diana arrived next with my cousin Greg's wife, Susie and then Melinda who had visited me in the hospital twenty years before. Melinda was a mother herself now and no longer worked in street outreach, but we remained in touch over the years and enjoy a wonderful friendship. The Gays arrived before Mom and me and were already setting up the boat. Frankie came not too much later and came right over to me to see what he could do to help.

Everything was pulled together and we started walking down the pier to the boat. There was a steep set of stairs to be climbed for entry onto the deck, so Frankie began helping my elderly family. It was comical to me as I wondered if my extended family had ever seen a black man before. Everyone was gracious. He was an authentic gentleman. They asked my mother who he was.

"Frankie is Justin's dear friend from childhood."

If they only knew… I couldn't help but laugh inside.

With everyone on the boat, we launched out onto the water. The ride was smooth and everyone interacted wonderfully. After sailing for an hour we came up to an inlet with a small island in an area called Chuckanut Bay. It is one of the nicest scenic areas on the water in Northern Washington. My brothers and I played here when we were kids. Above on the land, I could see the very park we used to frequent.

We anchored down and I placed the remains, which had prepared in biodegradable packaging for the service on the table.

Everyone gathered around and I moved close to my mother who was crying lightly.

We began the service with a song I selected for its beautiful lyrics:

Another day,
Chance to make another chance,
A fragile place,
Running on empty
A smile so faint
Barely even breaks the space
World's on shoulders now.
Don't be afraid,
He who knows will make a way
His word alone is what has kept me.
Born the Son,
King of eternal peace,
Lay your burdens down…
If you catch me dreaming,
Please don't wake me till I'm done
Just leave me sleeping,
Until the morning comes

Just pass me over,
Make believe that I'm not there
Just leave me be

Until the Savior comes…

"Pass Me Over", Anthony Hamilton

Everyone went around and shared a few words and memories and when my turn came, I pulled out George's emotional apology, and began to read it aloud:

Dear God:
Let me first start by saying that I am sorry. Sorry for being a drug addict and sorry for dying of AIDS. Although I am in pain right now, I know that I won't be when you come for me. Please take care of my family who I love very much, my Mom and Dad and my brothers, Cameron and Justin. Please watch over them and forgive me for everything I have done to hurt them and you. As I write this letter I know that you are with me and I thank you God.
Thank you for taking care of me now.
Love, George

It was an enlightening experience, as no one in my family knew that George had died of AIDS. It had all been kept a secret. The minister led us in a beautiful prayer. I wasn't sure how she would be received since most in my extended family were from a more conservative church background. Here was a female minister – from a trans-denominational spiritual group – with an obvious liberal leaning. She began the prayer with "Mother, Father God." I was always fascinated by most religions intolerance for each-others practice – but there were no judgments this day. My aunts, uncles and cousins were all perfectly accepting, loving and supportive. They were awesome.

I removed my shoes and climbed over the boat onto the hanging ladder. I was secure and ready to do what I had waited many years to do. My brothers were being celebrated, as was my father, and they were going to be together and be remembered as God's children and our family.

Not for their faults but for their gifts.

Frankie handed me my family and I gently placed each one into the calm blue ocean.

As the ship of mourners and celebrators headed back to land, I looked into the sky, which was still clear and beautiful. Everyone was enjoying the beautiful weather and the guests were quiet and comfortable. The wind in my face and the fresh ocean air was healing – and I felt good about what we were doing. I looked over at Frankie, who had been looking at me intently. His loving face was angelic as he stared at me, concerned how I was holding up. He nodded his head upwards one time, asking me silently if I was okay.

I nodded back once to my old friend, letting him know that I was. I was finally beginning to heal.

As the world turns, and the moon fades,
and the sun begins to shine
Like the flowers, and the trees grow,

you're always on my mind.

"Think of You" – Ledisi

Chapter 46

THE AFTERMOM

ife in Los Angeles got back to normal as it ever would. I worked and continued on my professional career path while still learning and growing in ways I never imagined. I would love to say that I have done everything perfectly. I haven't.

I remained in contact with my mother on a more frequent basis and visited her every few months. There was always a question of when and where we would have to proactively embrace her elderly progression and the phone call came almost four years after the memorial.

"I am not sure what I'm going to do," she said distressed on the verge of tears, "I don't think I can maintain this house anymore. It's too much for me." Not one to ask for help, I knew she had hit a defining moment in her life. I booked a flight and went to see her.

When she picked me up from the airport I noticed dents and scratches on the front, side and back of her red Suzuki mini SUV. I didn't say anything because I could tell she was a little out of sorts from driving on the freeway to pick me up. When we pulled into her driveway, I saw what had been abusing her car. "Mom, were you playing bumper cars with the house and garage?" I was trying to be funny to make light of a serious situation, and mom laughed, but there was a big hole in the house near the gas meter and she had also bumped into the sides of the garage – several times.

We made it into the house and I started going through the mountains of paperwork – and unpaid bills that covered the dining room table. I didn't want to shame her, but I needed to get to the bottom of this mess. "What are all these bills doing on the table Ma?"

"Since your father died, I can barely make ends meet. My eyesight is so bad I can only drive during the day and I can't read the damn bills well enough to pay them!" She started to laugh as if it was funny, but we both knew that it wasn't. She needed help. Now she was in survival mode.

It took two full days, but I was able to go through several trees of paperwork. Some of the bills had been paid twice and some weren't paid at all. We got everything organized and straightened out and then I decided it was time to have "the talk".

"You know it may be time that you think about selling this house and moving somewhere more sensible. You can't live alone without assistance anymore."

She started look around and fear took over the room, "Look at all this stuff! I don't know what to do with any of it! Almost fifty years of useless crap! I can barely walk and can't even pack it into boxes."

I would help in any way I could, but wasn't sure where to start. We talked about an apartment in downtown Bellingham where she could walk and shop and be mostly self-sufficient. We looked at assisted living facilities, but all of them were out of her reach financially. The thought of my mother living with me crossed my mind, but what would that be like? I did have a three-bedroom condo – but an over forty-year old (single!) man living with his mommy? I wasn't sure about it but I was sure that she should at least liquidate her belongings, sell her car and the house. She could stay with me in Los Angeles until it was all worked out responsibly.

It took a few months and we were able to sell most of her furniture. She kept some odds and ends and an antique bedroom set, which was given to her and dad by Baba and Nana – as a wedding gift. I wanted to make sure that it was packed up safely and properly so I assigned myself the task of emptying the drawers – the same drawers where I had found my brothers remains years prior. The same secret drawers where I had seen more stuff and hadn't had the chance to be nosy enough to go through the rest of it, yet.

I was enjoying my Early-family history lesson and tore through the timeless items that had been stored for safekeeping. There were baby books and art pieces that had been created by my brothers when they were youngsters and pictures of all of us boys from Grade School. I got distracted by the interesting artifacts and spent a couple hours picking through all the gems I had never seen before. Cameron's Baby Book, George's Baby Book, my mom and dads Baby Books. I had picked through all of them and noticed another book at the bottom of the drawer, underneath what looked like a sheet of wallpaper. It too, was a book. A white padded book cover with an illustrated silver tree and block-lettered words that read, "Wee Me". I opened the book to the first page and saw the name of the child whose birth was being celebrated: mine.

Many people would never relate to such a find but the excitement that I felt when I opened the page and saw my name was overwhelming. My family loved me – and they celebrated my birth. My mother kept a journal with my weight and my height, when I spoke my first word and took my first steps. Even as a toddler, I remembered some of these wonderful and happy times in my life.

I thumbed through the book and felt a sense of individuality and gained a new appreciation for my family – even though most of them are gone. I belonged and I am a part a family ancestry.

I am.

When I turned to the last page of my baby book, I saw four loose pieces of paper folded neatly in half. The letter was typed on an old typewriter – from my very first fan.

Friday, 12:04pm, September 5th - 6lbs. 13oz.

Dear Justin Reed:

When you are older you may be interested to know a little of what was happening on what we call "United States of America on Earth" when you arrived here. How about a few words about your fathers relatives, too! I will start with the eldest, which was proper then.

Your Grandfather, George David Early (called Baba) would be 79 years old on December 2, 1969, and still worked like a 30 year old; he spent the morning golfing and the afternoon picking fruit.

Your grandmother, Rose Ruth Fisher Early (called Nana) was 63 years old and couldn't even work like a 60 year old! We lived on 4 acres in Bothell, WA with a 15-year old German Shepard whom everyone loved (his name was Guard). He tried to talk to me a couple of times but I got so upset and pushed him away. Shame on me! We also had 3 grown and 5 baby quail left plus 2 grown and 5 baby chipmunks who raced and played around the back porch. I won't mention the 20 old hens and 75 black speckled chickens...

Your big brother Cameron was 6 years old and just starting First Grade in school. On the second day he came home and said he had learned to read! I received a phone call from him at 5:30pm today to tell me about YOU; he had dialed the number himself!

Your brother Lloyd George (called Georgie or George) was 4 years old. He was a husky, strong willed guy with a great personality. When he saw that your parents had taken his chest of drawers and put it in the nursery for you he went in and gave it a good kick! You can't blame him can you? His new chest is being painted red in the basement. They have a smart dog named Poncho.

Your fathers' sister Lynn and Husband Allan Rook had given you 3 cousins: Deborah was 12 years old and was a quiet and studious girl. Diana was 10 and loved to talk on the telephone. Greg was 6 and just started first grade.

1. *Richard Nixon was President of the United States.*
2. *Don Evans was the Governor of the State of Washington.*
3. *The 3 astronauts blasted off for the Moon on July 21st, returning safely on July 24th. Neil Armstrong and Edwin Aldrin were the first men to step on the moon while Michael Collins kept the rocket in orbit.*

4. *Rock and Roll was the big fad in music, which didn't do the nerves or eardrums of the older generation any good! The most famous group were the "Beatles" from England who have just dis-banded.*

5. *Negroes, or as they preferred to be called "Black" were being integrated into schools, television and all walks of life faster than ever before in our history!*

Now, if you should become famous (which isn't important), or make this world a better place for mankind, you will have a small chapter for your autobiography! Be happy.

Welcome to your family!

Love,

Nana.

Pictured: Nana and Baba

Chapter 47

OPINIONATION

Pictured: Justin Reed Early (Credit: Todd Franson)

Not many that experience such trials and difficult challenges will have the ability or the resources to have the happy ending that I am honored to write about. The purpose of this book is to raise awareness – and to prevent this story from repeating in following generations. America has made great strides helping children who suffer, but we must continue to grow and to become more accepting of her people – our people. We must also share the responsibility of raising our children and give them access to basic necessities to ensure that their lights shine brighter than ever before. They must be fed and treated equally no matter what. There is no reason for a hungry child in this great nation – the richest country in the world.

They must be educated, empowered and inspired to be greater than we ever imagined them to be. We mustn't allow them to be bullied and punished because they are different.

Children are One Hundred percent of our future. We need to invest in all of them as such.

Mental illness, depression, domestic violence, alcohol and drug addiction are some of the more common factors that contribute to homelessness. Children who age out of foster care often will not have the support structures to carry them and they too will end up sleeping on streets.

It is estimated that any given time, 1.6 million unaccompanied children are homeless and are living the same life and going through much of what you have just endured reading this journey. They come from very diverse social status backgrounds and different walks of life. Many have been discarded simply because they are LGBT (Lesbian, Gay, bisexual, transgender). Many religious organizations encourage such abandonment. These beliefs are harmful and contribute to staggering instances of bullying and suicide.

There are up to 2 million children affected by homelessness every year in the United States alone. More than 80% of these kids will be physically or sexually abused.

Their tumbling spirits will become so injured that they will need to use mind-altering substances to sooth their slowly dying souls. Drugs will be the medicating solution to effectively cope with the harsh reality of deteriorating ethics and moral character. They will start to develop and expand upon criminal records. They will be arrested and convicted for minor survival crimes and will be introduced into a Justice System that lacks compassion and hope. They will be tossed around and will be introduced to other negative behaviors where their chances of success will continue to dwindle. When they turn 'of age' usually eighteen, they will 'age out' of the juvenile system and graduate into a life of further crime, which will land them into the adult prison system. A now mostly privatized prison system, which considers inmates as an asset to generate revenue, which I characterize as a modern-day form of slavery. A disproportionate amount of incarcerated Americans are of color (African American), because the current system continues to marginalize and punish them unfairly.

As many of these people progress in negative environments, hope for better circumstances will dissipate. Many of them will die, like the many you met and lost on this journey because they haven't been inspired or guided to change. Many will remain incarcerated and will continue spinning in the revolving door of inadequacy. It is important to know and be reminded what we go through and no matter how young or old, we *can* heal our lives and we *can* get through these challenges.

My experience in the aforementioned is more valid than an opinion because it is my *experience* that a spiritual path or awakening is required for a man or woman to break the cycle of drug addiction and emotional insufficiencies. This spiritual awakening is talked about in all 12-step programs. It happens by waking up to the fact there is a power that created this universe – and you aren't it. Some people call the power God or a Higher power. I call it Spirit. Some people don't call it anything at all – they just acknowledge that it *is*.

When I look up and see the stars glisten or go to the ocean and listen to the waves – I offer gratefulness to this source. I pray in the morning for good things for others and for myself. No matter what happens in my life – my perspective is always better because of this (which means if life sucks, and I pray – I begin to feel better. Life still may suck, but I feel better, until it does get better. Which it always does)!

We will all need to stand up for these kids – at least a little, in any way we can. Whether we donate or volunteer, we are now the generation of heroes that many people who have no means will rely on to inspire success.

Humans can heal physically, emotionally and spiritually and we can also heal negative teachings and belief structures. Racism, homophobia, sexism are oppressive forms of hatred that are passed down generationally and are intended to marginalize their victim. These odious teachings are social diseases that must be treated and healed spiritually in order for us to attain true freedom and be positive examples to everyone we meet. There are many of us, myself included that consider our time a much better place. But the infrastructure that is in place still passively marginalizes minorities (based on race, religion, sex, class, status, identification).

I am not a metaphysical genius or a popular spiritual leader or anyone known or credible. I just continue to heal my life and try to remain humble when it comes to learning new things. I continue to make mistakes – but learn from my lessons when it can better my life and the lives around me. I share my story because a miracle happened within me – it was a gift from the universe that is available to anyone who reaches for it. Anyone can attain this miracle.

I made a decision when I woke up this morning, as I typed this very word, to tap into the good that the world and universe have to offer – and I offer it back in as many ways as I can.

Good things and the simple perception of them continue to manifest in my life as a result of this basic knowledge.

I highly encourage readers to give back and to be of service in and *outside* of your respective communities. Be a mentor, deliver meals, volunteer at a professional level or donate financially to a non-profit organization. Your intention, your action and your contributions make a powerful difference. It will also help guide you in a direction that you may find edifying. These activities have played a significant role in my corrective and reparative accomplishments.

Though I am not here to disclose a miraculous spiritual breakthrough path, there are many enlightening conduits that can be guides to attain a greater spiritual understanding and it will present if you let it.

Most of this knowledge is already within us.

Chapter 48

EPILOGUE

My mother still lives with me and is my biggest fan and source of inspiration. She has supported the STREETCHILD project and has also purchased books to donate to homeless children in shelter in the United States. She is an amazing cook but unfortunately, doesn't like to clean or do my laundry (I tried!). We have an amazing relationship that I am grateful for. When she is not watching Kathy Griffin she is a comedienne in her own right and keeps me - and all my friends – laughing. Although her hearing and vision are deteriorating, she has learned how to use an iPhone and texts me her shopping lists (which mostly consists of Milk, Bourbon and Cigarettes). She also has an iPad she uses for Facebook, Mahjong and Solitaire. She said she would like to start dating again, as long as the man is much older than her, closer to death than she is, and very, very rich.

∞∞∞

Lou Lou still doesn't have a headstone, but I hope one day she will. I honor her memory and know she would be proud of me, and Frankie.

How amazing it is that after all these years her story is still making such a profound difference in peoples lives.

Like she did in mine.

∞∞∞

Frank (the miracle formerly known as Frankie) has been clean and sober for many years. He went to college and obtained his Bachelor's degree. He began working in the field of addiction and went to Graduate School where he obtained a Masters Degree. He is a specialist in his field and I am very proud of him and even more proud to still call him my friend.

My love for Frankie helped define my life and this book. It was an amazing experience that allowed me to grow in many ways, which were articulated in this memoir.

After I wrote the first draft of STREETCHILD, we 'gave it a go' as a couple, and decided that we were not a romantic match. He continues to live in Seattle, WA.

∞∞∞

Roberta Joseph Hayes was finally confirmed as the 42nd victim of the Green River Killer, Gary Ridgeway. He was sentenced in 2003 to 48 life sentences without the possibility of parole.

Roberta's children were all adopted and I never had any contact with any of them – until now.

Lonnie Lamont (Josh) is a father and we have made contact. When we first spoke he told me, "I know you knew my mom – because no one ever knew me by my birth name."

Kai – lives in Oregon and we have had several conversations pertaining to his mother. He is definitely his mothers' child – and was happy to learn a bit more about her.

Roberta's older sister, Kandice (Kandi), found out about StreetChild and was very leery about reading it. After doing so, she contacted me through Facebook. She wanted to give me her blessing and thanked me for capturing her sisters' intimate and sweet personality.

∞∞∞

Lou Lou and Frankie's sister Lisa, who I stayed with as a youngster, died while I was writing this memoir. She was smoking crack while on oxygen and it burst into flames. She breathed fire from the explosion severely burning the inside of her lungs. Combined with other major drug related illnesses, she never recovered.

Her daughter Di Di (Diane Parr) left home in 1989, the year I left Seattle.

No one ever heard from her again.

∞∞∞

Erin (Tiny from Streetwise) recently gave birth to her tenth child. Mary Ellen Mark has followed her and taken pictures throughout the years. We remain friends and are in contact through Facebook.

You can see Erin in many of Mary Ellen's exhibits and on her website. www.maryellenmark.com

∞∞∞

Tom Dunne (the outreach man) married another outreach worker Vicki Wagner who runs the National Network for Youth. They adopted the baby of a street child who is now grown and amazing.

∞∞∞∞

Judy Hightower is a doting grandmother and remains on the bench in Seattle. She lovingly refers to herself as my black mama and has become my greatest supporter. She is my mentor and has been a high source of empowering love and guidance.

∞∞∞∞

Detective Benson is retired and graciously assisted and contributed factually to StreetChild.

∞∞∞∞

I never heard from Gary King (the Preacher Man) again. I never wanted to.

∞∞∞∞

Lisa C. (my New York lesbian) owns Henrietta Hudson's, a popular Manhattan Bar in New York City. We are still best friends and take turns traveling to each other's coast. I am also very close with her family and sister Linda – who is an amazing cook!

∞∞∞∞

I keep in touch with several of my Walden House friends (Shannon Bennett, Karen Redus, D.K. Haas, Donna Hilliard, Erric White, Davey White and Barbara Nolan just to name a few).

∞∞∞∞

Michael McDavid lives in Miami with his awesome partner and we remain dear friends.

∞∞∞∞

To the reader: THANK YOU. This book was self-published and is a grass roots project with no 'Hollywood' assistance or financial backers. We have done it all ourselves (writing, editing, artwork, Public Relations) with *your* help and the help of many dear friends – and we would appreciate it if you continue to spread the word about StreetChild on your social networking sites – as well as sharing this title in your book clubs and online reviews.

Chapter 49

IN HONOR OF...
THE GREEN RIVER VICTIMS

"It's not easy being Green…" Storme D'Laverie (Stonewall Riots)

I dedicate this chapter to the forty-nine lives - that were so mercilessly stolen from their families by a very evil and horrible serial murderer - whose name I will not mention ever again.

May all of you - at least now - Rest in Peace.

Chapter 50

THANK YOU

MARILYN KENTZ, thank you for your assistance while walking the first draft of this journey. You nurtured me though some difficult memories and I appreciate your love and patience. www.themommies.com & www.fearlessaging.com

My country AMERICA – God, and the Spirit of the universe for guiding me into perfect love and completion. To my family, Cousin Diana (Teagan, Anders and Rylee!) and Curt Schnaible (Katelyn, Jack and Scott!) Aunt Lynn Randall "Auntie Mom"... Greg Rook, Susie Rook, Dustin Barnes. Cousin Debbi & Paul Brainerd, you are true examples of giving.

My mother, who continues to drop knowledge, love and humor.

Laval Jones... I continue to pray in love.

Rob Woronoff for adopting a grown Streetchild (and his book!) and for helping me, help others.

John Ogren (the original outreach man), Tom Dunne, The Outreach Man and wife Vicki Wagner. Tony Ross, Ronn Burns (for helping me get back in shape!), Von and Lori Shuler, my favorite neighbors. Uki Amaechi for being such a dear friend and the highest example of motherhood I have ever seen – you are perfection (I love you Isaiah and Iniko!). Danny Glover, I would "dream" when you would walk through Walden House and come watch football with us. You contributed as an example to my success and your brother Reggie Glover contributed directly. Carlos Dennis, you were there and I enjoy our friendship. Luis and Danyail Sotomayor. Teresa Crespo, Georgie Crespo, I still wish you were my son... Sean Sasser, you are a good friend and I love you... Antigone Hodgins and the entire BAY Positives family... Dr. Janet Shalwitz, Pam & Judd Ling-Winnick. Eric Ciasulo, My step daddies Scotch Ellis Loring and Todd Holland; you're both amazing. Steven Okasaki your talents are endless and thank you for your kind words. Martin Jouflas, Susan Jouflas, Melinda Schill-Teeny, Rita, for taking care of the Street Kids and for staying in contact with most of the surviving success stories. The Bailey Family (Beck, Mel, Marty, and mother Sharon, RIP), my neighbors from childhood. George Lozano and the entire Covenant House staff and programs; it is because of your tenacity and dedication of people like you that I am alive to write this book. Jeffrey Drew, Greg Cardona, Sal Rullen, Mike Fahed, Don Norman, Manny Rodriguez, Eddie "X" Irrizary, you are in my heart! Frankie Knuckles, thank you for letting me hang in your booth for all of those years... Larry Flick you always believed in me and supported me before knowing any of this, thank you for your friendship, for being a great pen pal and for being the first to read STREETCHILD (and for the blurb!) and Keith Price and the entire Sirius XM family! Pete Avila, thank you. Lisa Sculti Williamson (Jessi, Sofie, Ryan and Autumn) for witnessing the worst and now the best (and Bob) Richard Moon, you are a dick! The Cannistraci family (and Betancourt kids) - my New York family. Thank you for loving me. Lisa C., my best friend and sister, my lesbian lover! My little nephew Enrique Jesus Hernandez, for reading and giving feedback. Mama Lizette, you are amazing. Kevin "Buffy" Morris, my Morris "Mom and Dad" and of course David "Muffy" Mosby. DJ Mike Cruz and Fernando, David Henney (RIP). Joanne Coraci, for supporting and inspiring me to do this and for reading the first "whacked" draft. L.P., available on iTunes... Earl Pleasure, JoJo Odyssey, Carolyn Corrado. Ken Breeding, for helping save my life... Grandma D., you too (RIP)! Mary Ellen Mark and Martin Bell, for raising awareness to homeless youth with your movie Streetwise. Thank you for making me a little part of Streetwise. Meredith Lue for your patience and assistance. Ananda Edmonds, Donna Hilliard, Dr. Marsha Mouton for fixin' my grill... Little John Fletcher, Erin "Tiny" Blackwell, Ann Bredice, Lynlee, Kevin Wayne "Black Junior" Jones, Ronald Leroy "White Junior" Cady, Eddie Thomas, Marlys and Laura Greer, Paula, Alice, Dora Norland, Wanda, Gayle "Pinky" Turner, Kenny Appletoff (Senior and Junior), Frank Woody, Bill Betten, Bobby & Myrna Larson, Marcy, Black Justin, Kim and Steve, Gina and Brent, Tina, Mikey, Beverly,. Rob Winrader, I thank God (and Frank) for you. Jaime too! Andrea Fleming, I am so proud of you! GLAAD for making sure we are perceived responsibly and honestly. The gay community and the role models who go above and beyond (too many to list because everyone is so amazing!). Nicole Broduer, The Seattle Times, Metro Weekly, Heath Daniels, Paul Gendreau. Cathy Renna (Renna Communications), Cindi Creager and Rainie Cole (Creager Cole Communications), Jen Bergman, Josie Coleman, and everyone who contributed professionally to the success of StreetChild.

Krystle Luv Lamphere, Justina Mia Rose Couch and Frankie Luv Jasmine Couch. FDC, Thank you for a lesson learned. I wish you all the above and beyond the best on your journeys

National Network for Youth – the Board of Directors, member agencies - it was an honor serving on your governing board and I wish you all the best and support your future.

President Barack Obama, First Lady Michelle and the entire Obama Administration who work tirelessly to improve the lives of Americans. Your work is manifesting many positive changes not only for all Americans, but everyone all over the world!

Please don't be afraid to talk about this story because it is edgy or uncomfortable – use it to help a child that might otherwise end up on the streets – or the parent who doesn't know what to do with a child. We can prevent homelessness if we try – and most importantly, we can prevent stories like mine from ever having to be written.

I hope to see you around.

IN MEMORIUM

Again, I would like to dedicate this book to the memory of my dear friends, Lou Ellen Couch, Roberta Joe Hayes, my brothers, Cameron David Early and Lloyd George Early and to all of the street-kids and heroes that continue to define my life.

You are my world.

The Street Child

43996050R00142

Made in the USA
Middletown, DE
25 May 2017